GREEN CANE

AND

JUICY FLOTSAM

GREEN CANE

A N D

JUICY FLOTSAM

SHORT STORIES BY
CARIBBEAN WOMEN

Carmen C. Esteves and
Lizabeth Paravisini-Gebert
Editors

Rutgers University Press   *New Brunswick, New Jersey*

Second paperback printing June 1992

Library of Congress Cataloging-in-Publication Data

Green cane and juicy flotsam : short stories by Caribbean women /
 Carmen C. Esteves and Lizabeth Paravisini-Gebert, editors.
     p.   cm. — (Rutgers Press fiction)
   Translated from Spanish and French, some originally in English.
   Includes bibliographical references.
   ISBN 0-8135-1737-0 (cloth) -- ISBN 0-8135-1738-9 (pbk.)
   1. Short stories, Caribbean. 2. Caribbean fiction--Women authors.
 I. Esteves, Carmen C., 1952-   . II Paravisini-Gebert, Lizabeth.
 III. Series.
 PN849.C32G74 1991
 808.83'1089287--dc20   91-4788
                                                                     CIP

British Cataloging-in-Publication information available

To our mothers

Carmen Elena Montesinos Vda. de Esteves

and

Virgenmina Rivera de Paravisini

and to the memory of our fathers

Antolino Esteves de Jesús

and

Domingo Paravisini

CONTENTS

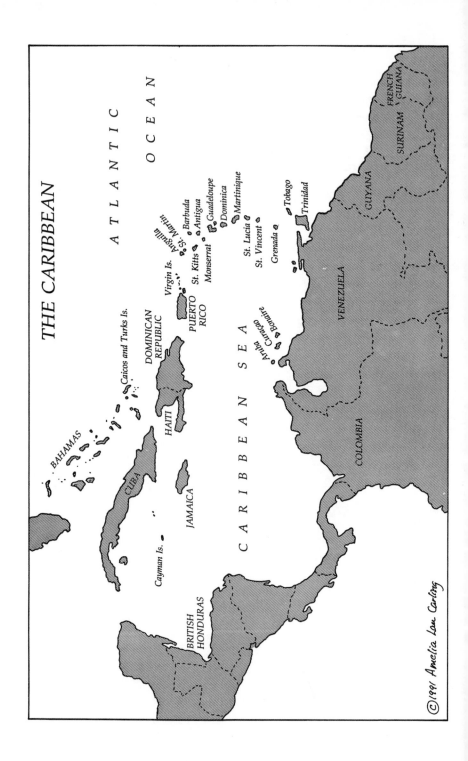

THE CARIBBEAN

ATLANTIC OCEAN

BAHAMAS

Caicos and Turks Is.

DOMINICAN REPUBLIC

HAITI

CUBA

Virgin Is.

Anguilla

St. Martin

St. Kitts

Barbuda

Antigua

Monserrat

Guadeloupe

Dominica

Martinique

St. Lucia

St. Vincent

Grenada

Tobago

Trinidad

PUERTO RICO

JAMAICA

Cayman Is.

BRITISH HONDURAS

CARIBBEAN SEA

Aruba

Curaçao

Bonaire

COLOMBIA

VENEZUELA

GUYANA

SURINAM

FRENCH GUIANA

© 1991 Amelia Lau Carling

INTRODUCTION

and first upon the hillside where bare feet
in a goat's wake avoiding the small brown pebbles
know earth as it was made and men in fields
releasing cotton from the mother tree
milking tits heavy with white wholesomeness
or riding wave on wave of green cane till
the swell abates and the warm wind
finds only calm brown surfaces
thick with the juicy flotsam of the storm
make poems

and men who speak the drum
bembe dundun conga dudups cutter
or blow the brass or play the rhumba box
or lick croix-croix, marimba or tack tack
and women who record all this
making the tribe for start in blood
and sending it off to school to factory
to sea to office, university   to death
make poems

Pamela Mordecai,
"Poet's World"

The last two decades have witnessed a veritable explosion in the literary production of Caribbean women. Gone are the days when every generation or movement would have one representative woman writer who would signal by her presence the very absence she was called upon to negate: that of women's voices in the mainstream of literary activity in the region. Beginning in the 1970s, the growing international reputations of Caribbean writers such as Maryse Condé, Rosario Ferré, Jamaica Kincaid, Jean Rhys, and Simone Schwarz-Bart, among others, have focused attention on women's literary activity in the region and on women's particular contribution to our understanding of Caribbean societies through literature.

The increasing popularity of Caribbean women writers has been sparked by a growing interest in voices from the Third World, where issues of gender and feminism are compounded by labyrinthine questions of race, power, colonialism, poverty, and the correlations between national and personal identities. Since their work often addresses some manifestation of gender, class, racial, or colonial "Otherness," it has served as the catalyst for critical exchange on these issues. The exploration by Caribbean women writers of the remnants of plantation-bred socio-economic structures, and of the concomitant lack of sisterhood between black and white women in Caribbean societies, for example, has made a valuable contribution to the ongoing revision of traditional feminist thought.

Thus far, critical attention has centered almost exclusively on Caribbean women novelists. Short story writers (and poets) have received at best moderate notice, primarily because their work has appeared most frequently in local journals, newspapers, and magazines, severely limiting access by readers and critics. The short story, however, is a genre of unique importance in the Caribbean, with roots dating back to rich Taíno/African folk traditions of which women have often been the custodians. It has been as short story writers that a large number of Caribbean women have established their literary reputations—Dora Alonso, Rosario Ferré, Olive Senior, and Jamaica Kincaid are cases in point. But there has been until now no collection of short stories where the student of literature as well as the general reader could experience the richness and variety of the genre as practiced by Caribbean women.

The stories included in this anthology have been selected to show the broadest spectrum of themes, styles, and techniques. This diversity can be seen in Jamaica Kincaid's brilliantly eloquent portrayal of a mother-daughter relationship in "Girl"; in Jeanne Hyvrard's poignant depiction of the alienation of a Caribbean woman in Parisian exile in "Opéra Station. Six in the Evening. For Months . . ."; in the eroticism of Dora Alonso's description of an old woman's frustrated sexual desires in post-revolutionary Cuba in "Cotton Candy"; in the symbiotic relationship between the tormented plantation mistress and the parasol who narrates Olga Nolla's "No Dust Is Allowed in This House"; in Ana Lydia Vega's parodic reversal of male erotic discourse in

"ADJ, Inc."; in Myriam Warner-Vieyra's affectionately humorous tale of the triumph of folk-belief over Church bureaucracy in "Passport to Paradise"; and in the solidarity between the privileged light-skinned girl and the victimized black servant in Michelle Cliff's "Columba," to offer some examples.

In their search for their individual voices as Caribbean writers, women have had to address the traditional themes and tropes of Caribbean literature—slavery, the plantation economy, colonialism, the complexities of class, race, and language—from their own particular vantage point, that of women from emerging nations where patriarchal/colonial institutions have sought to silence women's voices in general—and colored women's voices in particular. Therefore, in resisting their double oppression, their work both echoes and subverts these themes and tropes, often calling into question accepted notions and well-established "truths," revealing aspects of the Caribbean experience not previously gleaned from literary or historical accounts.

Perhaps the most obviously resonant theme is that of the writer's relationship with the written word, with her very ability to write, with her discovery of the often awesome power of the text—a recurrent theme in these stories. This is a theme of particular importance given both the widespread illiteracy in the region and women's limited access to formal schooling and higher education. Thus writing itself becomes an audacious act, one tantamount to an usurpation of the potential for literary creation, which had been previously the sole province of males. Claude, protagonist of Maryse Condé's "Three Women in Manhattan"—transplanted from Pointe-à-Pitre to the inhospitable landscape of New York City—awaits the moment when the audacity to write "would come back to her, that her hips, her sex, her heart, her head would set off in motion once again and that she would give birth to her world."

Claude's quest for her lost "audacity to write" allows Condé to address women's situation vis-à-vis literary establishments which have sought to suppress female voices. The quest itself is mediated in the text by Claude's relationships to two women writers: Elinor, whose fashionable apartment Claude cleans; and Vera, an old Haitian activist who has offered her shelter and protection. The two women stand on opposite poles of the literary world: Elinor is a successful young African American novelist torn between black and white literary establishments, eagerly courted by white critics who find in her work the epitome of "the folklore of the Old South and [of the] collective black patrimony," and harshly censured by black critics who want her "to speak once more about slavery and the slave trade, and racism," and to adorn blacks "with the virtues of victims"; Vera is a Haitian novelist whose unpublished manuscripts bear witness to the suppression of the voicing of the Haitian historical plight. Vera's tragic inability to find a publisher for her many-times-returned manuscripts, juxtaposed against Elinor's position as a writer in vogue, prompts Claude to ask vital questions about women's relationships to the very literary establishment they seek to penetrate: "Why were they condemned to this inglorious end? Who defines Beauty? Who decides upon success? Why was Elinor basking in the full sun? Vera in darkness?" Claude's own eagerness to write is fed by her desire to tear down the barriers that have silenced Vera's Caribbean voice. She dreams of writing a work that would present Vera "not such as she was—an octogenarian in a pitiful wool cardigan, raising her pathetic voice in a tumult of distress—but such as she dreamed her to be: Erzulie Dantor, flaming torch clenched in her fist."

Ramabai Espinet's "Barred: Trinidad 1987" strikes a similar chord, suggesting that the "tumult of distress" in which Vera finds herself is rooted in the "newness" of the Caribbean condition, in the historylessness that marks newly-independent island societies emerging from centuries of colonial control. Espinet's tale articulates the uneasy relationship between the East Indian immigrant and his or her new landscape—and the silence to which it leads—a theme that has widespread resonance in cultures founded upon the horrors of slavery and the Middle Passage. In the story, a young East Indian woman agonizes over her people's frustrating relationship to words in "the peasant newness of this settlement": "We are lost here, have not found the words to utter our newness, our strangeness, our unfound being. Our clothes are strange, our food is strange, our names are strange. And it is not possible for anyone to coax or help us. Our utterance can only come roaring out of our mouths when it is ready, set, and can go."

This preoccupation with the utterance, and with the underlying pain it must sooner or later express, is shared by the disembodied voice in Jeanne Hyvrard's "Opéra Station. Six in the Evening. For Months . . . ," tortured by its inability to negotiate "the river of words in the mangrove thicket of writing": a voice adrift in the underground maze of the Parisian Metro searching for a way to "dance the broken voices reemerging from everywhere." Hyvrard expresses the anguish of a writer overwhelmed by a history of slavery, death, and deportation so devastating that it leads to silence, or at best to the fragmented utterances of the dispossessed. Her story bares the word's power to unleash the frustrations of the disinherited into revolt.

A different aspect of the dangerous potential of the written word is exemplified by Rosario Ferré's "The Poisoned Story," where the printed page becomes an instrument of death and revenge. Through its central character's questioning of the authority of the male interpreter of her story, "The Poisoned Story" exposes the way literature can distort history to deny a voice to the black and the poor, as well as to women. Ferré's fiction to date has focused precisely on the problem of the voicelessness of marginalized groups in Caribbean societies, and it has attempted, through the medium of the short story, to demythify official history and to open avenues of communication—voices—through which women and the poor can question the otherness that has been imposed on them.

This preoccupation with finding ways to give voice to experiences not explored before in Caribbean literatures emerges poignantly in "Cotton Candy," where Dora Alonso, one of Latin America's most highly regarded short story writers, examines the voicelessness of repressed desire and its piteous consequences.

Lola, the forlorn heroine of the tale, wastes her life away, torn between her pathetic attempts at proclaiming a burning sensuality constantly doused by male fears of her torchlike desire, and by her mother's suffocating control. Lola's inability to express the wealth of feelings bursting within her is representative of women's preoccupation with the silencing of their voices that characterized the Caribbean literary tradition until well into the 1960s. This tradition's concern with the creation of a body of literature that articulated authoctonous interpretations of history and developing definitions of national identity led to the neglect and devaluation of women's writing, as the themes acceptable within the context of national formation—political development, agricultural reform, breaking the race barriers to education and the professions—often fell outside the boundaries of women's socio-historic experiences.

As Alonso's exploration of a woman's erotic silencing shows, Caribbean women writers have appropriated the erotic as a favored avenue for the articulation of their own socio-historic and political concerns. This is indeed the case in Ángela Hernández's entrancing "How to Gather the Shadows of the Flowers," where a woman's yearning to verbalize her erotic fantasy life—and progressively to withdraw into it—is narrated by her bewildered lower middle-class family. Hernández's often-humorous juxtaposition of Faride's erotic poetry with the family's middle-class dictums of propriety is characteristic of the treatment of female sexuality in these texts. Her fantasies provide Faride with the opportunity to transcend the narrow confines of her village society. In them she emerges as a sophisticated, worldly traveler, an ardent lover, a brilliant student, a theater-goer, all the things that her being female in a traditional Caribbean village has precluded. This very incongruity between her surroundings and her dreams provides the bittersweet humor of the text.

This use of humor surfaces again—with a heavy touch of irony—in Hilma Contreras's "Hair," the chronicle of a middle-aged man's growing obsession with his curvaceous young neighbor and her mane. Contreras's own juxtaposition of Luciano's feverish fantasies against his wife's matronly placidity lays the foundation for the somewhat unsettling punchline that marks the end of the story, which Contreras uses to satirize the many layers of male objectification of the female body in the text.

The story's humorous debunking of the role of women as sexual objects is representative of a growing openness in the themes acceptable in Caribbean literature, a recent development which parallels the emergence of women's movements in the region in the late sixties and early seventies. Ana Lydia Vega is a fitting heir to Contreras's humorous use of the erotic to articulate feminist content, as her story "ADJ, Inc." attests. The characters in "ADJ, Inc." parody male erotic language and postures, unveiling the absurdity of what is accepted as normal behavior in matters of gender relations and vividly revealing the class and race underpinnings that govern male/female relationships in the Caribbean. Vega's award-winning fiction offers countless examples of irreverently funny depictions of women's subversion of patriarchal, middle-class sexual mores. By often choosing as her characters lower middle-class or working-class women—traditionally excluded because of their race and class status from the chivalric protection afforded the virtue of white women of the upper classes—Vega subverts the accepted notions of respectability that have perpetuated patriarchal control: the very notions that had informed the tragic fate of the tormented virgin spinster of Dora Alonso's "Cotton Candy."

Caribbean women's claim of the erotic as a favored means of expression is an integral part of their demand for unrestrained access to the world of writing and books. This claim is the theme of Jean Rhys's "The Day They Burned the Books," the story of a young girl seeking to save books from the pyre to which they have been condemned by the unenlightened mother of her "special friend." The late Mr. Sawyer's library—a quintessentially English gentleman's library transported to a Caribbean setting—is also quintessentially a male space, and Mrs. Sawyer's dismantling and burning of a library that had been a more powerful rival than any mistress could have been is fueled by a hatred akin to that of the protagonist of "No Dust Is Allowed in This House" toward the wall built to confine her. Mrs. Sawyer's hatred for her husband's books, however, reaches fever pitch when faced with books by women. "[B]y a flicker in Mrs. Sawyer's eyes," the narrator tells us, "I knew that worse than men who wrote books were women who wrote books—infinitely worse. Men could be mercifully shot; women must be tortured."

The protagonist's yearning to be part of a world of books that transcends the racial and class constraints of Dominica's minuscule white society is mocked by her inability to find in the French book she manages to save from the pyre—a book she cannot read or understand but which bears the tantalizing title of *Fort Comme La Mort*—the key to admission into the well-guarded male realm of literary creation. Rhys's ironic, ambivalent playfulness concerning the relationship between women and the creation and understanding of texts—Mrs. Sawyer, for example, is described as "an awful liar" who can't make up a story to save her life, but who "makes up lies about people all right"—points to these writers' demythification of the supposed voicelessness of Caribbean women, a voicelessness that the irrepressible tales presented here resoundingly deny.

A significant number of the tales included in this collection are narrated from the vantage point of the folk or fairy tale, traditions to which women have had ready access in the domestic sphere. Of great importance to the development of a women's literature in the region is their manipulation and often reversal of the tropes of the indigenous folk tale and the European fairy tale.

The oral tale is represented in the collection by the anonymous "Tétiyette and the Devil," a funeral tale recorded as narrated by a young Guadeloupan woman in 1971. "Tétiyette and the Devil"—a story of a young girl who marries a devil despite her family's warnings and must be rescued by her brother when the devil attempts to eat her up—is reminiscent of the European tale of Little Red Riding Hood, complete with the slashing of the devil's belly from which the girl emerges "all whole." As a cautionary story, the narrative is fraught with ambiguities about women's sexual initiation and female independence, and is characteristic of the frequent depictions of women in the oral tradition as having to be rescued by males from the consequences of their imprudence and foolhardiness.

These assumptions of the folktale are laid bare by Rosario Ferré in her rewriting of stories from the Puerto Rican folk tradition. Ferré, an avid listener and reader of folk and fairy tales, has published several books for children which reinterpret the many stories she heard from her nanny as a child. Interested on the one hand in rescuing these stories from the threat of extinction, and on the other hand in rescuing her readers from the patriarchal and misogynistic elements of the oral tradition, Ferré's rewriting of folktales inscribes them in a new tradition, that of Caribbean feminism. Through her artful combination of traditional plots and narrative devices with unfamiliar, often anachronistic elements, she subverts the accepted views on women and the oppressed characteristic of the oral tradition. For Ferré, as for many Caribbean short-story writers of earlier generations—Florette Morand-Capasso, Virginie Sampeur, Lydia Cabrera, Ester Feliciano Mendoza, to name a few—the richness of the oral tradition has constituted the mainspring of literary creation. In one of her autobiographical essays, "The Writer's Kitchen," she narrates how, following the failure of her first attempt at writing a story, she used the remembered oral tales of her childhood as the source of her first successful text, "The Youngest Doll."

In "The Poisoned Story," the story included in this collection, Ferré draws upon two related traditions, the European fairy tale and the tales of the Arabian Nights. From the fairy tale Ferré borrows the familiar trope of the wicked stepmother seeking to separate the child from the father and his possessions. The story is complicated by its being transposed to a planter society where the age-old antagonism between stepmother and female child of the fairy tale is compounded by the race and class antagonisms which are the legacy of slavery and the plantation order. From the tales of the Arabian Nights Ferré borrows the trope of the printed page that poisons the reader when it comes in contact with the skin or the lips as the stepdaughter's means to destroy the lower class, pragmatic, materialistic stepmother who threatens to bring an obsolete, ruined planter and his family down to earth. Ferré's interest in incorporating the tales of the oral tradition, be they Caribbean, African, or European, into her literary work finds an echo in Myriam Warner-Vieyra's "Passport to Paradise" and Paulette Poujol-Oriol's "Red Flower," two stories that remain very close to their roots in the Caribbean oral tale. "Passport to Paradise," which narrates the victory of a group of Guadeloupan villagers over a Church bureaucracy that sought to restrict access to paradise to the rich and powerful, belongs in style and structure to the Anancy/trickster tradition—the Juan Bobo and Pedro Urdemalas tradition of the Spanish Caribbean—where the establishment's own rules are turned against it to accomplish its defeat. Among the elements the tale shares with that tradition are the villagers' faith in their own resources when faced with an external threat, their denunciation of the hypocrisy of the powers-that-be, their solid roots in the small plots that sustain them, the oneness of a community whose survival depends on their ability to act in concert, and their deeply ingrained optimism and humor.

Paulette Poujol-Oriol's story, different in tone and style from "Passport to Paradise," belongs to the tales of Guinea so prevalent in the Francophone oral tradition. A touching story of a young African man whose wife and fellow villagers are captured for transportation into slavery in the Caribbean, "Red Flower" is the only example in the collection of a story dealing with the ominous Middle Passage, and it draws on the rich store of tales of the lost African paradise disrupted by the white man that has played such a central role in maintaining alive, for an often illiterate audience, the vital connections of Caribbean peoples with Africa.

Similarly, Mirta Yáñez's "Of Natural Causes," though not drawn directly from the oral tradition, is dependent on the reader's familiarity with the legendary stories of the Haitian leader Mackandal and of his campaign of terror against the

French planters of the colony of Saint Domingue in the late eighteenth century. Yáñez's placement of the story's key scene during an old Haitian coffee picker's retelling of Mackandal's legends to a group of avid listeners gathered around a camp stove underscores the centrality of the tale to her story. The scene focuses on a well-off white planter's challenge to the veracity of the tales told by the old black man. There is in the story a clear thematic link between the oral retelling of the stories of Mackandal's triumph over the exploitative French planters—stories central to the Haitian, and indeed the Caribbean oral traditions—and the celebration of the triumph of the Cuban Revolution. Cuco Serrano's open challenge to that tradition mirrors his previous attempts to subvert and betray the Revolution, so that his destruction becomes symbolic of the triumph of both the people represented by Mackandal and the Cuban villagers who find such comfort and inspiration in his legend.

Marie-Thérèse Colimon-Hall's "A Pottage of Lentils" epitomizes Caribbean women's eclectic combinations of the oral, folk, fairy, and, in this case, biblical narrative traditions in their tales. "Borrowing" from multiple tropes from these traditions—the three sisters, the rambling dilapidated mansion, the recovery of the family's lost fortunes, the humble suitor turned charming prince coming to the rescue, the masking of the heroine's identity—Colimon draws the reader into a familiar world, which she then defamiliarizes through their placement in the non-fairy-tale-land of impoverished Haiti and through the open-ended conclusion, which leaves the traditional happy ending much in doubt. Colimon's framing of her narrative within the context of the biblical tale of Esau's relinquishment of his birthright for a pottage of lentils serves a similar purpose, as, next to the oral/folk/fairy tale tradition, the Bible is perhaps the only other narrative universally familiar to a Caribbean audience.

The Bible is indeed the only book in June-Plum's house in Opal Palmer-Adisa's "Widow's Walk," a book that she reads to her dying mother as a source of hope and courage, but also a book that underscores society's injunctions to women to conform and accept, as June-Plum's meditation on her many pregnancies in light of the Bible's exhortation to be fruitful and multiply indicates. In "Widow's Walk," however, folk culture is represented as a more vital force than the Bible in guiding the characters' lives. Through the representation of Yemoja, mistress of the sea, as the powerful rival to which June-Plum may have to surrender Neville, Palmer Adisa vividly renders the power of folk wisdom to reconcile humans to the beauty and violence of tropical nature. Fearing that Neville has drowned, but still hopeful that Yemoja may return him if properly appeased, June-Plum bows, as if in penance, to the sea: "She does this three times, then scoops up a handful of sea water and drinks it. She is beginning to understand Yemoja, more powerful than any person, including herself. She is a force of nature that prevails. Surrendering to her is not defeat; it's wisdom. June-Plum breathes more easily as she heads home."

Underlying these uses of the folk- and fairy-tale tradition is the preoccupation of Caribbean women writers with the problems of race and class that are the legacy of colonialism and slavery. In these stories, these conflicts are apparent in the representation of the solidarity between female characters, regardless of their class status, and the dispossessed peasantry. Such is the import of Michelle Cliff's "Columba," where the young female narrator eschews the privileges of the white and wealthy milieu of her guardian in favor of the company of the young black servant with whom she shares a perspective of disempowerment. "Columba" encapsulates the themes we have come to associate with Cliff's fiction: the denunciation of race and class privileges with their resulting exploitation of the black and poor, the anger at the impotence of being female and young, and the young female protagonist's concomitant alienation from her world. The comforting embrace of the young girl and the servant that ends the story is emblematic of this solidarity, a solidarity echoed movingly in Olga Nolla's "No Dust Is Allowed in This House."

In Nolla's story, the parasol/narrator's identification with her mistress finds a parallel in the mistress's seeking the mute comfort of her servants Eusebio and Margarita when confronted with their shared powerlessness before patriarchal power. A feminist story of overwhelming anger, "No Dust Is Allowed in This House" centers on a privileged plantation mistress who comes violently in conflict with a husband's power to isolate her and her beautiful family from any soiling contact with the underprivileged. As told by the loyal parasol whose responsibility has been that of preserving her mistress's "special paleness"—an uncontrovertible proof of her status as a lady—the story underscores white women's precarious position in Caribbean societies, poised as they are between the power of the white male to whom they are inextricably linked by race and class, and the peasantry and working class with whom they stand linked by their relative powerlessness. The negation of myriad aspects of her personality bursting to be expressed finds an outlet in her imagined bursting of the walls that isolate her, an explosion which prefigures, but does not promise, the possibility of freedom from patriarchal, racial, and class constraints.

More characteristic of the reality of the relations between Caribbean women is Phyllis Shand Allfrey's "Little Cog-burt," which depicts a white woman's unempathetic distress at seeing herself surrounded by black faces whose beauty she can only very unwillingly acknowledge. Allfrey's slow dissection of her character's racism is underscored through Moira's mirroring in her crippled soul of little Cog-burt's crippled hands—hands and soul that "will never grow any larger or stronger"—and through her uneasy relationship to Cog-Burt's uninhibited mother Ma'am Jovey. The story, with its sentimental albeit hard-hitting unveiling of the psychological nuances of racism, is but one example of the depiction of the seeming impossibility of relations of sisterhood between black and white women, separated by class as well as by race. It is a theme present in many of the stories included in the collection, whether as a central theme—as in Aida Cartagena Portalatín's "They Called Her Aurora" and Olive Senior's "Bright Thursdays"—or as an vital element of the characters' social landscape—as in Bea Vianen's "Of Nuns and Punishments" and Ramabai Espinet's "Barred: Trinidad 1987."

These stories—Olive Senior's "Bright Thursdays" particularly—

address the complexities of race relations in the Caribbean, where great significance is attached to relative skin color, and where the polar categories of black and white that characterize race relations in the United States are replaced by a broad spectrum of racial categorizations that runs the gamut between black and white. Laura, the protagonist of Senior's "Bright Thursdays," is a child whose destiny is sealed by the "whiteness" of her features: "Laura had come out with dark skin but almost straight hair which Miss Myrtle did her best to improve by rubbing it with coconut oil and brushing it every day, at the same time rubbing it with alcohol to keep it soft and make it 'clear.' Miss Myrtle made her child wear a broad straw hat to keep off the sun, assuring her that her skin was 'too delicate.'" Laura's "straight nose" and "long dark hair" are her tickets of admission to the relative affluence of her white grandparents' home, where she contemplates the white faces in the photograph gallery and "silently beg[s] pardon for being there." Her alienation underscores the survival of patterns of social relationships rooted in slavery and the plantation which still mar the possibilities of sisterhood in Caribbean societies.

Laura's victory over this alienation at the conclusion of "Bright Thursdays" recalls Hazel D. Campbell's "See Me in Me Benz An T'ing," with its intimation of a possible break of the deadlock of post-slavery, post-colonial relationships between women. The embrace extended to the Lady in the torched Mercedes Benz by the working-class women who had witnessed the mob's assault on her and her "Status Symbol"—an embrace that shelters her "into the safety of their humanity"—is emblematic of the possibilities of transcending the residues of colonial-bred relationships between black, colored, and white women. Campbell's story heralds a hoped-for era of sisterhood until now not evident in relations across class and race between Caribbean women.

These problems of class and race have been the result of plantation-bred economic structures that Caribbean societies have yet to transcend and which still hamper Caribbean socio-economic development. The myriad economic and political problems that have plagued these island-nations, the collapse of the sugar industry in many Caribbean islands in the 1940s and 1950s being perhaps the most obvious, resulted in a diaspora that brought millions of Caribbean migrants to settle in large metropolitan centers like New York, Montreal, London, and Paris, which were to become the centers of literary activity for the new migrant communities. Countless Caribbean women writers have experienced this diaspora and as many as half of the writers represented in this collection have lived for extended periods away from the island-homes where they spent their formative years. Some of them—Jamaica Kincaid, Michelle Cliff, Liliane Dévieux, Opal Palmer Adisa, Ramabai Espinet, Myriam Warner-Vieyra—appear to have permanently settled in their host countries.

The migration experience has consequently become a theme of special resonance for Caribbean writers, male and female, and is represented in several of the stories included in this collection, some of which begin to chart and analyze the delicate and complex process through which an island-oriented literature written from the perspective of exile becomes a literature of migration which responds to the experiences of Caribbean migrants in their new environments. Marie Thérèse Colimon-Hall's "A Pottage of Lentils" explores the push/pull factors leading to Haitian migration to New York City; Aida Cartagena Portalatín's "They Called Her Aurora: A Passion for Donna Summer" and Maryse Condé's "Three Women in Manhattan" depict the experiences of Caribbean women as domestic workers, and of their class-and-race-bound relationships with their white female employers, a theme that Jamaica Kincaid explores in her most recent novel, *Lucy*; Liliane Dévieux's "Piano-Bar" explores the ways in which women have found in the experience of migration the means to break away from the patriarchal aspects of Caribbean cultures which hampered their full development while remaining true to the nurturing values of their native cultures. In her refusal to return to Haiti from her exile home in Montreal, Eva, the aptly-named protagonist of Dévieux's story, embodies the spirit that gave birth to the dynamic Caribbean communities in exile. The process of adaptation to their new social environments may eventually cut individuals such as Eva, Aurora, and Claude from their Caribbean roots—that is too often the cost that exile exacts—but their voices articulate essential aspects of what has been a vital element in twentieth-century Caribbean history.

Seen as a whole, perhaps the most salient feature of the stories collected here is their presentation of the multiplicity of voices of Caribbean women: the mother in Jamaica Kincaid's "Girl," the aunt in Velma Pollard's "Parable II," the parasol of Olga Nolla's "No Dust Is Allowed in This House," the adolescent of Bea Vianen's "Of Nuns and Punishment," the ambivalent university student of Magali García Ramis's "Cocuyo Flower," the passionate, distressing voices of Ramabai Espinet's "Barred: Trinidad 1987." They stand in these texts as representatives of women observed, pitied, imagined, hated, and loved, and they linger with us long after our reading is done, reminding us of the accomplishments and the promise of Caribbean women's writing.

ACKNOWLEDGMENTS

We would like to express our deepest appreciation to the authors of the stories included in this collection for their interest in our project and their generosity; and to our translators—Daisy Cocco de Filippis, Thomas Spear, Hilda van Neck-Yoder, Diana Vélez, and Betty Wilson—for their professionalism and respect for deadlines. Special thanks are due to Olga Torres-Seda for the bibliography that accompanies this text, as well as for her handling of dozens of interlibrary loan requests and her expert assistance in locating journals and magazines for us. Amelia Lau Carling prepared the map of the Caribbean.

We are indebted to Fred Nichols of the CUNY Graduate Center for his assistance in identifying authors from the Dutch Caribbean; to Carol Boyce Davis of SUNY Binghamton, Maximilien Laroche of Lavalle University, Betty Wilson and Marie-José Tzengo-Tayo of the University of the West Indies, Elaine Savory Fido of New York University, Hilda van Neck-Yoder of Howard University, and Thomas Spear of Lehman College for their help in locating authors; to Robert Loomis of Pace University for his assistance in locating copyright holders; and to Julie Comella and Gene Homicki of Data Methods Incorporated for their generous technical assistance. We are grateful to our friends and colleagues: to Evelyn Ackerman of Lehman College for bringing our work to the attention of Rutgers University Press; to Joan Dayan of the CUNY Graduate Center and Reginetta Haboucha of Lehman College for their willingness to listen and share their knowledge of Caribbean literature and folklore respectively. We are grateful to Pamela Mordecai for her permission to use the poem that inspired the title for the collection; to El Museo del Barrio, especially to Petra Barreras and Arlene Dávila; and to María Jara, who keyed in the manuscript so diligently.

Thanks are due to a special young woman, D'Arcy Alise Gebert, for her endless walks to the post office, and for photocopying, collating, and performing countless other tasks that freed us to work on the manuscript.

Our deepest thanks go to Leslie Mitchner, Executive Editor at

Rutgers University Press, for her enthusiasm for the project.

Most of all, we thank our husbands, James Kraus and Gordon Alan Gebert, for their encouragement, support, patience, and constant help—from reading and sharing their feelings about the stories with us, to cooking, shopping, cleaning, babysitting, and myriad other tasks. Thanks.

For their permission to reproduce copyright material we thank: Pantheon Books, a division of Random House, Inc., for Dora Alonso's "Cotton Candy," from *Fragment from a Lost Diary and Other Stories* (1973); Hazel D. Campbell for "See Me in Me Benz An T'ing"; Michelle Cliff for "Columba"; Ramabai Espinet for "Barred: Trinidad 1987"; the University of Nebraska Press for Rosario Ferré's "The Poisoned Story," from *The Youngest Doll and Other Stories* (1991); Jamaica Kincaid and Farrar, Straus and Giroux, Inc., for "Girl," from *At the Bottom of the River* (1983); Pamela Hitchins Mordecai for "A Poet's World"; Opal Palmer Adisa and Kelsey Street Press for "Widow's Walk," from *Bake-Face and Other Guava Stories* (1986); Velma Pollard and The Women's Press for "Parable II," from *Considering Woman* (1989); Wallace Literary Agency for Jean Rhys's "The Day They Burned the Books," from *The Collected Stories of Jean Rhys* (1987), copyright 1974 by Jean Rhys; Longman Group UK for Olive Senior's "Bright Thursdays," from *Summer Lightning and Other Stories* (1987); and Aunt Lute Books, Ana Lydia Vega, and Diana Vélez for "ADJ, INC.," from *Reclaiming Medusa: Short Stories by Contemporary Puerto Rican Women* (1988).

For translation rights we thank: Éditions Nubia for "Tétiyette et le diable," from *Contes de mort et de vie aux Antilles* (1976); Aida Cartagena Portalatín for "La llamaban Aurora (Pasión por Donna Summer)"; Marie-Thérèse Colimon-Hall for "Le Plat de lentilles"; Maryse Condé for "Trois femmes à Manhattan"; Hilma Contreras for "La cabellera"; Liliane Dévieux for "Piano-Bar"; Magali García Ramis for "Flor de cocuyo"; Ángela Hernández for "Cómo recoger la sombra de las flores"; Présence Africaine for Jeanne Hyvrard's

"Station Opéra. Six heures du soir. Pendant des mois . . . ," and Myriam Warner-Vieyra's "Passeport pour le paradis," from *Femmes Echouées* (1988); Olga Nolla for "En esta casa no puede haber polvo"; Éditions Seghers for Paulette Poujol-Oriol's "Fleur rouge," from *Les Fantômes de Philomène* (1989); Astrid H. Roemer for "Lola of het lied van de lente"; In de Knipscheer Publishers and Bea Vianen for "Over Nonen en straffen"; and Mirta Yáñez for "De muerte natural."

For permission to print previously unpublished material we thank the Estate of Phyllis Shand Allfrey for "Little Cog-burt."

All translations done for this book are copyrighted in the names of the translators.

GREEN CANE

AND

JUICY FLOTSAM

This tale from Guadeloupe, recorded by Ina Césaire and Joëlle Laurent for their collection Contes de mort et de vie aux Antilles, *belongs to the rich oral tradition of Caribbean funeral tales. Narrated during the long wakes characteristic of the region, they differ from other types of tales in that they address an adult audience and are almost exclusively told by male* conteurs. *"Tétiyette and the Devil," however, has the distinction of having been recorded as told in Creole by a seventeen-year-old Guadeloupan girl.*

ANONYMOUS

Tétiyette and the Devil

Once upon a time there was a woman who had only one girl-child.

That child was very hard to please, and found no one to her taste. One day a goat came to the woman's house for a drink of water. He said: "Good morning, Madame, a bit of water to drink, if you please." The woman called her child, whose name was Tétiyette, and said: "Tétiyette, give the goat something to drink."

The young girl came out, picked up the most beautiful of her silver cups and gave the goat to drink from it. Afterwards the mother said to the young girl: "Tétiyette, Tétiyette, that goat wants to marry you!" The young girl replied: "I want nothing to do with him, I want nothing to do with him, make him go away, he eats grains!"

The following day a pig went walking by, came in, and said: "Good morning, Madame, a bit of water to drink, if you please." The woman went out, picked up the most beautiful of her daughter's silver cups, and had him drink from it. The pig asked if he could see her daughter. The woman said: "That's not up to me, but to her." She said: "Tétiyette, Tétiyette, a pig is asking for you, a pig is asking for you." The young girl said: "Make him go away, make him go away, I want nothing to do with him."

But there was a devil roaming the neighborhood. For a long time he had been wanting to eat up the young girl. He put on very, very, very beautiful clothes. He decked himself in gold. He wore all the gold he owned. He wore his best suit. He came to the house and said: "Good morning, Madame, a bit of water to drink, if you please." The woman went out, picked up her daughter's most beautiful silver cup, and gave the gentleman water to drink. The man asked the woman if she had a daughter. The woman said she did. He asked if it was possible to see her. The woman replied: "That's not up to me, but to my daughter!" The woman said: "Tétiyette, Tétiyette, a young man is asking for you." The young girl looked down to see the young man, and found a good-looking gentleman.

She was pleased. She said: "Have him come up, have him come up, I want him!" The man came up and they sat in the living room. They talked. He asked her to marry him. She said yes, she'd be pleased to, and the man said to her: "If you'd like, we can choose a date for the wedding immediately." The girl agreed. They chose a date for the wedding.

After that the devil left. The woman said: "Tétiyette, no man can be that beautiful! Here, your mother is going to give you a pin and a handkerchief. At night, after you go to bed, you will stick your husband with it. If blood flows, he's a human being, but if slime oozes out, he's a devil."

They got married, and that night, while the man slept, the young girl did as her mother had told her. When she stuck her husband, slime oozed out. She took the handkerchief, washed it carefully, and the next morning she stuck herself with the pin. Blood flowed. She said to her mother: "You see, I didn't lie to you. There's the blood!" The mother replied: "Fine! that's good!"

Several days went by. They lived pleasantly together until one night the husband started to eat up the young girl. The man had a seven-story house. The girl lived on the seventh floor and the rest of the people lived on the second floor. That night, the devil started eating up the young girl. She started to cry out:

Oh, Mama! Oh, Mama! Bel-air drum!
The man to whom you married me, Bel-air drum!
Is a terrible devil! Bel-air drum!
He's eating me up! Bel-air drum!

Her husband replied:

Oh, Mother-in-law, Mother-in-law! Bel-air drum!
Your daughter doesn't know what she's saying, Bel-air drum!
I'm only playing with her, Bel-air drum!
It's just that she doesn't love me, Bel-air drum!
It's just that she doesn't like my caresses, Bel-air drum!

The mother was in bed. She did not say a word. Her daughter cried out:

Oh, Papa! Oh, Papa! Bel-air drum!
The man to whom you married me, Bel-air drum!
Is a terrible devil! Bel-air drum!
He's eating me up! Bel-air drum!
He's swallowing me! Bel-air drum!

The mother said: "Harry, Harry! Don't you want to go see what's happening to our daughter?" Her husband replied: "Agh! I don't give a damn! I had already warned her to beware." But during that time, the devil continued to eat up the young girl. The only thing left for him to eat were her last two toes. But the girl also had a brother. She sang out:

Oh, Little Brother, Little Brother! Bel-air drum!
The man to whom they married me, Bel-air drum!
Is eating me up! Bel-air drum!
Is swallowing me! Bel-air drum!

The brother was lying down. He wanted to get up but at the same time he didn't want to. He went to wake up his mother and his father: "Papa, Mama, little sis' voice has changed; she sounds very different from before." The father replied: "Agh! I don't give a damn! I had already warned her to beware." The mother said: "As far as I'm concerned, I had also warned her to beware."

The little brother said: "Oh no! Oh no! She's my sister, she's my only sister and she's being eaten up! Oh no! Oh no!" He went to the kitchen and there he grabbed a very big and very sharp knife. He climbed up the staircase, twenty steps at a time. When he reached the room, the devil had swallowed half of his sister's last toe. He slit the devil's belly with one single blow, and his sister emerged all whole.

Translated by Lizabeth Paravisini-Gebert

Phyllis Shand Allfrey was born in Dominica in 1908. While in England in the 1920s she joined the Fabian Society and the British Labour Party. Back in Dominica in the 1950s, she founded the Dominican Labour Party. She was Minister of Labour and Social Affairs for the short-lived West Indian Federation, and was editor of the Dominica Herald *until 1965, when she began publication of an opposition paper,* The Star, *which cultivated local writers. She is best known for her 1953 novel,* The Orchid House. *"Little Cog-burt," of which Allfrey was extremely fond, has been repeatedly broadcast on West Indian radio, and is published here for the first time. Allfrey died in 1986.*

PHYLLIS SHAND ALLFREY

Little Cog-burt

She held the scissors out to him, and her fingers (like her lips) drooped and looked peevish. "Cut off at least six inches," she said, as if the effort of speaking, even to a husband, was too great. He obediently gave a preparatory snip-snip, pausing to study for the last time vivid sunlight on her shoulder-length hair.

"At least six inches!" She was impatient. "I'm so *desperately* hot."

"For the Christmas tree fairy . . ." the minute he'd spoken, he could have snipped off his own tongue. Why had the word Christmas risen like that, out of his rather matter-of-fact subconscious? Ah, because of the poinsettia trees: only a minute before he'd walked across the enclosed garden and seen their green sturdy promise. A fine blaze of poinsettias for Christmas, and there will be a full moon, too, had been his involuntary inner comment: he remembered those expensive silver and vermillion cards, the ones reserved for non-religious older friends. Of course in those days he'd never seen poinsettia bushes growing practically wild beneath a stone wall.

By the tense look of her neck as he lifted the blond sheaf, he knew how he had hurt her. But after all it was an accustomed ritual, and ritual always means memory. In England the same thing had happened every year, at the end of the children's summer holidays. "Cut off a few inches of my hair, please, Richard." (She didn't trust hairdressers.) He would perform the shearing, carefully, reluctantly; and when he stood away from her with the lovely writhing in his hand, she would gaily cry: "For the Christmas tree fairy!" Every year they made a new doll with a pink silk face and pleated cellophane dress, and Moira had sewn the living tress to its little head, binding it with a silver fillet: the children had cut out a star for its forehead and made a tiny wand.

This year, of course, the children were three thousand miles away, invisibly and implacably growing away from childhood.

"Curse it!" he exclaimed. "These scissors must be blunt." But he really meant that *he* was blunt; and proceeded to underline his bluntness in the most appalling manner.

"I think we ought to give a party for the children on the estate," he said with a sort of tender brutality. (If you are smashed in a plane crash, you should go up again immediately. If you're afraid of horses, just step up and stroke one, praying that it won't kick you: that was the way he had been brought up.) Because he had reached the stage of straightening-up operations, when tiny clippings fell like gold ash on the veranda, he pretended not to notice her shudder.

But she shook her hair free, and it was so thick that it looked squared; she faced him, the petulance in her eyes burning somber. "I won't do it," she said. "Why should we?"

"Because we no longer live in Esher, and I'm no longer a bank manager. Running this peculiar old copra plantation has its obligations. Everybody else gives a party for their laborers' children. It's considered patriotic."

Anyone could see by the wrinkling of her nose what she thought of the laborers' children and of patriotism.

"Well, I won't," she said again, firmly; and in the words which she did not add, but which he so clearly heard her thinking: "I won't give a party for those dark children, those dark children, those dark children . . ." She leaned her elbows on the railing and looked towards the poinsettia bushes, seeing perhaps two healthy Anglo-Saxon girls dash across the terrace and disappear into emerald shade. "Mother!" they cried, "Mother! Don't forget us, suffering at boarding school, making aunts and cousins suffer during the holidays! Don't give a party for the dark children, whatever you do!"

He handed her the shining relic. "Very well, darling," he said with deceptive acquiescence, going indoors to pour them both a drink, for it was nearly sunset; they kept the rule about not drinking until sundown, but made up for such restraint during the evening.

Moira straightened herself with the languid ease which excessive heat gave her a right to indulge. Before she would drink with him she'd burn the hurtful sheaf in her hand. But where? She went into the kitchen: there was no fire. One can't burn either incriminating letters or locks of hair on an electric cooker. The house did not possess a single fireplace. There was a lavatory, of course, but that was degrading. Besides, it was such lovely material . . . she stroked it, as women stroke silks when they are out shopping. On her dressing table there was a wooden box full of ribbons. She lifted the lid and settled the thing there, like a sleeping tortoise-shell cat. "Now I can forget it," she said, running a comb through her lightened locks, feeling liberated. She went down to him, and they lifted their glasses. Somehow she had not expected him to look so sad. "Am I letting you down?" she asked softly.

He did not reply, but laid his cheek against her shorn hair.

She turned and kissed him. "It's just their horrid swarthiness," she sighed. "Ours are so fair—and so far."

"Ours are as fair as toothpaste and honey and theirs are like lumps of toffee," said Richard.

"But perhaps they're not such bad little things. I expect their parents dote on them," she murmured in a false surrendering voice. "All except that revolting little Cog-burt," she could not resist adding honestly. Right at that moment the idea came into her head that because Cog-burt was so horrible she would give him the biggest present of all, a huge rubber ball which Aunt Jane could send out with the new linen: but she would only do this because she couldn't let Richard down.

Cog-burt's mother was their laundress, a great broad mahogany woman who had several lovers (gossip reported) and whose other children had died in infancy. Cog-burt had actually been named Cuthbert in appreciation of a new governor, but although the nobility of his naming might have aided his survival, it did nothing else for him. He was a miserable whining little boy with a potbelly and matchstick legs, who dragged along behind his enormous mother. "I do think," Moira said to Richard, "that a laundress ought to wash her own child, don't you?" Ma'am Jovey didn't waste any of her sewing skills on him either, though she seemed fond of the boy. While she sat on the veranda step and helped Moira to stitch name-tapes on the new sheets (doing it so deftly that one forgot her monstrous sausage fingers), little Cog-burt would crouch several yards away, clothed in a couple of split seams, peeping up mistrustfully now and then—he was afraid of Moira. "Cog-burt looks rather sickly," Moira (who had once been a hospital nurse) would say to Ma'am Jovey. "Cog-burt suffer," said Ma'am Jovey. "What does he suffer from?" "Oh, he suffer from worms, or so they say," Ma'am Jovey would reply: and Moira would shrink into the house, repelled.

She did not let Ma'am Jovey and Cog-burt or even Richard and the maids see her making the Christmas tree fairy. Actually she was ashamed of herself for giving in. She made its pink face beautifully, embroidering a tolerant smile on it, and though she could hardly understand the dialect of the dark children, she thought that on the afternoon of the party she would hear their admiring excited voices exclaiming in wonder that the fairy had *real hair*. Richard, of course, did all the penultimate preparing; he had the tact not to say anything as he tied the fairy with a reef knot to the tip-branch of the casarina tree, that tree which was so nearly like a frost-nipped Christmas tree, and yet not quite like one.

[The sun's] yellow radiance was streaming in (nearly time for our drinks, thought Moira—what a nuisance!), and soon the laborers' children streamed in too, through the back door. A few familiars had the nerve to plod up the front stone steps and cross the polished floors to huddle beside the wonderful tree, its arms full of little knobbly shining gifts, its trunk nearly hidden by larger and plainer parcels. They marched in like swarthy gnomes in their best clothes, but they did not say anything at all: they were either struck dumb or had been told roughly to behave themselves and keep quiet. Really Moira was forced to admit that some of them were very handsome when they were washed and dressed. But their silence made her jittery; she began to look unhappy, to think of the fair children who always danced and shrieked on these occasions, dragging their friends into a tangle of festivity. Richard, feeling her misery, came up with a glass of sherry. "Turn on the radio, darling," she asked him. But the only station he could get was a Spanish-American one broadcasting on conditions in the Panama Canal. Switching it off, Richard addressed the children, like a headmaster on opening day.

They knew his voice: it reassured them; the brown maids, smiling, were passing around glass saucers of ice cream; the party began at last to get going; but until the time came for the giving of presents it didn't seem like a party at all.

With the opening of the presents, everything was excitingly different. "This is for you, it came all the way from England in a ship." What a father's gift Richard had for saying the right thing! "For me?" They untied the knots carefully. Little girls hid packages under their skirts, unwilling to bare them to the public eye. Little boys tore at crackly paper and flung it on the floor; they began to race across the room and compare gifts, quite like the fair children after all; some of them even laughed.

The radio, appealed to again, emitted some wavering carols from the United States. Mothers waiting in clusters at the front door started humming. "Give them a drink—get out the rum!"

cried Richard to the maids. He went over to Moira. "Well, my darling, don't you think they're all happy now?" "All happy except me," was what she hadn't the heart to say to him; her heart in fact was in a suburban English house and her mind was on a local cocktail party they promised to attend—as soon as the dark children were out of the way.

"Yes, as happy as anything," was what she said, compelling herself to look around the room again, noticing little Cog-burt dressed in a tremendous cut-down suit, moping behind the stripped tree. She forced herself to go forward. "Cog-burt, haven't you had your present—your lovely present?" she asked him. But he was not used to that wheedling tone in her: his shoes were painful; he shrank away. She could have burst with the idiocy of it all. Picking up the great round package tied in crimson, she held it out to him: but he kept his hands clasped behind his back. She looked around for Ma'am Jovey. "Fetch his [mother," she said to Richard, and he led Ma'am Jovey] up the stairs, a tumbler in her great hand.

"Give little Cog-burt his gift, please," Moira commanded, disclaiming responsibility for that other being whose misery (judging by his huge pitiful eyes) so nearly outstripped her own. Ma'am Jovey had to stoop to get at the little boy, and her drink dripped onto his mute face. She chucked him under the chin with the large parcel, but he did not respond. "See, Cog-burt," said Richard reasonably (for Moira was bidding goodbye to the other satisfied smiling children), "See, Cog-burt, this is a grand ball. Let me unwrap it for you." But awkwardly Cog-burt began to cry, as he often did, a horrid snivelly little noise and a wetness of eyes and nose. His mother, gulping her rum, bent to him again. He bleated out a few plaintive unintelligible words, and Ma'am Jovey gave a mountainous shrug. "He say he don't want the ball, sir." "Well, you take it home. He may want it later. Perhaps he's shy," said Richard, knowing that the word shy was a fantastic understatement. "No, sir, he not shy, sir. He talk funny."

"What *does* he want, then?" cried Moira, coming to them through the emptying room, stealing up like an irritable ghost as the first moonlight shone on a blaze of poinsettia petals in the garden.

"He say he want the angel off the tree. The angel with hair like madam's," Ma'am Jovey blurted out in an excess of reproachful amusement.

Richard looked at Moira; Moira looked at Cog-burt; Ma'am Jovey looked at her empty glass, and Cog-burt looked with his sad dripping eyes at the Christmas tree fairy. "Let him have it—shall we?" Richard ventured, not wanting to upset Moira, feeling in a trouser pocket for his penknife; but Moira had already climbed on a chair and cut off the fairy, twig and all, with her pair of scissors. "After all," she said severely, as if to a critic, "he was the only child who really *noticed* it." But she hated to give it to him. She genuinely hated to pass it over to the horrible little boy. She hesitated, and for all the world would have thrust the delicate wisp into Ma'am Jovey's sausage hand and run from the room, out into the warm moonlight. No, she had to go through with it, she couldn't let Richard down, Richard who was watching her so oddly.

"He had foot-cramp," said Ma'am Jovey.

What a small Negro boy he was, to cause all that fuss! He was so small that Moira had to kneel on the floor to make her ridiculous presentation. She tossed back over her shoulder: "I'm not surprised he wouldn't accept the ball. He could never have got his arms around it." For now, stiffly as a child in a trance, little Cog-burt had unpinned his arms from his spine and held them halfway out; the coarse sleeves were like tents.

Moira gave the hair of her Christmas tree fairy a last stroke to remind little Cog-burt how precious it was; then she laid the light glistening thing competently in his minuscule hands—hands (as she now saw, being close to him at last) that would never grow any larger or stronger.

Dora Alonso was born in Matanzas, Cuba, in 1910. She has been an active contributor to many Latin American journals. A prolific writer, Alonso has published novels, short stories, and children's literature and has won numerous literary awards thoughout Latin America. Her first novel, Tierra adentro, *won the Premio Nacional de la Dirección de Cultura, and she received the 1961 Casa de las Américas Prize for* Tierra inerme. *Alonso's fiction, particularly that written before 1959, offers poignant and powerful depictions of marginalized characters struggling against an alienating reality or a corrupt society, and have often focused on the exploited Cuban peasantry.*

DORA ALONSO

Cotton Candy

The butterfly was dancing above the trees. It would fly down, lighting on a radiant morning glory; gather its wings, making them vibrate with a delicious quiver, and at the same time, move its light legs over the wine-colored petals. In flight again, it would land on the edge of the cotton candy machine.

Lola, fascinated, watched the yellow butterfly. At once she took in the juicy acrid smell of the cubalibre branches, which she parted with her childish hands. The butterflies were falling under the green whip, dying, astonished, and young Lola was gathering her fragile harvest to offer to her first love. Donato was ten years old; he rode a bike and whistled in a strange, compelling way because of his cleft palate. Donato, recipient of dead butterflies given by the girl in an occult rite, which not even Donato knew about.

From butterfly to butterfly. Donato, Domingo, Dionisio, Daniel, Danilo, David. And more and more. Lola had her fifteenth birthday, sighing under a steady rain of winged corpses, on her hair, her hands, her budding breasts. At night the sheet that covered her was a shroud seeded with wings and a luminous powder which threatened to soar in flight, taking her up in the air to where cats meowed among angels and owls.

A growing young woman under the domination of a tyrannical mother, Lola grew wild in the quiet settlement of Minas, gathering dreams which went back to Donato when she was seven. At twenty, the accumulated names shouted among bands of butterflies drove her crazy.

Every day, under the weight of a repeated and unconsummated guilt, she wanted to go with the cats and the angels; but her hot flesh got tired just with the sewing machine pedal and the rags which necessity made her sew. At midnight she would leave her bed to go out, like a sleepwalker, onto the patio. Hearing the buzzing of the feverish beehives, Lola burned among the honey and the gyrations, wanting to sink her teeth into the sweetness full of stings. Almost insane, she would invoke the names of the telegraph operators, train conductors, rural guards, circus men, traveling salesmen, cousins, and friends whom she tirelessly loved in great secrecy.

Every week the only prostitute in town would come secretly to see the tormented seamstress; she always came very early, tired and smelling of bed and tobacco. Between them they chose attractive patterns from fashion magazines. Their relationship was established on the basis of the respectability of the loose woman, who employed manners and words of an exaggerated refinement, and on feigned ignorance on Lola's part. When they finished choosing a pattern for a dress, they would exchange recipes, or talk about the existence of spirits and their apparitions, while also gossiping about weddings and baptisms. The seamstress's mother was present during the visit, taking part in the innocent gossip which smelled of cumin and bright light. And when the time came for the dress to be tried on, the eyes and nose of the virgin would seek traces of guilt in the naked flesh of her best client.

The constant tightening and loosening of dreams and realities were gradually deforming the young woman. Laden with adornment triplicated by her anxiety—necklaces, old ribbons, rouge, long rhinestone earrings—showing off her small feet, she would go to dances where few men asked her to dance. An instinctive defense drove them from the ardent virgin, as a devouring and persistent pyre is avoided.

The monotonous years, for her repetitions of frustrations and renewed desires, killed her grandparents and uncles, and forced her relatives to emigrate. Her lonely forty years fought then, like a dog biting its chain, and her mother agreed to move to Havana. The two women would soon understand that Luyano was no better than Minas. For ten more years Lola struggled to have a man in either of two ways: "Marry me," or "I'll set you up in a room." But her mother, going against nature, hung onto her with equal obstinacy and drowned Lola's last murmurs of necessity.

On her mother's death, the spinster felt an alleviating remorse which made her dissolve into tears. She was alone now, but it was late. Lola would have struggled a little longer with the sewing, but her eyes refused to go on. In order to earn a living she sold fabrics and cosmetics door to door, but she offered such good terms that she ended up selling lottery tickets. Her hair was gray by then, and the wrinkles began to devour her face.

Giving reasons to herself, she became used to the circumstances, accepting the hard buffetings of life without suffering too much. Her bread arrived wrapped in an Official List, and each Saturday the voice of a child from the orphanage, or of a young blind man, who would choose the lucky number while turning the lottery box filled with numbered balls, would announce the winner. She ended up picking a site near the zoo, as a handy place for buyers of single or whole sheets of lottery tickets. Kind, smiling, with a big pocket in her skirt where she kept her change, she would cry out the numbers with her nasal voice. At the end of the day she would ride the bus to Luyano, to the same shack where she had always lived.

As removed from politics as Simon the Dwarf, she did not have to fight in any way to get the benefits of the new era. She entered through the same door that solved the economic anguish and the unfortunate life of the humble vendors in the zoo. Lola was assigned a stall to run the cotton candy machine. For the first time she felt secure and could look around her peacefully. The old lady ate her bread without having to worry about the next day.

Every morning she very politely greeted the other employees; the hundreds of them who went hurriedly on their way to the different businesses in the park. She was by now nothing but wrinkles and bags, crowned with an ugly mane tarnished by a permanent. A big woman with a thick waist and straight, fat, pianolike legs, arms with hanging flesh, and feet that walked twisted like a wild parrot. But in spite of herself, there was a certain virginal aspect about her disheveled figure: a seal of something well-kept, aging without rendering any service.

The routine work allowed her to free her secret parades, which followed her throughout her long spinsterhood like a consuming plague. While filling the metal spoon with sugar, pouring it in the electric centrifuge, and forming a great cone by curling the white threads around a stick, she would indulge in unending daydreams.

Old already, she built a refuge with all she had not been allowed to live. As others recall their actual memories, Lola unearthed phantoms and butterflies.

The large human family of the zoo took a liking to her and enjoyed embarrassing her by telling her dirty jokes. Being a good woman, she would render small services and gossip about work and events of the park.

Lola needed several years to discover the background and the different relationships of the life surrounding her. It was in the spring that she glimpsed it in its limited fullness. She didn't tell anybody, but she tuned her ears, her eyes, on trees, beasts, birds. Always in wait, with each pore like a hungry mouth.

She would go to sleep wishing it was time to go back to work. When she finished work, she would use any pretext to stay longer and go slowly through the zoo in order to look with newborn pupils at the cages.

A new existence seemed to animate the animals, and she

discovered and felt love in every corner and over her head. The inexpressible, contagious atmosphere fascinated her. With the beginning of the spring cycle the beasts became beautiful like the trees and the light. And the favored season inflamed the caresses of the turtledoves and the light blue of the tiny birds from the village of San Diego; it brought together the claws of the eagles and the crowns of the herons.

Whistles, like darts, rent the air. The exalted tenderness preceding desire began and the old woman, with her parrot feet, was a wandering elf in its pursuit.

The music of the ringdove was heard at all hours, and of the white, red-breasted dove. Hummingbirds nested in Lola's ecstatic eyes.

The zoo buzzed like the distant beehives in Minas, with the bellows of the deer, reborn in his bristling hide, lapping his timid female. In the cave, forgetting her captivity and the noisy avenue, the gray bear, sitting on her haunches, attracted and kissed, sucked her mate, from the forehead to the mouth, the mouth . . .

The ancient virgin of the cotton candy looked blindly for any encounter with whatever sang or roared limitless love. She would be still for long periods, scrutinizing her newly discovered feelings. In the well-kept prison was born the unmatched joy of heat and mating.

Lola waded though the lukewarm preludes, searching with unsure steps for the deep water of unhampered sex. The forgotten dizziness of her youth returned with the strength of a llama, who mounts his female for a very long time, hurting her. With the lasciviousness of the chimpanzees before the monstrous flower of the female; with the modesty of the spider monkey who tantalizes the imagination. With the incredible variations of the orangutans, masters of the science of the brothel; contortionists, enjoyers, human in the art of extracting from sex its rich variations. They would roll on the ground intertwined, a ball of pleasure, distilling it, silent, surrendered. Lola, followed by the furious ghost of a mother, wanted to flee, but she would stare and stare, tense, full of anguish, her mouth metallic, her knees buckling, and her face red with shame.

Her quiet blood would grow to a high tide with the repetitions of the acts. They were weeks of communal delirium in which she went from bough to cage, from one animal to the next; to the ferocious surrenders of the coupled lions who, roaring, would tear at each other, to the crosses between tiger and lion, which gave birth to ligers and tiglons.

It was the time when the guards were afraid—of the new rhythm, the delirious fights, of the seeding.

The season of love transformed the intimate hours of the spinster. Lola returned to her two-strand necklaces; to her long, glittering earrings; to her rouge; to her small, high-heeled shoes stuffed with her overflowing feet. She would pin flowers on her blouse and use French perfumes.

During the last spring she craved a hand mirror and went to look for one in the knickknack shops, among an extravagant scramble of dust-covered objects. The mirror was a beautiful piece of embossed silver, with cupid and fawn motifs and a beautiful glass surface. She kept it in her purse, and looked at herself covered with makeup and trinkets like a barbarian queen.

Last May, after eight years of mixing the sugar threads, of sighing with the birds and the beasts, of mixing her history, her ghosts, her butterflies with the colors of the birds' plumage and the breath of the beasts in love; one Dionysian morning in which the four thousand inhabitants of the zoo seemed to copulate in unison, in which the feverish pupils seemed to sparkle, sexes palpitate, and the painted Egyptian touracos, which the rains discolor, were floating in nuptial flight, Lola had an encounter with the Jockey.

The Jockey found her by the food stalls, and Lola saw a young man: smooth face, his teeth intact, sparkling eyes, muscular neck without jowls or wrinkles. . . . She blinked in surprise. So afraid . . . ! He said something like, "You're drunk," and she shrugged her shoulders without answering. She was looking straight at the old black man in charge of the kangaroos and the llamas, who was approaching on the other side of the path. Julián seemed to be made of light and ebony. New from head to toe, the beautiful black man.

Lola hurriedly opened her purse and her hand shook as she took the mirror out.

From the polished moon surface the girl from Minas smiled at her.

Translated by Myrthe Afelia Chabran

Hazel Dorothy Campbell was born in Jamaica and has worked as a teacher and public relations officer. Her first published story appeared in the Sunday Gleaner *in 1970. Since then she has published two collections of stories—*The Rag Doll and Other Stories *(1978) and* Woman's Tongue *(1985)—and has won numerous literary prizes. Campbell's deceptively simple fiction explores the function of religion in the shattered cultures of the Caribbean. It is a fiction characterized by an ambiguous sense of doom and resurrection under a veil of social commentary.*

HAZEL D. CAMPBELL

See Me in Me Benz An T'ing

Like the Lady Who Lived on That Isle Remote

The Lady of the house sucked her teeth angrily as she put down the telephone.

"Carl knows I can't stand driving down to his factory," she complained loudly.

"Why doesn't he just send the driver for the car!" She gestured in annoyance. "In a hurry, my foot!"

The maid dusting the furniture nearby didn't comment as she knew her place better than that. In any case she wasn't being directly addressed.

"Don't forget the upstairs sitting room," the Lady ordered, suddenly turning her annoyance on the maid. "Yesterday I ran my finger over the TV up there. Absolutely filthy! Don't know why it's so difficult to get you people to do an honest day's work."

Carl had absolutely ruined her day, the Lady pouted. She would be late for the session with the girls and miss all the nice gossip. Furthermore Carl knew that she hated driving through the section of the city where he worked. So much violence, and all those people glaring at her in hostility as if she were personally responsible for the squalor in which they lived. Like wild animals some of them with their uncombed heads and crazy talk. Watching her as if any minute they would attack. No wonder the papers were always full of horrible stories about them. Now she wouldn't even have time to do her nails and she had so wanted to show off the new shade Sylvia had brought back from Miami for her. Damn that Carl!

Quarrelling with the maid, the gardener, and the two Alsatians blocking her path to the car, she gathered her purse and her keys and got into the sleek black Status Symbol which had been resting in the double carport.

The 4.3 liter, V8 engine sprang alive and settled into a smooth purr before she eased into reverse, turned it around, and put it into drive to make the long trip from home on the hilltop to workplace by the seashore. It gathered speed as she rolled down the hill, and, as always, she felt a tiny moment of panic at the strength of the horsepower growling softly under the bonnet, controlled only by the swift movement of foot from accelerator to brake as necessary. Carl had promised her this car if ever he was able to buy a newer one, but since 1972, no new models had been allowed into the island so she had to be content with the Mazda, which didn't satisfy her vanity half as much as the Status Symbol did.

Annoyance returned sharply as she imagined how the girls would have exclaimed when she drove up in the Benz.

"Eh! Eh! How you manage get Carl to part with his car?" they would tease. And she would explain that the Mazda was in the garage so she had to borrow the Benz, pretending with them that it was these great big problems which made life so difficult. Then they would settle down to a nice chat about the Number of Things they were having to do without! And Who had just gone, or Who had decided to! And pass a pleasant hour or so laughing at the kinds of things some people were packing into trailers. And had they heard that Jonesie was working in a shoe store in

Miami as a sales clerk! No! God forbid! And my dearing, and oh dearing each other, they would with large eyes contemplate life in the '70s in Jamaica, each realizing, but not saying that they did not know how to come to grips with it.

As the Lady skirted the Sealand trailer parked at the foot of the hill, she remembered that she wanted to renew her campaign to get Carl to migrate. After all he could even pack the factory machinery in the trailer, she thought, and they could relocate in Florida. Lots of other people were doing it. Things were really getting impossible. Imagine, not even tampons in the shops. Good thing she knew many people who were still commuting between America and Jamaica, so she could get a ready supply of the things she absolutely couldn't do without.

As she passed through Half-Way-Tree, the Lady collected her wandering thoughts. She would need all her concentration to get safely through the congested parts of the city she would soon be entering. Just last week a friend of theirs had been pulled from his car and savagely beaten because he had scraped somebody's motorcycle with the car.

She made sure all the doors were locked, touched the power button for the windows, and turned on the air conditioning. She was always grateful for the ability to lock up herself in the car. Lock out the stenches of gutters and overcrowded human flesh. Lock out the sounds of human distress. From the cool, slight dimness of the red interior of the Status Symbol, even the sight of distress took on a sort of unreal appearance, so she could pass through uncontaminated.

A little past Half-Way-Tree, she hesitated a moment before deciding to turn down Maxfield Avenue. She hated cutting across Spanish Town Road, but this way was shorter, and Carl had said to hurry. That was why he hadn't sent somebody for the car. The double journey would take too long. She had wasted enough time already, so she would have to hurry. She was afraid of Carl's bad temper. He would lash out at her even in front of the factory staff if he was sufficiently annoyed. She was sure it wasn't all that important for him to get the car. Probably some luncheon or other for which he needed the Status Symbol to impress somebody. He wouldn't dream of driving one of the small company cars. Not him. No matter how it inconvenienced her.

By the time she reached the first set of lights, the traffic had already begun to crawl. Not much use her ability to move from 0 to 60 miles per hour in ten seconds flat, here. Not much use all that horsepower impatiently ticking under her restraining foot. Thank God for the air conditioning, she thought again.

As she waited for the green light, the billboard on top of the shop at the corner caught her eye; "LIFE IS A MUTUAL AF-FAIR," it read. Somebody ought to tell Carl that. Instead of dragging her through this horrid part of town he should be protecting her. Any moment now a bullet could shatter the glass and kill her.

She spent a moment indulging her overactive imagination, seeing her blood-splattered breast and she leaning back as still as she had seen a body in some film or other. The impatient horn behind her made her suddenly realize that the lights had changed.

She moved off quickly, smiling at her melodramatic thoughts. Actually she wasn't feeling too afraid. After all, didn't Carl do this trip every day? And if there were problems outside, she couldn't hear.

That group of people milling around outside that shop, for instance, she couldn't see what was creating the excitement and since she couldn't hear either, what did it matter? They were like puppets in a silent movie. In fact she could not decide what they were doing. Was it a dead man they were looking at?

Christ! Her imagination! She really must do something about it, she thought. Wonder if she was getting off. Lots of people getting crazy these days, because of all the stress and strain, she'd heard. They were probably just fassing in somebody's business as usual, idle bitches that they were. Look at those on that other piazza. Winding up themselves and gyrating to some beat loud enough to penetrate her castle of silence. That's all they were good for. And those others milling around the betting shop, race forms in hand. How could the country progress with so many idlers never wanting to do any work? And even those who said they worked couldn't do a thing. Her annoyance deepened as she thought how she couldn't get Miriam to clean the bathrooms properly. No amount of telling did the trick. No matter how often she told her what to do. No matter what amount of cleaning things she bought.

The traffic began to crawl again as she neared Spanish Town Road. Just at the part she would have liked to pass over quickly. Now she had plenty of time to look out through her smoky glass at unreality.

Another billboard. Advertising Panther. Good-looking youth, she thought. Not like the dirty bums cotching up the walls, the lampposts, and any fence strong enough to bear their weight. The Panther boy looked like somebody who would care about life and not spawn too many children. But what did he have to do with these dirty creatures passing as men around the place? Giving all those worthless women thousands of children by the minute. Silly ad, she thought. Silly place to put it.

Ah! There was her favorite on the other side. Beautiful clouds and a jet taking off into the sunset—FASTEST WAY TO CANA-DA—She liked to think about that. Escape from the closing-in feeling of Jamaica. It was only a matter of time, her friends were saying, before all of Kingston and St. Andrew looked like these dumps around her. Zinc fences hiding poverty and nastiness, hate and crime. Smells she could only imagine now. People living, no, not living, existing on top of each other. God forbid that she should ever live like that. That she should even live close to this. Bad enough to have to drive through.

Suddenly she realized that none of the cars was moving, neither up nor down, and that there was an unusual amount of people on the streets even for this crowded area.

What could be the matter? she thought in alarm.

Then she noticed the driver in front of her turning up his car windows in haste, seconds before she saw the first part of the crowd running between the cars. Running in her direction.

Oh God! She prayed softly. Had it finally happened? Were they going to get her? Stories she had heard about riots and those who got caught in them raced through her thoughts.

But even in her panic she still felt fairly safe. Wasn't she protected in her air-conditioned car? People were swarming around like the cartoon figures on Spider Man, the TV show her children were always watching. And she was looking on at the action, as if she were in a drive-in movie, with a larger-than-life screen surrounding her. But even as she watched, the sounds of their distress began to filter into her castle.

She wondered what was happening, but dared not open her window to find out. To do that would be to let in reality which would force her to think and act. Better to stay locked up in the car and hope that whatever it was would allow her to get moving soon.

In the distance she saw something like a wisp of smoke and thought perhaps it might be a fire. But why would the people be running away from it? And why did they look so frightened?

And even as she noticed their fright it turned to anger right before her eyes. One minute they were running away from something, wave after wave of them. The next, like a freeze in a movie, a pause, long enough to allow anger to replace fright. A turn around. And then hell breaking loose.

She could tell by the shape of their mouths that they were angry. By their swoops for weapons that they were angry.

From nowhere, it seemed, sticks, stones, and bottles appeared and began to fly around.

The car, she panicked. They would scratch the car, and what would Carl say? That the damn ducoman wouldn't match the shade and he would have to do over the whole car—if there was any duco available? Funny how Carl's anger about a scratched car was more real to her than the anger of the mass of people milling around about her, getting hurt, hurting and going mad with anger for what reason she didn't even know.

The traffic going in the opposite direction had somehow managed to move on, and those behind her were frantically trying to turn around to escape the mob.

The Lady tense and nervous put the car into reverse and put her finger on the horn hoping that they would clear the way for her to turn around. But all she did was to bring down their wrath on her. The reality of their anger began to reach her when she felt the human earthquake rocking the car. A human earthquake fed by anger. Anger now turned against the Status Symbol in their midst. The out-of-place Symbol.

The driver before her had abandoned his car. The doors were wide open with people like ants tearing off the wings of an injured beetle. Oh! God! There was one of the madmen trying to open her door to pull her out. To destroy her. She didn't need to hear them yelling, "Mash it up! Mash it up!" She shut her eyes in pain as the shattering sound reached her and the stone which had smashed the windscreen settled on the seat beside her, letting in reality. The reality of angry sounds, angry smells, demented faces, and nightmare hands grabbing her.

She didn't hear herself screaming as they dragged her from the car, roughly discarding her to fight as best she could. They weren't interested in her. Only in the Symbol. The Symbol must be destroyed. The insulting Symbol, black as their bodies, inside red as their blood.

Mash it up! Not just a scratch. Damage it beyond repair. Rip out its red heart. Turn it over. And just to make sure, set it on fire. Destroy it forever.

The Lady stood in the crowd, assaulted by forgotten humanity, and she still didn't feel their reality. She was remembering the day her husband had brought the car home. The first year the factory had made a profit he had ordered this car to celebrate. "This is the symbol, Baby," he'd said. "The symbol that we've arrived." That was why, between them, they jokingly referred to it as the Status Symbol.

Her feelings now were tied up with the Symbol's destruction. Her blood scattered in the streets. Her flesh being seared by the fire. And the sudden roar of the flames as the Symbol caught fire, pulled a scream of animal rage from the very bowels of her.

But the roar of the sacrifice quieted the mob's anger. As quickly as they had come they began to melt away.

The Lady didn't notice. The Lady didn't hear herself bawling. Neither did she feel the gentle hands of the two old women steering her away from the scene of her destruction.

"Thank God is only the car!" they whispered, as they hurried her away from the street, down a lane, and into a yard. They took her behind one of the zinc fences, into the safety of their humanity. "Sometimes the people them not so fortunate," they murmured as they bathed her cuts and bruises and gave her some sweet sugar and water to drink. "You is lucky is only this happen to you."

And they didn't ask her name. For them it wasn't important who she was. She needed help and they gave what they could without question, fear, or favor.

Born in Moca, Dominican Republic, in 1918, Cartagena Portala-
tín pursued advanced studies in music and theory at the School
of Plastic Arts in Paris. During the early period of her career she
was a member of the poetic group "La Poesía Sorprendida." She
was a valiant supporter of intellectual freedom during the harsh
period of the Trujillo dictatorship, and founded the press Brigadas
Dominicanas to publish the works of local authors. She has served
as director of the Museo de Antropología in Santo Domingo.
Keenly interested in the marginalization of women and blacks in
Caribbean societies, Cartagena Portalatín has chosen as her
themes the constraints of women's traditional roles and the
struggle against racial and class injustices.

AIDA CARTAGENA PORTALATÍN

They Called Her Aurora

(A Passion for Donna Summer)

Mom used to call me Colita. Colita García. But Mistress Sarah
enrolled me in school under the name of Aurora. Forget the
name Colita, she screamed. Deep inside I was still Colita, but to
others I became Aurora. I'm never going to forgive her the way
she laughs sarcastically when she calls me Aurora, putting me
down, because she who has renamed me Aurora has never seen
the light of dawn. No. Noo. And nooo. I'm not going to stay here
with her, in her house, it's true she pays for my studies, that she
tells everyone I'm so talented, but I'm fed up with her and with
the sisters at school, that Sister Fátima, a skinny beanpole like
that Twiggy on TV, and the Mother Superior, wise but with looks
like those of Sancho's Aldonza, constantly nagging me with her
theorems, her triangular rectangles, her parallel lines, and her

punishments and phone calls—screw you Colita-Aurora—to make Mistress Sarah hound me like a pack of mad dogs. No. Noo. And nooo. No!

I said no. I don't love Mistress Sarah and I don't care about her beautiful home, I'm not growing old inside her four walls like a tree without juices, rotting away. No. I'm not going to stay with her like a tree burning up during the dog days of summer. No. I'm not going to stay sad, crestfallen, like the leaves on the trees pounded by gales and thunderstorms, within these four walls surrounded by green lawns and fruit trees. Nor am I going to put up with that broken record about how Aurora is a smart little black girl, or about how Negroes amuse me, or about Negroes with their jazz and their rhythm, or about how Negroes bring joy to the world, and go to the store and bring me Donna Summer's latest album, after all Negroes must have something to do, and it's just fine for them to entertain whites. No. Noo. And nooo. I like Donna Summer's never-ending music, all that nonstop wailing and howling, cascading like a vibrant and exciting waterfall. But it's not true that Mistress Sarah is going to keep me forever inside her thrilling jukebox, of jazz and boogaloo, of ragtime, beguine, etc. She is too old for that crap. She thought I wasn't going to leave, I'd like her to see me rushing to the bus stop, dragging a heavy bundle with my clothes and my books. Stop here, driver, I'm getting off in Haina. I walk a little, breathing sugar-cane air. I sit at Candita's Restaurant, where I have a very cold Seven Up. Hunger, that's what's wrong with me, and I move on to La Enana's Bar, where I have a Pepsi and eat two rolls. I leave in a hurry. Donna Summer's music fills the hut and spreads over the entire neighborhood. How well I remember that never-ending cascade of howls. The music and her voice fill the hut and the entire neighborhood, that very same beat that convulses and excites Mistress Sarah. To hell with all that, but here I am, exactly fourteen kilometers from the capital. It's seven o'clock in the evening, I enter the church and hide behind the altar of San Isidro, the farmer's son who controls the water and the sun. Let the saint cover me, let them not discover me. Holy, Holy, Holy. The streets are teeming with the unemployed and the homeless. La, La, La, La, Yeah, Yeah, Yeah.

Leaning against one of the walls at La Enana's, a young woman sways. Donna's voice swells as the lottery ticket seller raises the volume in the jukebox. Once again Donna's voice fills the bar, the neighborhood, the town. I try to put up my hair, kinky, stiff, if that's what I was born with, that's the way it'll stay. What doesn't make sense is how they can put me down while at the same time they brag about my smarts, because I'm almost done with high school. No. Noo. And noo. No! It kills me to see how many millions of whites enjoy listening to Donna Summer, the exciting young black singer. Once they were crazy about Armstrong, later on it was Makeba. All that jazz and all that rhythm which springs up so happily! Congratulations! But if I was Donna Summer, I'd pick up all the records from the stores, the dance halls, cabarets, hotels and motels, and the homes of the beautiful people.

I take off to work as an au pair, talked into it by the missis of a sugar technician, and here in New York, on this eleventh floor, I cook, wash, iron, run errands, put up with the bullshit that the deli owner, that Italian son of his mama, dishes out while he pulls my hair and calls me an ugly little black girl . . . asking me where I come from, and that and the other. Or the gringa's Colita, what took you so long? I explain to her that the son of his mama delays me or that I stopped to watch a Giordano stabbing a Manfredi, all over whether a body should be taken to the Manfredis' funeral home, while the policeman calmly explains that the stiff is a Giordano.

I decide to gather my thoughts like in those classified ads by Denis W. published in papers all over the world. They filled my head with ideas about this being the Free World, and I find myself here exploited like a slave by that gringa from Ohio. I don't understand this business of a Free World or of Exploitation, Colita, you're so ignorant, yes, I knew nothing of monopolies—I just buy my bras at Woolworth's, with their 300 stores, their manufacturing and sales—I knew nothing of the comings and goings of the police, policemen here, policemen there, policemen everywhere, I scream, stop it you, to someone who is touching my—Do you know what I mean? I'm sick and tired of watching you drink shots of tequila behind the old Mexican's counter, and this happens here where there are so many policemen, so many ITTs, here, from where they spread CIAs all over the world—daily violence, daily tortures—an unemployed, homeless guy, dazed as if he was high, beaten up just because he's acting funny, and he lets them beat him up, that's not the way Dominican machos behave. The policeman is acting tough, as if this was a cowboy movie. If this is the Free World, overabundant, overexploited, I'd rather be alienated. And no, noo, and no! I leave and I go back to Mistress Sarah and her constant music, Donna Summer's music, to face the same shit, the same put-downs: you're talking nonsense. And she screams and howls when I read in the paper about the injustices they commit against blacks in South Africa. Not happy with the lynchings in Soweto and Johannesburg, they mutilated Steven Biko in a prison cell in Pretoria. Mistress Sarah grabs me by the hair, and she screams as hard as she can: you're talking nonsense, you're talking nonsense. And she drags me to the record player, and raises the volume as high as it will go. Now I can't even hear myself cry. And Donna Summer's voice, her black woman's voice, fills Mistress Sarah's house, jolting it with its rhythm.

Translated by Daisy Cocco De Filippis

Michelle Cliff was born in 1946 in Jamaica. She is the author of two collections of prose and poetry, Claiming an Identity They Taught Me to Despise *and* The Land of Look Behind, *and of two highly regarded novels,* Abeng *and* No Telephone to Heaven. *She has been the recipient of several fellowships in creative writing, and is internationally known for her essays, articles, and lectures on racism and feminism. Her latest book is a collection of short stories,* Bodies of Water *(1990). Among the central concerns of Cliff's prose and poetry are the issues of race, class, and color that have played such a negative role in women's lives in the Caribbean and the United States.*

MICHELLE CLIFF

Columba

When I was twelve my parents left me in the hands of a hypochondriacal aunt and her Cuban lover, a ham radio operator. Her lover, that is, until she claimed their bed as her own. She was properly a family friend, who met my grandmother when they danced the Black Bottom at the Glass Bucket. Jamaica in the twenties was wild.

This woman, whose name was Charlotte, was large and pink and given to wearing pink satin nighties—flimsy relics, pale from age. Almost all was pink in that room, so it seemed; so it seems now, at this distance. The lace trim around the necks of the nighties was not pink; it was yellowed and frazzled, practically absent. Thin wisps of thread which had once formed flowers, birds, a spider's web. Years of washing in hard water with brown soap had made the nighties loose, droop, so that Charlotte's huge breasts slid outside, suddenly, sideways, pink falling on pink like ladylike camouflage, but for her livid nipples. No one could love those breasts, I think.

Her hair stuck flat against her head, bobbed and straightened, girlish bangs as if painted on her forehead. Once she had resembled Louise Brooks. No longer. New moons arced each black eye.

Charlotte was also given to drinking vast amounts of water from the crystal carafes standing on her low bedside table, next to her *Information Please Almanac*—she had a fetish for detail but no taste for reading— linen hankies scented with bay rum, and a bowl of soursweet tamarind balls. As she drank, so did she piss, ringing changes on the walls of chamber pots lined under the bed, all through the day and night. Her room, her pink expanse, smelled of urine and bay rum and the wet sugar which bound the tamarind balls. Ancestral scents.

I was to call her Aunt Charlotte and to mind her, for she was officially *in loco parentis*.

The Cuban, Juan Antonio Corona y Mestee, slept on a safari cot next to his ham radio, rum bottle, stacks of *Punch*, *Country Life*, and something called *Gent*. His room was a screened-in porch at the side of the veranda. Sitting there with him in the evening, listening to the calls of the radio, I could almost imagine myself away from that place, in the bush awaiting capture, or rescue, until the sharp *PING!* of Charlotte's water cut across even my imaginings and the scratch of faraway voices.

One night a young man vaulted the rail of a cruise ship off Tobago and we picked up the distress call. A sustained *SPLASH!* followed Charlotte's *PING!* and the young man slipped under the waves.

I have never been able to forget him, and capture him in a snap of that room, as though he floated through it, me. I wonder still why that particular instant? That warm evening, the Southern Cross in clear view? The choice of a seachange?

His mother told the captain they had been playing bridge with another couple when her son excused himself. We heard all this on the radio, as the captain reported in full. Henry Fonda sprang to my movie-saturated mind, in *The Lady Eve*, with Barbara Stanwyck. But that was blackjack, not bridge, and a screwball comedy besides.

Perhaps the young man had tired of the coupling. Perhaps he needed a secret sharer.

The Cuban was a tall handsome man with blue-black hair and a costume of unvarying khaki. He seemed content to stay with Charlotte, use the whores in Raetown from time to time, listen to his radio, sip his rum, leaf through his magazines. Sitting on the side of the safari cot in his khaki, engaged in his pastimes, he seemed like a displaced white hunter (except he wasn't white, a fact no amount of relaxers or wide-brimmed hats could mask) or a mercenary recuperating from battle fatigue, awaiting further orders.

Perhaps he did not stir for practical reasons. This was 1960; he could not return to Cuba in all his hyphenated splendor, and had no marketable skills for the British Crown Colony in which he found himself. I got along with him, knowing we were both there on sufferance, unrelated dependants. Me, because Charlotte owed my grandmother something, he, for whatever reason he or she might have.

One of Juan Antonio's duties was to drop me at school. Each morning he pressed a half-crown into my hand, always telling me to treat my friends. I appreciated his largesse, knowing the money came from his allowance. It was a generous act and he asked no repayment but one small thing: I was to tell anyone who asked that he was my father. As I remember, no one ever did. Later, he suggested that I say "Goodbye, Papá"—with the accent on the last syllable—when I left the car each morning. I hesitated, curious. He said, "Never mind," and the subject was not brought up again.

I broke the chain of generosity and kept his money for myself, not willing to share it with girls who took every chance to ridicule my American accent and call me "salt."

I used the money to escape them, escape school. Sitting in the movies, watching them over and over until it was time to catch the bus back.

Charlotte was a woman of property. Her small house was a cliché of colonialism, graced with calendars advertising the coronation of ER II, the marriage of Princess Margaret Rose, the visit of Alice, Princess Royal. Bamboo and wicker furniture was sparsely scattered across dark mahogany floors—settee there, end table here—giving the place the air of a hotel lobby, the sort of hotel carved from the shell of a great house, before Hilton and Sheraton made landfall. Tortoise-shell lampshades. Ashtrays made from coconut husks. Starched linen runners sporting the embroideries of craftswomen.

The house sat on top of a hill in Kingston, surrounded by an unkempt estate—so unkempt as to be arrogant, for this was the wealthiest part of the city, and the largest single tract of land. So large that a dead quiet enveloped the place in the evening, and we were cut off, sound and light absorbed by the space and the dark and the trees, abandoned and wild, entangled by vines and choked by underbrush, escaped, each reaching to survive.

At the foot of the hill was a cement gully which bordered the property—an empty moat but for the detritus of trespassers. Stray dogs roamed amid Red Stripe beer bottles, crushed cigarette packets, bully-beef tins.

Trespassers, real and imagined, were Charlotte's passion. In the evening, after dinner, bed jacket draped across her shoulders against the soft trade winds, which she said were laden with typhoid, she roused herself to the veranda and took aim. She fired and fired and fired. Then she excused herself. "That will hold them for another night." She was at once terrified of invasion and confident she could stay it. Her gunplay was ritual against it.

There was, of course, someone responsible for cleaning the house, feeding the animals, filling the carafes and emptying the chamber pots, cooking the meals and doing the laundry. These tasks fell to Columba, a fourteen-year-old from St. Ann, where Charlotte had bartered him from his mother; a case of condensed milk, two dozen tins of sardines, five pounds of flour, several bottles of cooking oil, permission to squat on Charlotte's cane-piece—fair exchange. His mother set up housekeeping with his brothers and sisters, and Columba was transported in the back of Charlotte's black Austin to Kingston. A more magnanimous, at least practical, landowner would have had a staff of two, even three, but Charlotte swore against being taken advantage of, as she termed it, so all was done by Columba, learning to expand his skills under her teaching, instructions shouted from the bed.

He had been named not for our discoverer, but for the saint buried on Iona, discoverer of the monster in the loch. A Father Pierre, come to St. Ann from French Guiana, had taught Columba's mother, Winsome, to write her name, read a ballot, and know God. He said he had been assistant to the confessor on Devil's Island, and when the place was finally shut down in 1951 he was cast adrift, floating around the islands seeking a berth.

His word was good enough for the people gathered in his seaside chapel of open sides and thatched roof, used during the week to shelter a woman smashing limestone for the road, sorting trilobite-form rock. On Sunday morning people sang, faces misted by spray, air heavy with the scent of sea grapes, the fat purple bunches bowing, swinging, brushing the glass sand, bruised. Bruises releasing more scent, entering the throats of a congregation fighting the smash of the sea. On Sunday morning Father Pierre talked to them of God, dredging his memory for every tale he had been told.

This was good enough for these people. They probably couldn't tell a confessor from a convict—which is what Father Pierre was—working off his crime against nature by boiling the life out of yam and taro and salted beef for the wardens, his keepers.

Even after the *Gleaner* had broadcast the real story, the congregation stood fast: he was white; he knew God—they reasoned. Poor devils.

Father Pierre held Columba's hand at the boy's baptism. He was ten years old then and had been called "Junior" all his life. Why honor an un-named sire? Father Pierre spoke to Winsome. "Children," the priest intoned, "the children become their name." He spoke in an English as broken as hers.

What Father Pierre failed to reckon with was the unfamiliar nature of the boy's new name; Columba was "Collie" to some, "Like one damn dawg," his mother said. "Chuh, man. Hignorant smaddy cyaan accept not'ing new." Collie soon turned Lassie and he was shamed.

To Charlotte he became "Colin," because she insisted on Anglicization. It was for his own good, she added for emphasis, and so he would recognize her kindness. His name-as-is was foolish and feminine and had been given him by a *pedophile*, for heaven's sake. Charlotte's shouts reached Columba in the kitchen. He was attempting to put together a gooseberry fool for the mistress's elevenses. The word *pedophile* smacked the stucco of the corridor between them, each syllable distinct, perversion bouncing furiously off the walls. I had heard—who hadn't?—but the word was beyond me. I was taking Latin, not Greek.

I softly asked Juan Antonio and he, in equally hushed tones, said, "Mariposa . . . butterfly."

Charlotte wasn't through. "Fancy naming a boy after a bird. A black boy after a white bird. And still people attend that man. . . . Well, they will get what they deserve," she promised. "You are lucky I saved you from that." She spoke with such conviction.

I was forbidden to speak with Columba except on matters of household business, encouraged by Charlotte to complain when the pleat of my school tunic was not sharp enough. I felt only awkward that a boy two years older than myself was responsible for my laundry, for feeding me, for making my bed. I was, after all, an American now, only here temporarily. I did not keep the commandment.

I sought him out in secret. When Juan Antonio went downtown and while Charlotte dozed, the coast was clear. We sat behind the house under an ancient guava, concealed by a screen of bougainvillea. There we talked. Compared lives. Exchanged histories. We kept each other company, and our need for company made our conversations almost natural. The alternative was a dreadful loneliness; silence, but for the noises of the two adults. Strangers.

His questions about America were endless. What was New York like? Had I been to Hollywood? He wanted to know every detail about Duke Ellington, Marilyn Monroe, Stagger Lee, Jackie Wilson, Ava Gardner, Billy the Kid, Dinah Washington, Tony Curtis, Spartacus, John Wayne. Everyone, every name he knew from the cinema, where he slipped on his evening off; every voice, ballad, beat, he heard over Rediffusion, tuned low in the kitchen.

Did I know any of these people? Could you see them on the street? Then, startling me: What was life like for a black man in America? An ordinary black man, not a star?

I had no idea—not really. I had been raised in a community in New Jersey until this interruption, surrounded by people who had made their own world and "did not do business" with that sort of thing. Bourgeois separatists. I told Columba I did not know and we went back to the stars and legends.

A Tuesday during rainy season: Charlotte, swathed in a plaid lap-robe lifted from the *Queen Mary*, is being driven by Juan Antonio to an ice factory she owns in Old Harbour. There is a problem with the overseer; Charlotte is summoned. You would think she was being transported a thousand miles up the Amazon into headhunter territory, so elaborate are the preparations.

She and Juan Antonio drop me at school. There is no halfcrown this morning. I get sixpence and wave them off. I wait for the Austin to turn the corner at St. Cecilia's Way, then I cut to Lady Musgrave Road to catch the bus back.

When I return, I change and meet Columba out back. He has

promised to show me something. The rain drips from the deep green of the escaped bush which surrounds us. We set out on a path invisible but to him, our bare feet sliding on slick fallen leaves. A stand of mahoe is in front of us. We pass through the trees and come into a clearing.

In the clearing is a surprise: a wreck of a car, a thirties Rover. Gut-sprung, tired and forlorn, it slumps in the high grass. Lizards scramble through the vines which wrap around rusted chrome and across black hood and boot. We walk closer. I look into the wreck.

The leather seats are split and a white fluff erupts here and there. A blue gyroscope set into the dash slowly rotates. A pennant of the Kingston Yacht Club dangles miserably from the rearview.

This is not all. The car is alive. Throughout, roaming the seats, perched on the running board, spackling the crystal face of the clock, are doves. White-Speckled. Rock. Mourning. Wreck turned dovecote is filled with their sweet coos.

"Where did you find them?"

Columba is pleased, proud too, I think. "Nuh find dem nestin' all over de place? I mek dem a home, give dem name. Dat one dere nuh Stagger Lee?"

He points to a mottled pigeon hanging from a visor. "Him is rascal fe true."

Ava Gardner's feet click across the roof where Spartacus is hot in her pursuit.

Columba and I sit among the birds for hours.

I thank him for showing them to me, promising on my honor not to tell.

That evening I am seated across from Charlotte and next to Juan Antonio in the dining room. The ceiling fan stirs the air, which is heavy with the day's moisture.

Columba has prepared terrapin and is serving us one by one. His head is bowed so our eyes cannot meet, as they never do in such domestic moments. We—he and I—split our lives in this house as best we can. No one watching this scene would imagine our meeting that afternoon, the wild birds, talk of flight.

The turtle is sweet. A turtling man traded it for ice that morning in Old Harbour. The curved shell sits on a counter in the kitchen. Golden. Delicate. Representing our island. Representing the world.

I did not tell them about the doves.

They found out easily, stupidly.

Charlotte's car had developed a knock in the engine. She noticed it on the journey to the ice factory, and questioned me about it each evening after that. Had I heard it on the way to school that morning? How could she visit her other properties without proper transport? Something must be done.

Juan Antonio suggested he take the Austin to the Texaco station at Matilda's Corner. Charlotte would have none of it. She asked little from Juan Antonio, the least he could do was maintain her automobile. What did she suggest? he asked. How could he get parts to repair the Austin; should he fashion them from bamboo?

She announced her solution: Juan Antonio was to take a machete and chop his way through to the Rover. The car had served her well, she said, surely it could be of use now. He resisted, reminding her that the Rover was thirty years old, probably rusted beyond recognition, and not of any conceivable use. It did not matter.

The next morning Juan Antonio set off to chop his way through the bush, dripping along the path, monkey wrench in his left hand, machete in his right. Columba was in the kitchen, head down, wrapped in the heat of burning coals as he fired irons to draw across khaki and satin.

The car, of course, was useless as a donor, but Juan Antonio's mission was not a total loss. He was relieved to tell Charlotte about the doves. Why, there must be a hundred. All kinds.

Charlotte was beside herself. Her property was the soul of bounty. Her trees bore heavily. Her chickens laid through hurricanes. Edible creatures abounded!

Neither recognized that these birds were not for killing. They did not recognize the pennant of the Kingston Yacht Club as the colors of this precious colony within a colony.

Columba was given his orders. Wring the necks of the birds. Pluck them and dress them and wrap them tightly for freezing. Leave out three for that evening's supper.

He did as he was told.

Recklessly I walked into the bush. No notice was taken.

I found him sitting in the front seat of the dovecote. A wooden box was beside him, half-filled with dead birds. The live ones did not scatter, did not flee. They sat and paced and cooed, as Columba performed his dreadful task.

"Sorry, man, you hear?" he said softly as he wrung the neck of the next one. He was weeping heavily. Heaving his shoulders with the effort of execution and grief.

I sat beside him in silence, my arm around his waist. This was not done.

Marie-Thérèse Colimon-Hall was born in Port-au-Prince, Haiti, in 1918. She began her writing career as a playwright and published five plays between 1949 and 1960. In 1974 she published her first novel, Fils de misère. *She has also written essays, short stories, and children's literature. Colimon's keen observations of the Haitian people's struggle against poverty give a particularly poignancy to her work, as* Fils de misère *demonstrates. In* Les Chants des sirènes, *her collection of short stories, she explores the painful impact of the Haitian diaspora on both the individuals in exile and the Haitian community.*

MARIE-THÉRÈSE COLIMON-HALL

A Pottage of Lentils

And Jacob was making pottage: and Esau came from the field, and he was faint:

And Esau said to Jacob, "Feed me, I pray thee, with pottage, for I am faint . . . ."

And Jacob said, "Sell me this day thy birthright."

And Esau said, "Behold, I am at the point to die: and what profit shall this birthright do to me?"

And Jacob said, "Swear to me this day," and he swore unto him, and he sold his birthright unto Jacob.

Then Jacob gave Esau bread and a pottage of lentils.

Genesis, 25:29-34

"Pan American World Airways announces the arrival of Flight 427 from Miami!"

The airport quivered like a forest in the minutes preceding a downpour. Quick steps glided over the wooden floor. Voices calling out here and there merged with the roar of the engines on the runway nearby. And the suppressed sobs, the boisterous goodbyes, and the tearful recommendations composed a strange rhapsody.

There were those who were simply leaving. There were those who were flying away. There were those who were running away. There were those who were fleeing. Some of them, unemployment and misery; others, failure and disillusionment.

Those forced to leave by their relatives because they gave more trouble than they were worth mingled with those leaving in quest of the diagnosis of hope, the panacea of a last chance. Those looking for a place far away to hide their shame rubbed shoulders with those going to drink from the very wellspring of Science. There were those deceiving everyone, the indifferent as well as their loved ones, pretending to leave on a short vacation when they knew full well they were leaving for good. Those who were hungry; those who had had enough; those who had nothing; those who had too much; those who had sold every-thing; those who had sold themselves; those who had things to sell and were going to offer them to the white man, on his home ground; those who had stolen money to "steal away," so as to be able, at long last, to fly with their own wings.

Many of them had spent that very morning in their offices or shops, signing their log-in books, letting themselves be seen, calmly going about their business at their post, so that nobody would know they were leaving until the last moment. (It is a well-known fact: one is not sure one is leaving until one sets foot in the plane, and the tiniest wisp of straw can ground the fantabulous flight.) So, until the zero hour, mum's the word. Otherwise, goodbye calf, cow, pig, brood; envious people place obstacles in your way, and you find yourself stuck on your native soil, having, to top it off, lost your means of subsistence since, faced with rumors of your impending departure, your employer would have dispensed with your services.

Some of them were wearing their Sunday best as if to go to a cousin's wedding: their best suits, knock-'em-dead spiked heels; others, flaunting their disdain for travel outfits, sported the nonchalance of frequent travelers who no longer spare their clothing any thought. There were those who, prudently, or because they had been warned, carried heavy coats on their arms. But there were others who, ignorant or unconcerned, were leaving with bare heads, lightly dressed, to set foot to the ground in their shirt sleeves in the dead of winter. There were those leaving in search of a title or a name. There were those that sought to drown theirs in the great beyond of anonymity. There were those who spoke English like Shakespeare himself, and there were those who signed their names with an X. Those whose papers were not in order crouched in a corner, lying low, shriveled up. They had been told that once there they must lead a clandestine life, and taking that advice to the letter, had begun, while still on their native soil, to make themselves as inconspicuous as possible, trying to pass unnoticed.

Those who had just been married, those who were going to get married; those leaving determined to get pregnant—the sure guarantee of residency papers; those forsaking husbands and children, all for the single goal of being admitted, accepted into the Promised Land, had given themselves an appointment in the vast antechamber of the coveted country: the airport. Some of them anticipated the voyage in an airplane with apprehension; others affected a casual air as they faced the steel bird, symbol of their destiny.

But for all, poor or less poor, young and less young, men as well as women, this was the pinnacle of their hopes and dreams. All, in sum, could see looming in the horizon, at the conclusion of their flight, on the other side of the Atlantic:

"A pottage of lentils"

The captivating siren's song promised it to them in all shapes and forms. And these men, and these women, spellbound by those enchanting voices, rushed in pursuit of that fantabulous dish that would satisfy their hunger forever.

At the far end, on a bench by the wall, Aglaé Labédoyère and Mathilde Ardoiun kept their distance from the crowd. The latter wore the immaculate cap and uniform of a nurse. She was no more a nurse than you or I; but through one of those thousand subterfuges employed by candidates for travel, with a view to deceive or appease, they thought, the gods who distributed visas, she had some time before donned the uniform of that guild.

They had placed their luggage at their feet and awaited the announcement from the loudspeaker in silence; contrary to other voyagers, the two friends were alone. Mathilde, whose brothers and sisters were already in the United States, had few relatives left in the country. Besides, as a last precaution, so that the matter was not spread about and compromised as a result, she had taken great care not to let her relatives know the date of her departure.

For Aglaé it was something else: she had deliberately refused to be accompanied. That ridiculous cortège of a family in their Sunday best escorting one of their own with tears and cries had always displeased her. She did not want to play the role of Iphigenia being conducted to the altar. She wanted to come to terms with her fate alone up to the very last moment; she did not want to be embraced by deceivingly protective arms, surrounded by pitying faces, by eyes that, though brimming with tears, gleamed nonetheless with interested hope.

The Labédoyères lived in Bolosse in a large dilapidated mansion whose vast courtyard, with its outbuildings all standing lopsided, its verandas with their bare balustrades, its moldings on the doors, and its decorated panels, gave testimony to vanished splendors.

Of all the quarters of Port-au-Prince, Bolosse was among those whose glory had been most ephemeral. Toward the end of last century, a group of fat bourgeois on whom politics or commerce, those two great providers, had bestowed a comfortable income, had allowed themselves to be tempted by that suburb offering the attractions of both the mountains and the sea. They had planted a squat mansion here, a small manor house with slender turrets there, all symbols of opulence and well-being, right in the midst of the poor huts of the neighborhood. Even today, when one looks at the remains of these ancient residences, one can easily imagine the splendor of bygone days; one can imagine the sound of the horses coming back to the stables and the reawakened echoes of the birds under the blossoming tree-lined walks.

But the Bolosse neighborhood had not kept its promise. It was accused, perhaps unfairly, of being a breeding ground for malaria-bearing mosquitoes; the preference for Turgeau and other neighborhoods higher up on the mountains intensified. The disillusioned bourgeoisie decamped, and little by little the beautiful insolent residences emptied. There remained only a handful of ruined descendants of those well-to-do families. Those who were happy to find, at the right price, a house with immense but increasingly empty rooms, since the furniture and the last of the bibelots, all of which had ended up in pawnshops and bric-a-brac stalls, had for a long time been a source of solid revenue for them.

Platon Labédoyère was such a one. And it had been in those rustic surroundings that his eight children had grown. The river, where the laundresses jabbered all day to the rhythm of clothes being beaten against rocks, flowed behind the vast and high veranda surrounding the house. From the bedrooms, which one reached by way of a big central staircase with numerous landings, one could feast one's eyes on the charming view: the burgeoning greenness of the mountains on one side, the stormy waves of the Antillean sea on the other.

But, when the last candlestick and the last Limoges candy dish had been sacrificed, the marvelous landscape around the house revealed itself in all its ghastly dullness.

A fisherman of moonrays, a lover of chimeras, having spent his youth living off the debris of an inheritance long since depleted, Platon Labédoyère never acknowledged his impotence. Nourished now with false hopes, tirelessly awaiting the conclusion of fabulous court proceedings to recover illusive property, he did not seem pained by the mediocrity in which his family was mired.

Yet, in his own way he loved the eight children going to seed around him. He loved his unassuming wife, whose distinguished manners already belonged to an era long gone: that in which society women received as educational principles nothing but the following rules, which they applied all their lives:

"Always speak in a low voice, do not raise your voice under any circumstance."

"Above all speak French, a refined French at that. Don't speak Creole except to the servants, if at all."

"Look after the house after the fashion of the Roman matron, and if you can't spin wool, concentrate on your needlework. Whatever you do, avoid showing yourself outside the house except on rare and very specific occasions: masses, funerals, and obligatory visits."

"Be elegant, without excess, and never let any visitor see you scantily dressed."

"Practice dignity, discretion, reserve, and . . . complete submission to the husband."

"Bring a child into this world every two years, breastfeed it for a long time, wean it only while awaiting another, being careful not to neglect any aspect of the older children's education. Keep the children clean and well-dressed." (It would have been a disgrace for these mothers if on Sundays the young girls couldn't wear big new ribbons, four fingers wide, forming a cockade over their heads, or if the young boys couldn't show themselves on the veranda dressed in their white shirts with sailor collars trimmed with piping.)

Aline Labédoyère had been one of those women, of a breed now extinct. Charming and respectable women, forever corseted in the rigidity of outmoded principles which they had the responsibility to transmit to their children.

They could not perceive that the world around them was changing. Fervently believing the received dogmas, they felt themselves to be the vestal virgins of a certain way of life which, in their eyes, constituted a sort of decalogue of Haitian life. A decalogue that they could not transgress without demeaning themselves: God, Duty, Family, was their motto; Sacrifice, Dedication, Resignation, Dignity, their life's goal.

The austerity typical of their plain and simple existence, more concerned with the search for superior pleasures than with the satisfaction of material needs, conferred on them a sweet serenity. Then, meals were frugal and based solely on natural products. Jugs and jars of glazed earthenware took the place of refrigerators. Butter, meat, cheese were words reserved for holidays. Except for New Year's day, cola and cakes were seen only at wedding receptions and first communions. The feasts to which they were invited were described as "family parties."

When they turned eighteen, the sons and daughters had the right to participate, on Sunday mornings, in parties picturesquely denominated "feet shufflers."

A ball was the biggest event in these women's lives. One went about on foot. One knew nothing of cinemas. One saw only a few well-chosen friends who, having passed the test of time, had reached the status of relatives. One was happy with little money, sometimes with no money at all. And one awaited better days.

It would have astonished Aline Labédoyère to hear that her children nurtured other aspirations; that that idyllic picture in pastel colors did not fit the era's new decor. What could they want? They didn't eat their fill every day in the mansion on the hillock of Bolosse, but they enjoyed the respect and consideration of the neighbors. The big mango trees in the yard helped assuage the gnawing in their stomachs. Couldn't one be content with that? Wasn't their customary evening meal of a big pot of herb-bouillon and a bowl of tea made with good country leaves enough to calm their appetite? Wasn't it conducive to a good, restful sleep, bearer of forgetfulness? But the daughters (the Three Graces) soon started to worry their mother. It did not take her long to discover that they were made of a different stuff than she was, belonging to a new race whose desires she did not understand.

Aglaé, Thalie, and Euphrosyne! Not one of them had in her the spirit of docility, or the fatalistic acceptance of unhappiness that had branded their mother and grandmothers. They expressed all sorts of unfamiliar, unusual desires which clashed with the mother's habits and expectations. But she felt it was useless to battle against them, that here was a force against which her voice had proven a very weak weapon. She took fright in advance, however, when she thought of all the money it would take to satisfy all those multiple new needs. Money! The term itself was not customarily in her vocabulary. But nowadays it was the only word one heard at home. Money, they needed it to get those little bottles of polish without which hand and toe nails couldn't survive; it was needed for the at first monthly, then twice-weekly visit to the beauty salon; it was needed for those unnameable trinkets without which life seemed impossible. Confronted with daughters who refused to have any of the ground corn, the fruit with syrup, and the stewed peas of the daily menu, Aline Labédoyère found herself in unfamiliar territory; deep down she blamed herself for having been so adamant about giving them such a refined education (the only time she had exercised a firm authority in her home). She had believed she was doing a good thing bleeding herself white to place them and keep them in those renowned schools on which the eyes of all God-fearing parents converged. Undoubtedly, in contact with their rich classmates, Aglaé and her sisters had acquired extravagant tastes and a love of frivolities, the mother thought *in petto*.

But what did all matter now that poverty had installed itself so insidiously in their abode?

Not having anything more to sell of the ancestral inheritance, and taking refuge in a last burst of dignity which, he claimed, forbade him from asking the State for a job, Platon Labédoyère fled the house more and more often. He left early and returned late at night, not able to bear the silent reproaches in their gazes, the spectacle of faces and bodies ravaged by hunger.

Powerless, he had relinquished all his fatherly duties, and become sweet, smiling, indulgent, almost humble.

Moved to tears by the memory of that man disarmed in the struggle against a pitiless existence, Aglaé recalled his pathetic efforts, his withdrawal, and finally the paternal abdication.

The financial straits gave way to need, and need to depriva-
tion. The day arrived when the daily meals failed to materialize.
Little by little they lost the habit of sitting down at the table at
regular hours. They ate what they found, as they found it, when
they found it. The specter of consumption loomed in the horizon.
The family began to fall apart bit by bit: Théodule, Adrien, and
Nerva, the three boys whose ages ranged from eight to fourteen,
fled the empty and somber mansion in favor of the thickets in
the neighborhood. There they could still appease their hunger
with seasonal fruits and what they could find in orchards and
gardens. The daughters, older and more closely watched,
couldn't allow themselves to roam the woods. Their only
subterfuges to battle the gnawing in their stomachs consisted of
interested visits made at certain times either to a godmother or
a distant relative. But they were careful not to use those means
with the good people of the neighborhood. Before the latter, they
must, to use the mother's expression, keep a stiff upper lip, feign
affluence, not allow the merest suspicion of their need to arise.
Because the deepest shame would descend over all of them if a
member of the household were to accept help from anyone.
Death before humiliation: those were their marching orders.
Besides, it would be disgraceful for anyone to give the humble
neighbors of the district glimpses of their decline. Misery that
hides itself is just the more tragic.

One day, a day even more somber than others, "the letter"
arrived. No one wrote to the Labédoyère family anymore. It had
been ages since poverty had cut them off from the rest of the
world, from the rest of the country. Who remembered their
existence since the time when, lacking clothes, lacking everything,
they had stopped going anywhere society people went? Thus the
letter hit them like a thunderbolt from a clear blue sky. It was
signed: Simon. Simon was a very melancholy little neighbor of
Bolosse one had not paid much attention to when he vegetated
in the shack across the street with his mother, a servant or cook.
That young beanpole who always stared straight ahead as he
walked and seemed not to see anyone. That Simon, gone for ten

long years, that Simon who had not been heard from again, had now thought of those old neighbors across the street. On a page and a half he formulated a proper and duly written proposal of marriage after having stated very precisely the solidity of his present means. Anyway, he wrote in a French peppered with English phrases, after these ten years of hard existence, he had suddenly felt alone, yes, alone. There was no question of tying the knot with one of those girls he had encountered in New York! They are ideal for brief love affairs, these American girls, since they are so uncomplicated. Anyway, when it came to marriage it was definitely necessary to look back to the native country. It was there that Simon had decided to hunt down that rare bird, the true companion, that person with whom he could, each evening, after work, speak Creole to his heart's content, devour green plantains with herring-salt, and (he did not write this down, of course) hungrily kiss that flesh tanned by the sun, his childhood paradise finally regained.

The reading of this letter provoked what is usually called a mixed reception in the Labédoyère family. What is he driving at, this little Simon? Madame Aline went totally off the track, thinking that she would once again play the patroness, and was already searching her mind for a deserving innocent maiden in the neighborhood on whom to bestow this windfall. The boys couldn't give a damn about their former neighbor's heartaches. They only knew one thing: they were hungry. Euphrosyne and Thalie seemed far away. Only Aglaé understood everything, immediately.

The second letter, which arrived a week later, very quickly confirmed her suspicions, and having the satisfaction of that modest triumph, she said nothing, she never avowed that she had guessed a long time before that which was now laid before everyone's eyes in such flamboyant words. Euphrosyne, it was Euphrosyne he wanted, that boy! Euphrosyne, the beautiful daughter of the house; the brunette with long black hair and big startled eyes. Euphrosyne, who was only thirteen years old when he had left. How then had he come to think of her at the moment of choice, wondered the naïve? To remember her! How long had he lived with that image in his mind? Since when, since when? Since forever, it seemed. Since, as a child, he came to get water for his mother from the Labédoyères' pump and he would watch the little girl, eight years younger than he, walk across the yard, already exhibiting the nonchalant walk of all great coquettes. Maybe his desire to leave dated back to that day. To leave, to reach to the end of the world to find whatever it took to win that unattainable goddess. Now it was done. Simon, little Simon, the son of Lormélise, the servant, was, if not rich, at least very well off. He offered a furnished apartment and a big car. He offered passage, rescue, all that in exchange for nothing at all: a very tiny "yes" that needed to be uttered by the lips of a petite young woman. But that "yes" remained glued to Euphrosyne's throat, choking her. For two reasons: the first of which was that Euphrosyne's dream had had a name—William—for as long as she could remember. And then, Simon, the son of Lormélise, was not quite the thing. But that same name of William also haunted the dreams of each of the other sisters. William, another young neighbor, had been visiting the house for many years without ever declaring himself. Each of the three sisters (twenty-five, twenty-three, and twenty-one years of age) thought that he came for her, but he remained silent. A poor medical student, poorer even than the Labédoyères who at least had a roof over their heads, he couldn't allow himself to formulate plans for the future. Every evening, he, with a group of his classmates, would borrow the long veranda that surrounded the house and lose himself in his studies while the Labédoyère family sought to forget their sorrows in sleep. Those young women, their fingers worn out by the poor-quality, poorly-paid embroidery work which they delivered to shops, and which was their sole source of revenue, would sometimes prepare for him, when they could, either a fresh-fruit milkshake or some black coffee.

Everyone, starting with the young man in question, knew that William was destined for one of the Three Graces. Yes, but which one? Euphrosyne herself was certain that she was the chosen one, even if no one else knew it. Deep down she had no doubt that she belonged to that race of women who know that all they have to do is to be. That had been the case in her relationship with her sisters from the time they were tender babes. Aglaé could very well be the most intelligent and Thalie the most obliging and devoted to her family, but she, Euphrosyne, had always carried off all the spoils in every field. At the time when the family still could make an effort to take part in fashionable gatherings and other celebrations, the main roles had naturally been reserved for her. She had been enthroned on street altars during the Feast of Corpus Christi; had preceded the bride and groom in wedding processions; she had played, in turn, the role of virgin or fairy in children's plays; she had barely escaped the carnival float from the heights of which she would have had to throw kisses at the mob for three days. That time she had been overruled by her family. Queen of Carnival, a Labédoyère, it was unthinkable! But not for not having been realized had that project contributed less to consolidate in the young girl the conviction that all the honors so gleaned throughout her childhood were her due. So it was with confidence and serenity that she awaited the sure and certain moment when William would offer her the wedding band due her.

Thus it was that Simon's request jolted them like a deafening echo, causing an upheaval within the family circle.

The suitor's second letter remained unanswered for a long time, but Euphrosyne wasn't moved for an instant. She ignored her family's anguished vigil with a superb indifference, while they awaited her verdict like manna from heaven. After some timid attempts which resulted in nothing but rebuffs, no one dared talk about it. But everyone thought about it incessantly: Simon, Simon, the leper, Simon the Cyrenaic, Simon-Peter, and on this rock!—was forever present before the Labédoyère family. Everyone savored in advance the advantages to be had by all from that union. A daughter there, think about that! A member of the family in the Promised Land! Well! That was just as good as if the head of the family had been offered a high post. Goodbye poverty! A substantial steady check, parcels of useful gifts for all, and then, every year or so, the departure of others toward Eldorado. That was salvation! In the meantime, the boys would return to school; the other two daughters would quickly find suitors; the father, his sprightliness regained, would recover his zest for life; and the mother, who had felt her strength consume itself slowly, by force of hardships and griefs, would recover health and joy.

But there: Euphrosyne remained silent. Euphrosyne refused to be either scapegoat or savior. She was waiting for William and would not marry Simon.

It was then that the idea sprung in Aglaé's brain. She did not speak to her mother about it at the outset. Upright as she was, Aline would have spoiled everything with her lack of understanding. Aglaé had a long conversation with her sisters and the decision was made. Besides, the trick was so simple. It was so obvious that they were astonished not to have thought of it before. Ten years had gone by since their young neighbor had seen the object of his thoughts, or any of the other girls in the house. Their features could be but hazy in his memory. Without having the younger sister's beauty, Aglaé resembled her. The same complexion, same shape of the face, lips, eyes. For the rest: a more slender figure, shorter hair—all that could be changed.

That is how one morning the impatient suitor received the photo he had requested, accompanied by a letter signed Euphrosyne. In the joy that that tacit consent brought, he only saw fire. The correspondence was established between him and the chosen one. It was of short duration. Aglaé-cum-Euphrosyne hardly had the time to get to know her future husband well through the brief and burning missives that he addressed to her. The letters quickly took a more practical turn. The documents furnishing the Embassy with the requested assurances arrived. Then came the checks for expenses, the beginning of the trousseau. Swept away in that whirlwind, Aglaé no longer paused to reflect. The day a traveler brought a small jewelry box for Mademoiselle Euphrosyne Labédoyère, the architect of this little plot wanted to call the whole thing off. But it was too late. She had to slip the engagement ring on her finger in front of the visitor. One blamed her distress on the emotion of the moment. When evening came and the doors were closed, the three accomplices brought the family, who had watched the little ceremony in bewilderment, up to date on the plan. Madame Labédoyère couldn't get over it: What! With her younger sister's birth certificate, Aglaé had managed to change her identity. She was Euphrosyne now! But where were the principles of honor and integrity . . . They didn't give the mother the time to speak. The boys exulted, dancing with joy, blessing their older sister for having saved the family. Dear Euphrosyne, thoroughly reprieved, and well rid of a rival who, though not necessarily dangerous, could get ideas into her head about William and become a bit of a nuisance, the true Euphrosyne breathed easy. Aglaé had sold her the right to happiness. For a pottage of lentils.

Oh well! Everything was for the best in this best of all possible worlds. Fortune, which for one instant they had believed lost like those soap bubbles which soar and disappear after having made their iridescent colors sparkle in children's eyes, fortune had gently come to settle in the house.

The final preparations were quickly finished. The ticket for the voyage arrived.

Now "Aglaé-Euphrosyne," sitting on an airport bench, awaited the moment when the plane would lift her away from this land of misery. That was all she wanted for the moment. Later, well, later, she would see! The marriage ceremony was scheduled to take place in fifteen days. The date was set, the invitations sent, and the betrothed carried in her suitcase her white gown and her immaculate veil. Oh well! Once the marriage was consummated, if ever the trick was discovered, well, one would see.

"Pan American World Airways announces the departure of Flight 427 to Miami and New York . . . passengers please board . . . "

Aglaé got up, picked up her small carrying case, labeled "Euphrosyne Labédoyère" in big letters. Brandishing her passport and official documents, drawn up in that same name and address, very conspicuously before her, like a monstrance, she crossed the last gangway leading to the runway.

The steel aircraft stood there, supreme, triumphant. The sun made its cabin sparkle, and, hungry monster that it was, it devoured through its thin mouth the mob of passengers plunging into its belly.

Aglaé-Euphrosyne had one final pause. Shame, despair, disgust? She looked to her right at the mountains in the distance as if searching for a way out; then, bowing her head, as if to pull herself together before entering the arena, she walked with brisk steps toward the plane.

At the top of the boarding ramp she turned around: the taste of sacrifice, pungent, violent, bitter, climbed to her lips. She breathed the warm air of the country for the last time and, offering the flight attendant who greeted her her most dazzling smile, plunged into the heart of the gigantic bird.

Translated by Lizabeth Paravisini-Gebert

Maryse Condé was born in Guadeloupe, but has spent long periods in West Africa, France, and the United States. She studied in Paris, earning a doctorate in comparative literature from the Sorbonne in 1975. A prolific writer, Condé has enjoyed enormous literary success in France and the United States, and several of her novels, Segou I, Segou II, *and* Moi, Tituba, sorcière noire de Salem, *have reached best-seller lists in both countries. Condé's work, which includes fiction, drama, and criticism, has been published extensively in French and in translation. Her fiction displays a keen sense of irony, meticulous historical documentation, and a gift for evoking place and character.*

MARYSE CONDÉ

Three Women in Manhattan

To Wanda

"Did you hear me? Are you listening to me?"

Claude didn't raise her head. No, she wasn't listening to Elinor because she didn't need to. Every morning, Elinor would repeat the same instructions, pulling on her fine leather gloves or planting a bright-colored cap on her curly hair before disappearing, leaving behind a delicate scent.

"Wash, scrub, iron, water the plants. When you leave, don't forget to bolt the lock; it's very, very important . . ."

Since Elinor stared at her, hesitating as usual between tenderness and exasperation, Claude gave her a smile of apology and went into the kitchen.

The apartment into which Elinor had moved six months earlier was elegant. It was perfectly suitable for a young woman writer,

57

whose first novel, *The Mouth That Eats Salt*, had made the covers
of all the literary magazines. Not black magazines. Those, well,
you know what they're worth: as soon as a black man or a black
woman writes a few lines, they're treated as geniuses! Elinor had
been the subject of study in articles and had appeared on covers
of serious and objective white publications which culled her
references to folklore of the Old South and to collective black
patrimony while still emphasizing her beauty, burning like an
August night in Georgia. She had in fact given a copy of her
novel to Claude but her limited knowledge of English had
prevented her from reading it. She did nothing more than open
it up, looking fondly at the intertwining signs—which for her
meant nothing—before placing it on the only shelf in her bedroom
between her photo album and a copy of *Teach Yourself English*.
Through the kitchen window, Claude had a picture postcard
view: under a bright blue sky, the sparkling skyscrapers holding
in the perpendicular streets filled with yellow taxis. How
surprising New York is! Claude had not yet become used to this
beauty, which was as disconcerting as that of a face of which one
has never dreamed. Sometimes, leaving the dump where she
lived on 144th Street—where blacks and Puerto Ricans, united by
the same misery, clashed in the same hate—she wondered what
had led her from her nonchalant island to this city where
everything spoke of success, fortune. To her at nineteen, her past
seemed endless, confused, strewn with painful points of reference, already marked by failure. She had never known her father,
a native of Marie Galante who disappeared after his sad and
fruitful union with Alicia, her mother. Already overburdened
with children, her mother placed her in the hands of her
godmother, Mrs. Bertille Dupré, of an excellent Point-à-Pitre
family, who gave her the best education in exchange for domestic
work. Actually, she never got ahead of the domestic chores:
wash, scrub, iron, water the plants . . . on one side of the ocean
as on the other.

She looked back at the dirty dishes. The day before, Elinor had
given a reception. These days she had a lot of people over. This
is what she had to do in order to tend to her public relations.

After all, writing a book is not enough in and of itself: only the naïve think so. One must also promote it; and Elinor gave of herself. When she arrived for the first time at Elinor's house, Elinor overwhelmed her with questions in French which was both faltering and precise. First, Elinor thought Claude was Haitian, grown up in the humus that fertilizes all large North American cities. Then, she was surprised:

"Guadeloupe? Where's that? How old are you? What brings you at such a young age so far from home?"

Claude heard herself mumbling a true story as improbable as a web of lies. Who could believe that when she was of age, she left the Hotel of the Great Seas where she'd been hired after her Certificate in Tourism, had withdrawn the paltry nest egg that Godmother Bertille had built up for her in the Bank of Savings, and had packed her trunk? Why New York? Why not Paris through the migration scheme, the *Bumidom*, like all the others? Precisely because she was horrified by Paris. Several times a year, in the big house between the courtyard and the garden on Commandant Mortenol Street, Godmother Bertille's friends, returning from the French metropolis, would ecstatically go through their stories:

"My dear, we went all the way to the top of the Eiffel Tower with the children. Paris at our feet! What a sight!"

And Claude, careful not to knock over the glasses of coconut sorbet served to the guests, was smitten with hate for that city—overpraised harlot—and swore she'd set sail for another America.

At the end of the interview, Elinor had declared:

"So, everything is all right. You'll come for three hours every morning."

From that time on, a bond had tied them together, formed of compassion, scorn, at times hate, and love as well, for they shared a secret. Both of them knew it. Claude was an Elinor that the absent-minded sorcerer, destiny, had forgotten to gratify after having wrenched her from nothingness. Under the pretext of perfecting her French, Elinor had told Claude about her childhood in the Victorian house inherited from her mother's side.

The youngest of seven children, this number had always symbolized for her her predestination. When she described her mother, her aunts—especially her Aunt Millicent—Claude could picture them effortlessly. Add on a few curls, extra touches of eyeliner, jewelry both more austere and more rich, and you had Godmother Bertille, her sisters, her friends. As for the father, absent but forever present, quick to get angry over a wrong crease on a shirt front, he was Marcel Dupré, her godmother's husband, head of the Office of Direct and Indirect Taxation, who every Sunday had his nails polished by his eldest daughter. It was the same world, blown up to the proportions of a continent, that's all. Nonetheless, the resemblance ended there. In her buckled shoes, Elinor would skip from one person to another, presenting her cheek to be kissed. She was the prodigal child, the wild seventh who upset her teachers and who, at Martin Luther King's death, composed an ode in his honor, read in church and reverently listened to by everyone. She was not the godchild of humble origins, taken in by charity, raised without love, and turned ugly through indifference. Claude left the kitchen, crossed the living room—70 square yards of white carpeting, paintings by Romare Bearden, naïve painters, Salnave, Wilson Bigaud, Wesner la Forest, unusual and graceful objects brought back from Mexico that she dusted only with trepidation—then entered the office. This room was the place for a secret and remarkable alchemy. On a long drawing table placed against the window, the typewriter reigned. In differently colored folders, Elinor meticulously catalogued the manuscript of her novel in progress, the short stories, and the articles she was working on. Claude opened a file. What magic! These series of arabesques symbolized a thought, communicated an element of the imaginary which, through them, was more penetrating than reality. To write! To put her hips, her sex, her heart into motion in order to give birth to a world inscribed in her obscurity. To think that she'd had such audacity! In her garret in Pointe-à-Pitre, on evenings when the household slept, she used to scribble in spiral notebooks. An uncontrollable force within her. To whom could she show the fruit of those sleepless nights?

Miss Angélique-Marie Lourdes was her French teacher, a pretty *caprêsse*, a woman of mixed blood, all dimples, who still lived with her parents. Every morning, at the ten o'clock recess, her mother's servant would bring her a cup of hot milk and a croissant on a silver platter and she would eat in little bits like a bird. She was the only one who paid any attention to Claude, making her recite her tales, encouraging her with a smile. But to approach her? To put those clumsy scrawlings under her eyes? Claude had never dared; and when she left Guadeloupe she'd burned all of her notebooks, one by one. She sat down at the worktable, putting her hands heavily, clumsily, on the keyboard.

When she left Elinor's, Claude took the bus to Vera's, ninety streets uptown in the heart of Harlem. Here, there was no doorman in a sky-blue uniform with chevrons, no more security guard in a dark blue uniform and walkie-talkie, no more Oriental rugs, green plants, elevator taking you up to the 25th floor in one breath. In former times, however, with its heavy columns of mock marble, the building was probably not without a certain elegance. Alas, Harlem was no longer the capital of arts and pleasure where Zora Neale Hurston would show off her ankles dancing a Charleston. It was a dirty, desperate ghetto where most of the families survived thanks to food stamps. When Vera had moved in, fifteen years earlier, on several floors there had been doctors and Wall Street employees in their dark gray, three-piece suits. Since that time, everyone had fled to the suburbs where children weren't butchered and Vera, the last relic of the past, stayed where she was. Claude rang the doorbell—three long rings and one shorter one—heard the endless clinking of locks and bolts, then the door opened. How old was Vera? Sixty, seventy, eighty . . . ? She'd stayed slender, even slight. Not a single thread of silver in her crop of hair, but it was thinning, becoming more sparse, like a forest ravaged by too many fires. Her facial architecture was indestructible but her mouth and her eyes were wounded, defeated, destroyed from having feigned hope and courage for too long. She asked:

"Have you eaten?"

Claude shook her head. She insisted:

"Didn't she give you anything to eat?"

"She," of course, was Elinor. Claude was the bond between these two women who had never seen one another. One day she couldn't resist the pride of pointing to the cover of the literary magazine Vera was reading, and murmured:

"I work at her house, too!"

Vera was aghast; since that time, Elinor had become a subject of their daily conversations. Vera cut out every little review or article about her and made comments about them angrily:

"Beauty which burns like an August night in Georgia! Images, metaphors, symbols borrowed from Old South folklore, black voice, black rhythm. How can she put up with all of that? Doesn't she have anything better to do? No great cause, no great cause . . . !" The other subject of their daily conversations was, of course, Haiti, bleeding from all its wounds. Related on her mother's side to former president Omar Tancrède and on her father's side to former president Zamor Valcinq, Vera's family had been led to the slaughterhouse by the new dictator's orders, their land and possessions confiscated and their homes razed. If Vera had escaped the slaughter, it was because she had been in Europe where she had been beginning a double career as a concert pianist and a writer, and had let herself be wooed by a young Italian man. Abruptly, from one day to the next, she'd locked up her instrument and put her pen to the service of a great cause. Since that time, she contributed a column to an opposition newspaper which, like a phoenix, had disappeared dozens of times, and dozens of times reappeared. For someone who hadn't seen Haiti for twenty years, she knew everything that happened and analyzed everything people said there. The island was within her like a *poto-mitan*, the central pillar supporting her life. Tirelessly she would fly from one event to another—demonstration or march or supporters' party—administering comfort to everyone, then coming back to her glacial apartment where everything would go down the drain, like her hopes.

When Claude had met Vera, the latter hadn't eaten for two days and was looking at the world through a milky fog which made it more beautiful. She had been walking down Amsterdam

Avenue when she stumbled on a meeting room that was wide open, so rare in New York, that she had gone in. There—oh, surprise—people were speaking in French. Little girls with cinnamon-colored cheeks were passing around large platters of orangeade and pâtés. Had the face of God finally appeared? You could say so because, at that moment, Claude's gaze had met that of Vera.

Vera had no need of a cleaning woman; Claude didn't realize this right away. For the first months, she rubbed, polished, and made shine the worn and colorless objects, desperately trying to give them back their brilliance. Little by little, she discovered that this disorder—this state of ruin—suited Vera. Among the familiar companions of her furnishings, there was no longer any need to pretend. She came face to face with herself, already inhabited by death. Wrinkled up in a corner of the couch, she would page through her albums:

"Look at Mama, how pretty she was. I have her coloring. This here is my sister, Iris. There, that's Daddy! All of them are dead and I've never seen their graves . . ."

Tears rolled down her cheeks and Claude took the old hand in her own, gently kissing it. What could she say? She'd never known how to speak since no one had ever listened to her. Vera continued:

"This one here is Fabio! Ah, men! As soon as he knew I was no longer a rich heiress, he disappeared. After that point, I never again had confidence in anyone, anyone . . . " Next would begin the litany of those who had loved her and to whom, according to her, she'd refused to give herself. Letters stored in cardboard boxes she sometimes would recite with both mockery and great excitement. What had become of all these suitors? Married, fathers of families, prosperous bourgeois citizens, successful artists . . . or dead—they, too, like Vera's relatives, returned to the warm belly of the earth. Nothing of them remained but for these arabesques which had symbolized their passion. Fascinated, Claude poured over these pages which had so often been perused. The most precious moment, however, would arise when Vera would open the little briefcase that contained various manuscripts of her novels—all unpublished, all returned by editors from France, Belgium, Switzerland, and Canada. For hours on end, she would read chapters from them while Claude, hanging from her very lips, would try to find hidden, underlying faults in the words and sentences. For, after all, why were they condemned to this inglorious end? Who defines Beauty? Who decides upon success? Why was Elinor basking in the full sun? Vera in her darkness? Writing is but a trap, the cruelest of all, a snare, a sham of communication.

Every afternoon, after these long reading sessions in the only room the radiator would deign heat, Vera would fall asleep, her mouth open, and her snoring would sound like a death rattle. Claude would take her manuscripts from her hands: *The Battle of Vertières: A Historical Novel*; *A Haitian Woman's Heart*; *Angélita Reyes* . . . then she fell back into her daydreaming. Why had these two women, each in her own manner, become attached to her? Because of her youth? Her naïveté? Her kindness? She understood that she was their creation, that she was the papyrus roll upon which they freely drew the signs through which they had chosen to represent themselves.

But, by the same token, weren't they in her power? One act of refusal and the mirror in which Elinor saw herself so beautiful would break. One gesture of weariness and Vera could no longer breathe, exhausted, completely worn out.

At about three o'clock, Vera was still sleeping. Pulling on the goatskin jacket that she'd given her, Claude left. The bundled-up little boys who were playing in the street smiled at her. They knew her now. She was beginning to carry her own weight as a living person of the neighborhood. This was a good omen.

From Vera's apartment to City College, it wasn't very far to go. Claude had enrolled there, following Vera's repeated advice and her saying that education was the key to success.

"We used to be slaves. With patience, we've climbed every rung. And now, look . . ."

Claude would look, and what did she see? Men and women crammed into ghettos, humiliated in their minds, wounded in their flesh. Men and women subjects of dictatorship, wrenched to the cardinal points of the Earth. There still was Africa, about which Vera would often speak. It was so far away! Who knew what went on there? Nonetheless, the evening classes at City College were almost free. She was learning English. Bit by bit, the sounds of New York—which had frightened and deafened her—were becoming intelligible. She was able to decipher the puzzles of neon signs and posters . . .

At the corner of 140th Street, an old man huddled up under a porch looked up at her with his bluish, blind eyes. She offered him one of her last quarters.

Claude stopped, dumbfounded, in the hallway.

Draped in her sulfur-yellow bathrobe, Elinor was curled up, prostrate. She lifted up her haggard, virtually swollen face between the sad seaweed of her hair and moaned:

"Do you see what they're writing?"

In front of her were the magazines *Black Culture, Black Essence, Black World. . . .* But Claude didn't even glance at them. She was confused by this grief. It was as though, scorning the bloody hearts of the victims and the preachers' songs, the sun had refused to rise, leaving the world in its darkness.

"Just what is it they want? What do they want?"

She swivelled herself around:

"They want me to speak once more about slavery and the slave trade and racism, for me to adorn us with the virtues of victims, and to inspire hope . . ."

She sniffled, wiped her eyes with her two fists and, in such childish gestures, Claude once again saw in her the little girl that she had been.

"At forty, for the first time, my mother was allowed into a white restaurant in Colony Square. It was the big event of her life. Every morning, after giving praise to our great men who'd shed their blood for such a moment, we heard this story . . . I can't stand it any longer, do you understand?"

Claude wasn't sure she understood. Nevertheless, she assured her with a smile. Elinor got up. Her admirers wouldn't have recognized their idol on this particular morning. Yet already she was unfurling, getting back her grace, her bearing, as though ashamed of her disarray. Claude understood that nothing could stop her.

Left alone, Claude paged through the magazines, following a few lines with a finger, looking for familiar inscriptions. Why do words cause so much harm? What power is hidden in their design? How can it be captured and tamed to one's desires? In a certain way, Elinor, no more than Vera, had not succeeded in doing so. With a sigh, Claude turned toward the cluttered sink. A moment later, Elinor came and stopped next to her. You would have to have been quite shrewd to have made out the streak of tears under the flush of her cheeks. They smiled at each other and Elinor repeated:

"Wash, scrub, iron, water the plants. When you leave, don't forget to bolt the lock: it's very, very important . . ."

Nonetheless, these orders meant something entirely different. They symbolized the bond which tied them together, the secret they shared, the equilibrium reestablished . . .

The iron bit into the collar of the white blouse. Since childhood, Claude would hear people say that she had nimble fingers. It was the only charm she was recognized as having. When he'd finished inspecting the pile of still-warm shirts, Marcel Dupré would condescend to smile and would slip his fingers into his money-pouch:

"Here, buy yourself a piece of candy . . ."

Thursday afternoons, when she would visit her mother on the Canal, she would find her in the kitchen, her stomach perpetually distended by a pregnancy, wedged between the kitchen range and the table, and she would take the burning cast-iron from her hands. Relieved, Alicia would sit down heavily and then would begin a long tale of children's illnesses, fights with neighbors, blows and insults liberally dispensed by her husband of the moment, interrupting herself from time to time to exclaim, with a fleeting tenderness:

"How handy you are!"

Would she never be good at anything else? She looked at her

hands: small, slightly squared, still shaped by childhood. Since her arrival in New York, too busy in assuring her survival, she hadn't bought any spiral notebooks. She knew, however, that the audacity would come back to her, that her hips, her sex, her heart, her head would set off in motion once again and that she would give birth to her world. It was already moving within her. To whom would she show the fruit of her parturition? This time, she wouldn't hesitate: to Vera, who'd inspired her . . .

Vera would adjust her metal-framed glasses which added to the pathetic as well as comic form of her old face and would nod her head:

"This is good, it's good! Yes, it's very good . . . !"

The iron sputtered, the daydream ceased . . .

Toward noon, she went downstairs. In this haughty neighborhood, people focused on a point in space without ever meeting the eyes of others, nor ever touching upon cheeks, lips or hair; everyone seemed to be following his or her own ghost.

"She cried this morning!"

Vera could taste this news like a rare dish, then would overwhelm her with questions which she wouldn't know how to answer. It was best this way because Vera's imagination would then fill in all the gaps and compose a story to her own liking. Acting in this way, Claude wouldn't feel as though she'd betrayed a secret she should have kept. On the contrary, she would tighten the bond which had broken. In fact, since the time when the ship—blessed by God and H.R.H. the King—had withdrawn from the bay for the horrifying crossing, nothing more had brought them together. Places of residence had been assigned to them. Languages had compelled them to silence. Now, unity was being made anew.

On 140th Street, the cold had chased the old man from his wide doorway. In the shop windows—a jumble of Puerto Rican stores—mangos, avocados, and plantains spoke of the climate where misery at least can be clothed in rags of the sun. The sight of them gave rise in Claude only to a nauseous bitterness. She moved along more quickly because the cold felt sharper and more biting.

As she was reaching the corner of Amsterdam Avenue, her heart jumped. In front of Vera's building, an ambulance was parked: it was the materialization of a dread she'd carried with her daily. She knew that this moment would come. When Vera would fall asleep, she would lean over her, listening carefully for her breath. Not yet, not yet. Because, after all, even if she couldn't bring back to life all of the departed and Iris, the so dearly cherished sister, if she couldn't rebuild the villa in Bois Verna, high amongst its solitary cacti, or shoot down the dictator, glutted with blood, and scatter the various parts of his body over the intersection of the Croix des Bossales, at least she could offer her a story, a work which would present her not such as she was—an octogenarian in a pitiful wool cardigan, raising her pathetic voice in the tumult of distress—but such as she dreamed her to be: Erzulie Dantor, flaming torch clenched in her fist. She began to run but tree roots shot up through the pavement got in her way and made her stumble, preventing her from reaching her goal before the ambulance, in a powerful movement, drew away from the curb and took off up the endless, rectilinear street, uttering its long wailing of a mourning woman. A circle of bystanders had been formed and slowly disbanded. The Puerto Rican neighbor woman, the one whose children Claude had sometimes babysat while she ran to the supermarket to exchange her food stamps, stared at her sadly, whispering:

"Es la vieja mujer del quinto piso . . ."

Translated by Thomas Spear

Hilma Contreras was born in San Francisco de Macorís, Dominican Republic, and educated in Paris. She started writing while still in Paris in the 1930s. Contreras is said to be the first Dominican woman to write short stories and has published three volumes to date: Cuatro cuentos, El ojo de Dios, *and most recently* Entre dos silencios. *Her work covers a wide spectrum of themes and styles, ranging from her political novel,* La tierra está bramando, *to the fantastic tale.*

HILMA CONTRERAS

Hair

At twelve o'clock, just as they were about to close, a new and youthful voice asked:

"Can you sell me a bottle of Alka Seltzer?"

The two of them looked at the newcomer, surprised by such an anachronism.

"What beautiful hair," Doña Irene complimented her.

The girl smiled, shaking her chestnut mane with a haughty grace that seemed like a provocation.

The druggist wiped his face with his handkerchief.

"How can she stand it!" he exclaimed a few minutes later. "I die of heat just from looking at it. How dreadful!"

But she lived right across from them. Her name was Natividad. She would come home from school dressed in showy tight-fitting pants, flaunting her torrent of hair which reached down to her hips.

It brought him to despair.

"If they'd let me," he would repeat peevishly, "I'd cut it all the way to her nape."

To underscore his threat he brandished a pair of scissors, clicking them in the air.

One afternoon his gentle wife had a fit of laughter which dissolved into a feigned cough, because to make matters worse, the girl showed up with bangs down to her eyes.

Luciano began to live a terrible obsession. If he lifted his eyes from his work, there was the hair, on the street, on the balcony, at the window, on the terrace. There came a moment when, his understanding perturbed by the suffocating impact of all that hair, the prescriptions he handled lost all sense.

It wasn't summer yet. But summer's breath, like that of a puffing beast, filled the air.

"It's so hot!" Luciano said, sticking his head out the pharmacy door. "The air feels like fire."

"It's not that bad," commented Doña Irene, serenely seated in the undulating space in front of the electric fan. "But you're making yourself needlessly hot with all these comings and goings."

The pharmacist felt his wife's placid gaze on his back and could not repress an unpleasant prickly sensation.

"Well," he declared impatiently, "I'm leaving. Have the delivery boy help you close up when he gets back."

Doña Irene opened her mouth and placed her plump hands on the glass showcase, rendered speechless by surprise.

Men, she told herself thoughtfully, *are as complicated as entangled spools of thread. So it's hot . . . what else is new! Just like yesterday, like tomorrow, like always. The secret lies in not getting excited.*

Luciano turned the corner around the pharmacy in a great hurry, entered the first driveway, and practically ran up the stairs to the second floor, where they had lived since they had decided to open the business on the ground floor.

Fleshy, neither tall nor short, small-waisted, with Greek-vase curves, Natividad would come out on the terrace when the eaves sheltered it like a large visor of luminous shadow. She would pause for a moment on the only step on the threshold, glance olympically over her shoulder, arching her body, bending a knee to enhance the enticing line of her profile, and after shaking the dense beauty of her mane with a self-satisfied gesture, she would sit chastely in a native-wood rocking chair in the midst of her pots of geraniums. Between rocking her chair and glimpses at the book she was reading, her eyes would assess the effect that her self-display produced on passers-by.

That day one of her glances captured the admiration on the face of the pharmacist watching her from his apartment balcony.

Behind him Doña Irene called out.

"María! It smells like something's burning on the stove . . . María!"

Lying next to the body of his profoundly-asleep wife, Luciano experienced the torments of yearning for a dream that eluded him. He tossed and turned in bed, sweating, irritated by Doña Irene's wheezing breaths. Around midnight, having reached the point of exasperation, he got up and went out on the balcony, anxious for a breath of air.

The moon was shining brightly on Natividad's terrace. Its fixed and translucent light stained with black shadows the old oak tree in the garden. The girl rocked in her chair, apparently also unable to sleep. She noticed the pharmacist and smiled at him. The greenish nocturnal silence started buzzing in Luciano's ears. She was looking at him and smiling. She would rock for a few seconds and turn to stare fixedly at him. Luciano decided to go down.

When she saw him open the garden gate, she stood up, startled. The movement unveiled her naked body.

"What beautiful breasts you have!" he said admiringly, his eyes moist with emotion.

Instead of covering herself, Natividad tossed her head back with an arrogant gesture.

Luciano extended his arm. His hand filled with life.

She moaned in protest.

"No . . . let me go."

Ignoring her, he grabbed her brusquely by the shoulders to

kiss her. His fingers got tangled in her hair. He tried to gather it in a bundle on her nape but the locks escaped his fingers, winding themselves around his arms, brushing against his face. He felt suffocated with heat.

"I only want to kiss you," he panted. "Don't be upset. . . . Be good, I'm not going to hurt you . . ."

Frantic, he exclaimed:

"Damned hair!"

It was like a hot noose around his throat. He was choking as he kissed her, with no time to free himself from the never-ending hair, quivering with desire and fear.

The ardor of the struggle awakened Doña Irene.

"That nightmare again," she grumbled as her arm reached clumsily for her husband in the semi-darkness. "Don't drown, Luciano. . . . Wake up!"

Luciano sat up abruptly, half-crazed by anguish.

"The hair," he mumbled. "The hair . . ."

"What are you saying? . . . Come, lie on your side and it will be all right. . . . Where are you going?"

"To . . . I don't know. I'm soaked in sweat."

Once completely awakened, he said:

"Don't get up. I'll go get another pair of pajamas myself."

"Suit yourself. . . . But don't you start reading at this late hour . . ."

It was cool in the balcony. He breathed anxiously. All was still on the terrace, which was bathed in a moonlit brightness that made the chirping of the crickets reverberate. Leaning against the rail, Luciano stared for a long time at the exuberance of the geraniums. He was overcome by a furious desire to bite them so they would burst once and for all, driving away that unbearable feeling of lust.

Doña Irene changed position in her eagerness to resume her interrupted sleep. *This husband of mine,* she sighed, *is suffering from nerves. I hope to God it's nothing serious . . . I hope he's not going to go on like some men who go through crises at a certain age* . . . She made another effort to fall asleep, sprawling on her back on the bed while she chased away her worries and concentrated on the soporific task of mentally writing numbers on the dark night of her eyelids. A frenetic weight suddenly fell on top of her. She barely had time to utter:

"Ooh . . . Luciano . . ."

Translated by Lizabeth Paravisini-Gebert

Liliane Dévieux was born in Port-au-Prince, Haiti, in 1942, and was educated in Port-au-Prince, Paris, and Montreal, where she now lives with her family. She has published one novel, L'Amour, oui: La Mort, non, and various short stories scattered in literary journals and magazines. Her work explores Haitian economic and political migration to Canada and questions traditional patterns of gender relations. L'Amour, oui: La Mort, non is one of the few works of fiction by Caribbean women to explore the devastating impact of the Vietnam war.

LILIANE DÉVIEUX

Piano-Bar

Far behind us, the city of concrete, of glass and noise. A road plowed through the snow, far from the tiresome expressways, our headlights clearing the darkness bit by bit, and ahead of us a luminous point: piano-bar.

I dream that piano-bar like an Eden, this evening like an exorcism, against irreversible time, against love coated in verdigris. Against Daniel's silences, his bad moods, his big-shot airs, transforming me in turn into Eva-the-doll, Eva-the-little-girl, Eva-the-mad.

Piano-bar. Here, under the orange glints of the faint lights hanging on the wall, night becomes subdued light. A summer twilight eternally preserved. In a corner of the room, the Haitian pianist bends over his piano, over his music. A semi-sweet, semi-mad music which grabs you as soon as you come in, and which, as it grows late, goes to your head, like a cocktail. Piano-bar. The bar around the piano. The dance floor around the bar. Plenty of dancers. Mostly Haitians. Many of them with Quebecois women dancing Haitian-style, rhythmically swaying their hips.

I am now at the bar, sitting next to Daniel who does not yet want to dance. He remains silent, withdrawn, chasing I don't know what chimera in his cigarette smoke, seated before the glass he has emptied too quickly. Good, he finally emerges from his silence. He sighs:

"I am tired of living in Canada. Tired of being cooped up in an office, from nine to five, five out of seven days a week, tired of always getting there at the same time. And then, once you get home, you have to do everything yourself. Not to mention these shitty winters. I'm going back to Haiti, I can't take this country anymore."

"It's not only Haiti you miss."

"What's that supposed to mean?"

"You figure it out . . ."

It's my turn to grow silent. Facing the pianist who now sings.

"*Ayiti, Ayiti, mwen rinmin ou tout la vi* . . . , Haiti, Haiti, I'll remember you all my life . . ."

A tenor's voice, vibrant, bewitching, which blends perfectly into the sinuous melody and traces in my spirit the waves and undulations of the sea of the Antilles, the contours of our island, the bulging shapes of our mountains.

Daniel's sullen face disappears behind a screen of smoke, dissolving at the bottom of my glass where there's only juice and sun. The alcohol is in that music, in that song, in that voice . . .

The pianist-singer holds his last note for a long time, strikes his last chord and gets up. As if he had awaited that moment, like a spectator who relaxes at intermission, Daniel turns toward me with a broad smile and assumes a playful tone, almost like it used to be:

"Well, my doll, are you coming to Haiti with me? She who loves me follows me."

I draw my claws out:

"First of all, don't call me doll, you know how I hate it. Secondly, I will not follow you, I'm not your follower. Thirdly, even if I share your nostalgia, I have already told you that my life is here."

"Your life! You spend your days breaking your back over

tiresome brats, trying to keep them quiet with little drawings and little songs."

"I love my job, try to get that into your thick skull."

"Yes, Eva, but, if you were married, if you had children, you'd be less interested in taking care of other people's children."

Milord is in ad-mi-nis-tra-tion, he deals with important matters, he has a future. Whereas I . . . well, it's best to put an end to a discussion with no rhyme or reason:

"Listen, Daniel, I work all day, I still have some evening courses left to finish my education degree, right now I don't want to get married. Nor to return to Haiti. So don't insist. Besides, I don't want to have to explain to you one more time that I do more than just take care of children. Anyway, did we come here to argue or to dance?"

The music starts again. Records, while the pianist rests at the bar. Wow! A Cuban rumba, very rousing.

"Daniel, are we going to dance?"

Milord pouts. He doesn't feel like it. It doesn't matter, I'll dance alone. Thank God, things aren't the way they used to be, there are other women alone on the dance floor. And some of them—the Quebecois—are dancing together, because they go out "with the girls," and what's wrong with that? Thank God, it's not like in Haiti, long live the rumba! I spin, spin, spin, spinning to come face to face with the pianist, who landed I don't know when on the dance floor.

Good evening, smiles, of course, we had already met some-where—where? it doesn't matter—in any case, he, Christian, remembers me well. And besides, he has known Daniel since they were children, he had lost track of him for some time and was so happy to run into him again just now. Me? Daniel's wife? May God spare me! *Mande Bon Die padon!*

"No, he's a friend."

Said negligently, imprecisely. Nothing to add. And my memories, that euphoria of a few months ago, Daniel laughing, joking, a good dancer, ardent in love, my memories blur.

I make—or remake—Christian's acquaintance. He's at the piano-bar evenings from Thursdays to Sundays. The rest of the time he gives piano lessons and, when it rains, he composes. No, it's not easy to reconcile those two part-time jobs. The piano-bar isn't always amusing, not when people talk nonstop, when music is only a background noise. The piano lessons aren't necessarily lucrative when given at the pupil's home, and not without problems when given at home, when one lives in an apartment. But all that is still better than his first years in Montreal: days at the factory, evenings at the university, weekends playing the trumpet or the guitar in a small band, in half-deserted nightclubs. Not to mention his coursework.

"And you still managed to compose in the midst of all that?"

"For me that still remains the most important thing. I can only devote very little time to it, one morning a week at most. But they are wonderful hours, and that makes up for all the rest."

I understand. It's pleasant to hear all that enthusiasm. And I want to ask him lots of questions. But it is he who asks me the questions. What do I do? I am just delighted to tell him.

"Well, I'm responsible for a group of four-year-old children in a multi-ethnic nursery school. But I don't just mind them. We do all sorts of interesting things, we dance, sing, do artwork, play educational games. . . . All our activities have a goal."

"Like what?"

"Our dance sessions, for example, are geared to develop motor skills, to make them aware of their body, to help them place themselves in space."

Christian listens with interest, and asks what we do in music. I explain with pleasure, asking for his advice. It seems as if we have always known each other, as if we were old friends. We remain on the dance floor, the songs follow each other. Abruptly, he bends over my ear and speaks in a tone of intimacy, his voice full of emotion.

"You know, I just felt that you were the only person who ever truly listened to me."

I was astonished, I couldn't believe it, but one thing is true, I was listening to him with all my soul.

Christian returns to the piano. I look for Daniel, who's no longer at the bar. He has installed himself at a nearby table with some cronies he has run into, having recovered the fluent use of speech. He has livened up, he's getting all worked up. If it's not a debate over the independence of Quebec, it must be sports.

"Good evening, everyone."

The others greet me kindly but Daniel accosts me.

"You see, they just came in. You and your mania for wanting to go out early made me miss the Canadiens' victory."

When I said. . . . But I remain impassive. I smile and affect a cocky tone:

"What a pity you missed it. I am so sorry you didn't stay in front of the TV set. By the way, now that you're going back to Haiti, how are you going to manage without your Sunday-night hockey?"

Daniel glares at me, makes a resounding retort, and, on that note, I turn around on my heel. A quick hello in passing to friends I spot here and there, a bit of a chat, and I am back at the bar, facing Christian again. He's now singing that very beautiful song by Gilles Vigneault.

My country
In that country of blizzards
where the snow marries the wind . . .

Strange! Suddenly I feel as if the cold, the snow, and the blizzards had become tame, harmless. It is also strange to feel the impression—the illusion—that Christian is playing and singing just for me. Illusion? But he himself was thinking just now that I alone listened to him. And now, his smile, his eyes on me, are they masks and lies? Of course, singer, actor, liar, perhaps. But I, listener, spectator, accomplice. *Felix fictio.* Music to play-and-drink, delights and love-potions . . .

Christian attacks a Dominican merengue, I can't miss that. I try Daniel one last time, but he's still at the table with his cronies, drinking and carrying on. Dance that? That says nothing to him. So I go back to dancing by myself. Until the last break when Christian joins me. New tour of records. New musical tour around the world . . .

But Daniel is back at the bar, signalling for me to come. What does he want from me? I hope for his sake that there isn't a jealous scene brewing. In any case, the song is not yet finished, I reply with another hand gesture to wait, it won't hurt you.

The music ends, I walk over placidly, sit down very calmly, while Christian slips away. Well, what is it?

"This business of dancing to piano music . . ."

"Ah, Daniel . . . If you only knew how I would love to dance to an orchestra like those back home. With drums, trumpets, tchas-tchas, graj. Only all that is so far away. . . . Besides, they play records when the pianist rests."

"Anyway, this piano-bar is a dump. Let's go."

"Go if you want, I'm staying."

"You're staying just like that? How are you getting back?"

"I have plenty of friends here. I'm sure I'll find someone to give me a lift."

"But really, Eva, you can't stay behind dancing while I leave?"

"Why not? Are we glued together?"

"If you stay here tonight we're finished."

"Ha! . . . At any rate, when you return to Haiti . . ."

"Well, that won't be right away perhaps."

"You'd do well to hurry. Not to Haiti, not bloody likely, but to go find your mama, your godmother, your aunts, your maids, and all those other women who will agree to follow you, serve you, pamper you, pet you."

"You, at any rate, have no ambition. You'll spend you life wiping the asses of those little shits you take care of."

"Daniel, are you leaving, yes or no?"

"And you, are you coming, yes or no?"

"I'm staying."

"Very well!"

It comes out in a restrained tone, half-frustration, half-suppressed anger. I've had enough. I don't want to hear another word about it. And I get up. Daniel walks to the cloakroom, I toward the dance floor. Christian joins me immediately. Did he notice anything? If he did he's not asking any questions and I prefer to put it behind me.

Piano-bar, piano-alcohol, piano-dance. A bolero that very very gently goes to your head. Christian holds me tightly against him. Very tightly. I put my arm around his neck, place my head on his shoulder. Mad euphoria . . .

Later? We'll see. For the moment, life at the piano-bar is a musky rum.

Translated by Lizabeth Paravisini-Gebert

Ramabai Espinet, a scholar and poet, was born in Trinidad in 1948. She published her first collection of poetry, Nuclear Seasons, *in 1991, and had previously compiled an anthology of Caribbean women's poetry,* Creation Fire. *A scholar whose work has focused on Caribbean women's literature, Espinet has published articles on Phyllis Allfrey, Jean Rhys, and on the Indian woman writer in Trinidad and Tobago. Her concern with the emergence of the Indo-Caribbean voice is beautifully rendered in "Barred: Trinidad 1987," one of two fiction pieces Espinet has published to date.*

RAMABAI ESPINET

Barred

Trinidad 1987

I put a chair against the door of the room last night. Jammed it securely to the edge where the crib met the wall so that if the key turned in the lock and the door was pushed forward, a horrible grating noise would begin and I would wake up.

All of this because I lost my keys a few days ago. That and my wallet. All of my life I have flirted with the fantasy of losing these two things—a fantasy of being locked out and thrown absolutely upon my own primary resources. I remember standing above the Hastings Bridge in Vancouver, many years ago, high over the cold water and suddenly finding myself possessed by the mad urge to fling all valuables down. The valuables were pretty meager: a bit of makeup, a few dollars, the key to a shabby room in a little hotel. But what would I have done without them?

And that impulse has resurfaced over and over. All at once it happens without my consciously trying. All night long I hear a key turning in the lock downstairs, heavy footfalls on the stairs—an intruder confident and careless—what does this mean? And if someone has been dogging my footsteps and now possesses my keys, not to mention my wallet, what will I do when he appears?

I have no idea, but under my bed I keep a tin of insect repellent which I am told is good for spraying in their eyes. I also possess an old walking stick, a rape alarm with a light on it, and some candles and matches. Otherwise, there's only paper. Nothing much for a thief.

And, in between the waiting and his forced entry, I might die before the night is out of nerve-racking loneliness and anguish. All of my loves, fights, anxieties, and fears have crystallized into this mournful night where I am reduced to a purple jellyfish-like consistency. I can't sleep. And then I rise and throw open the doors to my balcony high above the ground. I look up at the peaks of the Northern Range—Morne Wash and El Tucuche. Unto the hills around do I lift up my longing eyes. Only I have no idea what I'm longing for, or if I do, it's still only an apprehension of something. I'm trying to approach closure, which for me is a completion of the whatever which is necessary for living and which remains like a door perpetually, uneasily, left ajar.

The mango tree is heavily fruited at this time of the year. I think: this is the land that spawned me, far from the continent of my origin. Can an island be someone's real home, I wonder? My ancestral roots are far from here and I don't even know, really, what they are.

I am Indian, plain and simple, not East nor West, just an Indian. I live in the West. My travel across the water to this land has not been easy and many a time I have squatted in the dirt of this or that lepayed hut, a few coins knotted in the corner of my ohrni, waiting, waiting—waiting to make the next move. There is fear, poverty, and sometimes a heavy hand striking at night. The enemy waits outside. Who is the enemy? Is it rum? The boy I married turns into a strange man who hits and curses at night. I bear much and one night I squat in the dirt waiting, the night black and quiet with only frogs singing in the bush where we live. I hear him coming home, drunk again, falling and cursing. The baby sleeping, the night quiet quiet. It is dark. I should move to go and light the lamp. But I don't move, I stay crouching on the dirt. After he is inside the house and stumbling around, then I follow and light the lamp. He is hungry.

"Way de food?"

He is enraged. I move to warm up the food and suddenly a cuff connects. And then he is deadly accurate—all over my head and breasts. The baby wakes and starts to cry.

I fall near the chulhah and he kicks me as I fall. I see him move towards the bedroom door mashing up everything on the way—a green-and-orange-flowered wedding lemonade set, a vision pot, and a blue and red plaque. His voice is deep and menacing, his boot heavy.

"Ah go kill dat chile tonight. Ah go dash out she focking brains. All yuh think is joke! All ah all yuh think I sorf. Well, tonight we go see. All ah all yuh go see."

The night dark and is only me and he and the baby in all this bush. He reach the bed and then he fall down near it. Where he going? Where the arse he think he going? He getting up, then he fall again straight on the new Slumberking. The springs start creaking again, he getting up. The baby bawling now and he getting up . . .

The cutlass by the fire, I chop some wood up this evening to cook the food. He on the bed and quick quick I chop him two, three times, me ain't know how hard. He give a lil sound and then he stop quiet. Me ain't really know how much time I chop he. He ain't get chance to touch the baby yet. I snatch she up and go outside and sit down in the middle of the road. No car don't come up here this hour. Is only high bush around. It getting cold but I can't move at all. All I could do is to rock the baby. And she, she sleeping. Light coming. I walk up the road—three milepost up—and call my brother-in-law. He come back to the house with me. They say the man dead.

All around us the cane fires are burning—rising and falling, smoke and soot. Nothing on earth has the live sugar smell of burning cane. And when the cane-sugar boils in the vats the smell is like all the holidays rolled into one fragrant ball—amber and crystalline on the outside and full of honeyed liquid in the center. We bought those balls at Ramdillah, later corrected to Ramleela. Which one is right, what the books now say or what we uttered in the peasant newness of this settlement? We are lost here, have not found the words to utter our newness, our strangeness, our unfound being. Our clothes are strange, our food is strange, our names are strange. And it is not possible for anyone to coax or help us. Our utterance can only come roaring out of our mouths when it is ready, set, and can go.

It has not been a happy arrival and we are still so morbid. There is a weed-killer sold to gardeners on this island. It is labelled gramoxone but everyone knows it as Indian tonic. The suicide tonic.

Indians ain't have no backbone, no stamina. You ain't see how at the slightest sign of stress they does run and drink Indian tonic? (Boy meets and loves girl but the arranged marriage gets in the way. Boy and girl drink **GRAMAZONE** and perish together—desire literally burning a hole through their bowels.) Indians ain't fraid to die. They does kill easy too. Is because they believe in reincarnation, don't doubt it. If you look in the hospitals is mostly Indians you go see. They there for accident, chopping, and poor guts. Is all the dhal and bhaji they does eat. And all the time the bitches and them have all kinda money hide up and save up. Yuh see all them saddhu and babu all yuh see walking the streets. Them is millionaires, man, millionaires. How yuh think Indians have so much business in this country? Them controlling the business community, you know, is only me and you stupid enough to think is white people. We born yesterday, we can't see what in front we eye. Them controlling ninety-five percent of the business in this country. They smart too bad. And all they children does do in school is study, study. I went to school with plenty Cramlal Booksingh and them yuh hear. And when they can't get in the good schools they does bribe man, bribe. Even in university they does buy the test paper. Is true they don't have no big job and money but them people low, they ain't bong for that. They ain't know how to live, they don't even spend money on food. Is only dhal and bhaji day and night.

After the birth of the second child there was no money in the house. Dass was working at a sweet-drink factory up on the main road, and one day they fired all the workers. Then he got a part-time end at the curry factory. But the little end never came home. He said it wasn't enough. He started to drink and gamble in the recreation club. We lived in the back in a low wooden house and I din't know how to manage. I couldn't cook good enough to sell and I had two children to mind.

One morning I got up. Dass had gone for the day already. He had forgotten a full pack of Anchor cigarettes on the table. And right where the window faced the road, I put an empty Klim tin, and two empty condensed milk tins turned upside down on either side of the Klim tin. Then I placed the pack of Anchor on the Klim tin. It wasn't long before a man came and bought the packet of cigarettes. He was my first customer. He was a tall thin Negro gentleman and I think he was a teacher. He said good morning before he bought the cigarettes and thank you when he left. I was nineteen years old. I bought two potatoes with the money to eat with roti for dinner. I didn't have to buy flour so I bought some sweeties with the change and put that in an empty bottle in the window. A Creole woman down the road showed me how to make sugar-cakes and tamarind balls.

Some time after Dass helped me to build a wooden counter just underneath the window. Later we put up a Coca-Cola sign, a Solo sign, and a newspaper sign. People came and bought in my little parlor. And only when Dass and his brother saw how I was making my way, they put together and we started the shop.

Outside now, the rain is pouring. Rain on a galvanized iron roof is the sweetest sound on earth. And when you lie with someone under the sheets in a safe bed while rain pelts down on the roof above, there is no other experience on earth like that. A crystal clear morning after the rain—dewfall, rainfall, footfalls of love. It is Sunday morning. I have lived through the long night.

Rosario Ferré was born in Ponce, Puerto Rico, in 1938. Her first book, Papeles de Pandora, *earned her recognition throughout Latin America. She has published four books of children's stories; a collection of poetry,* Fábulas de la garza desangrada; *a collection of feminist essays,* Sitio a Eros; *a novella,* Maldito amor; *and most recently another collection of essays,* El coloquio de las perras. *Through metafictional devices, Ferré explores the power of language to unveil the exclusion of women from a historical process she tries to demythify.*

ROSARIO FERRÉ

The Poisoned Story

And the King said to Ruyán the Wise Man:
"Wise Man, there is nothing written."
"Leaf through a few more pages."
The King turned a few more pages, and before long the poison began to course rapidly through his body. Then the King trembled and cried out:
"This story is poisoned."

A Thousand and One Nights

Rosaura lived in a house of many balconies, shadowed by a dense overgrowth of crimson bougainvillea vines. She used to hide behind these vines, where she could read her storybooks undisturbed. Rosaura, Rosaura. A melancholy child, she had few friends, but no one had ever been able to guess the reason for her sadness. She was devoted to her father, and whenever he was home she used to sing and laugh around the house, but as soon as he left to supervise the workers in the canefields, she would hide once more behind the crimson vines and before long she'd be deep in her storybook world.

I know I ought to get up and look after the mourners, offer my clients coffee and serve cognac to their unbearable husbands, but I feel exhausted. I just want to sit here and rest my aching feet, listen to my neighbors chatter endlessly about me. When I met him, Don Lorenzo was an impoverished sugar-cane planter, who only managed to keep the family afloat by working from dawn to dusk. First Rosaura, then Lorenzo. What an extraordinary coincidence. He loved the old plantation house, with its dozen balconies jutting out over the canefields like a windswept schooner's. He had been born there, and the building's historic past had made his blood stir with patriotic zeal: It was there that the criollos' first resistance to the invasion had taken place, almost a hundred years before.

Don Lorenzo remembered the day very well, and he would enthusiastically reenact the battle scene as he strode vigorously through halls and parlors—war whoops, saber, musket and all—thinking of those heroic ancestors who had gloriously died for their homeland. In recent years, however, he'd been forced to exercise some caution in his historic walks, as the wood-planked floor of the house was eaten through with termites. The chicken coop and the pigpen that Don Lorenzo was compelled to keep in the cellar to bolster the family income were now clearly visible, and the sight of them would always cast a pall over his dreams of glory. Despite his economic hardships, however, he had never considered selling the house or the plantation. A man could sell anything he had—his horse, his cart, his shirt, even the skin off his back—but one's land, like one's heart, must never be sold.

I mustn't betray my surprise, my growing amazement. After everything that's happened, to find ourselves at the mercy of a two-bit writer. As if my customers' bad-mouthing wasn't enough. I can almost hear them whispering, tearing me apart behind their fluttering fans: "Whoever would have thought it; from charwoman to gentlewoman, first wallowing in mud, then wallowing in wealth. But finery does not a lady make." I couldn't care less. Thanks to Lorenzo, their claws can't reach me anymore; I'm beyond their "lower my neckline a little more, Rosita dear, pinch my waist a little tighter there, Rosita darling," as though alterations to their gowns were no work at all and I didn't have to get paid for them. But I don't want to think about that now.

When his first wife died, Don Lorenzo behaved like a drowning man in a shipwreck. He thrashed about desperately in an ocean of loneliness for a while, until he finally grabbed on to the nearest piece of flotsam. Rosa offered to keep him afloat, clasped to her broad hips and generous breasts. He married her soon afterwards and, his domestic comfort thus reestablished, Don Lorenzo's hearty laugh could once again be heard echoing through the house, as he went out of his way to make his daughter happy. An educated man, well-versed in literature and art, he found nothing wrong with Rosaura's passion for storybooks. He felt guilty about the fact that she had been forced to leave school because of his poor business deals, and perhaps because of it on her birthday he always gave her a lavish, goldbound storybook as a present.

This story is getting better; it's funnier by the minute. The small-town, two-bit writer's style makes me want to laugh; he's stilted and mawkish and turns everything around for his own benefit. He obviously doesn't sympathize with me. Rosa was a practical woman, for whom the family's modest luxuries were unforgivable self-indulgences. Rosaura disliked her because of this. The house, like Rosaura's books, was a fantasy world, filled with exquisite old dolls in threadbare clothes; musty wardrobes full of satin robes, velvet capes, and crystal candelabra which Rosaura used to swear she's seen floating through the halls at night, held aloft by flickering ghosts. One day Rosa, without so much as a twinge of guilt, arranged to sell all the family heirlooms to the local antique dealer.

The small-town writer is mistaken. First of all, Lorenzo began pestering me long before his wife passed away. I remember how he used to undress me boldly with his eyes when I was standing by her sickbed, and I was torn between feeling sorry for him and my scorn for his weak, sentimental mooning. I finally married him out of pity and not because I was after his money, as this story falsely implies. I refused him several times, and when I finally weakened and said yes, my family thought I'd gone out of my mind. They believed that my marrying Lorenzo and taking charge of his huge house would mean professional suicide because my designer clothes were already beginning to earn me a reputation. Selling the so-called family heirlooms, moreover, made sense from a psychological as well as from a practical point of view. At my own home we've always been proud; I have ten brothers and sisters, but we've never gone to bed hungry. The sight of Lorenzo's empty cupboard, impeccably whitewashed and with a skylight to better display its frightening bareness, would have made the bravest one of us shudder. I sold the broken-down furniture and the useless knickknacks to fill that cupboard, to put some honest bread on the table.

But Rosa's miserliness didn't stop there. She went on to pawn the silver, the table linen, and the embroidered bedsheets that had once belonged to Rosaura's mother, and to her mother before her. Her niggardliness extended to the family menu, and even such moderately epicurean dishes as fricasseed rabbit, rice with guinea hen, and baby lamb stew were banished forever from the table. This last measure saddened Don Lorenzo deeply because, next to his wife and daughter, he had loved those criollo dishes more than anything else in the world, and the sight of them at dinnertime would always make him beam with happiness.

Who could have strung together this trash, this dirty gossip? The title, one must admit, is perfect: the unwritten page *will* bear patiently whatever poison you spit on it. Rosa's frugal ways often made her seem two-faced: she'd be all smiles in public and a shrew at home. "Look at the bright side of things, dear, keep your chin up when the chips are down," she'd say spunkily to Lorenzo as she put on her best clothes for mass on Sunday, insisting he do the same. "We've been through hard times before and we'll weather this one out, too, but there's no sense in letting our neighbors know." She opened a custom dress shop in one of the small rooms of the first floor of the house and hung a little sign that read "The fall of the Bastille" over its door. Believe it or not, she was so ignorant that she was sure this would win her a more educated clientele. Soon she began to invest every penny she got from the sale of the family heirlooms in costly materials for her customer's dresses, and she'd sit night and day in her shop, self-righteously threading needles and sewing seams.

The mayor's wife just walked in; I'll nod hello from here, without getting up. She's wearing one of my exclusive models, which I must have made over at least six times just to please her. I know she expects me to go over and tell her how becoming it looks, but I just don't feel up to it. I'm tired of acting out the role of high priestess of fashion for the women of this town. At first I felt sorry for them. It broke my heart to see them with nothing to think about but bridge, gossip, and gadflying from luncheon to luncheon. Boredom's velvet claw had already finished off several of them who'd been interned in mainland sanatoriums for "mysterious health problems," when I began to preach, from my modest workshop, the doctrine of "salvation through style." Style heals all, cures all, restores all. Its followers are legion, as can be seen by the hosts of angels in lavishly billowing robes that mill under our cathedral's frescoed dome.

Thanks to Lorenzo's generosity, I subscribed to all the latest fashion magazines, which were mailed to me directly from Paris, London, and New York. I began to write about the importance of line and color to a successful business, and not only for advertisement, but for the spiritual well-being of the modern entrepreneur. I began to publish a weekly column of fashion advice in our local gazette, which kept my clientele pegged to the latest fashion trends. Whether the "in" color of the season was obituary orchid or asthma green, whether in springtime the bodice was to be quilted or curled like a cabbage leaf, whether buttons were to be made of tortoise shell or mother-of-pearl, it was all a matter of dogma to them, an article of faith. My shop turned into a beehive of activity, with the town's most well-to-do ladies constantly coming and going from my door, consulting me about their latest ensembles.

The success of my store soon made us rich. I felt immensely grateful to Lorenzo, who had made it all possible by selling the plantation and lending me the extra bit of money to expand my workshop. Thanks to him, today I'm a free woman; I don't have to grovel or be polite to anyone. I'm sick of all the bowing and scraping before these good-for-nothing housewives, who must be constantly flattered to feel at peace. Let the mayor's wife lift her own tail and smell her own cunt for a while. I much prefer to read this vile story rather than speak to her, rather than tell her "how nicely you've got yourself up today, my dear, with your witch's shroud, your whisk-broomed shoes, and your stovepipe bag."

Don Lorenzo sold his house and his land and moved to town with his family. The change did Rosaura good. She soon looked rosy-cheeked and made new friends, with whom she strolled in the parks and squares of the town. For the first time in her life she lost interest in her storybooks, and when her father made her his usual birthday gift a few months later, she left it half read and forgotten on the parlor table. Don Lorenzo, on the other hand, became more and more bereaved, his heart torn to pieces by the loss of his canefields.

Rosa, in her workshop, took on several seamstresses to help her out and now had more customers than ever before. Her shop took up the whole first floor of the house, and her clientele became more exclusive. She no longer had to cope with the infernal din of the chicken coop and the pigpen, which in the old days had adjoined her workshop and cheapened its atmosphere, making elegant conversation impossible. As these ladies, however, took forever to pay their bills, and Rosa couldn't resist keeping a number of the lavish couturier models for herself, the business went deeper and deeper into debt.

It was around that time that she began to nag Lorenzo constantly about his will. "If you were to pass away today, I'd have to work till I was old and gray just to pay off our business debts," she told him one night with tears in her eyes, before putting out the light on their bedside table. "Even if you sold half your estate, we couldn't even begin to pay them." And when she saw that he remained silent, his gray head slumped on his chest, and refused to disinherit his daughter for her sake, she began to heap insults on Rosaura, accusing her of not earning her keep and of living in a storybook world, while she had to sew her fingers to the bone in order to feed them all. Then, before turning her back to put out the light, she told him that, because he obviously loved his daughter more than anyone else in the world, she had no choice but to leave him.

I feel curiously numb, indifferent to what I'm reading. A sudden chill hangs in the air; I've begun to shiver and I feel a bit dizzy. It's as though this wake will never end; they'll never come to take away the coffin so the gossipmongers can finally go home. Compared to my clients' sneers, the innuendos of this strange tale barely made me flinch; they bounce off me like harmless needles. After all, I've a clear conscience. I was a good wife to Lorenzo and a good mother to Rosaura. That's the only thing that matters. It's true I insisted on our moving to town, and it did us all a lot of good. It's true I insisted he make me the sole executrix of his estate, but that was because I felt I was better fit to administer it than Rosaura while she's still a minor, because she lives with her head in the clouds. But I never threatened to leave him, that's a treacherous lie. The family finances were going from bad to worse and each day we were closer to bankruptcy, but Lorenzo didn't seem to care. He'd always been capricious and whimsical, and he picked precisely that difficult time in our lives to sit down and write a book about the patriots of our island's independence struggle.

From morning till night he'd go on scribbling page after page about our lost identity, tragically maimed by the "invasion" of 1898, when the truth was that our islanders welcomed the Marines with open arms. It's true that, as Lorenzo wrote in his book, for almost a hundred years we've lived on the verge of civil war, but the only ones who want independence on this island are the romantic and the rich; the ruined landowners who still dream of the past as of a paradise lost; the frustrated, small-town writers; the bitter politicians with a thirst for power and monumental ambitions. The poor of this island have always been for commonwealth or statehood, because they'd rather be dead than squashed once again under the patent leather boot of the bourgeoisie. Each country knows which legs it limps on, and our people know that the rich of this land have always been a plague of vultures. And today they're still doing it; those families are still trying to scalp the land, calling themselves pro-American and friends of the Yankees to keep their goodwill, when deep down they wish they'd leave, so they would graze once again on the poor man's empty guts.

On Rosaura's next birthday, Don Lorenzo gave his daughter the usual book of stories. Rosaura, for her part, decided to cook her father's favorite guava compote for him, following one of her mother's old recipes. As she stirred the bubbling, bloodlike syrup on the stove, the compote's aroma gradually filled the house. At that moment Rosaura felt so happy, she thought she saw her mother waft in and out of the window several times, on a guava-colored cloud. That evening, Don Lorenzo was in a cheerful mood as he sat down to dinner. He ate with more relish than usual, and after dinner he gave Rosaura her book of short stories, with her initials elegantly monogrammed in gold, and bound in gleaming doe-heart's skin. Ignoring his wife's furrowed brow, he browsed with his daughter through the exquisite volume, whose thick gold-leaf edges and elegant bindings shone brightly on the lace tablecloth. Sitting stiffly, Rosa looked on in silence, an icy smile playing on her lips. She was dressed in her most luxurious opulent lace gown, as she and Don Lorenzo were to attend a formal dinner at the mayor's mansion that evening. She was trying hard to keep her patience with Rosaura because she was convinced that being angry made even the most beautifully-dressed woman look ugly.

Don Lorenzo then began to humor his wife, trying to bring her out of her dark mood. He held the book out to her, so she might also enjoy its lavish illustrations of kings and queens, all sumptuously dressed in brocade robes. "They could very well inspire some of your fashionable designs for the incoming season, my dear. Although it would probably take a few more bolts of silk to cover your fullness than it took to cover theirs, I wouldn't mind footing the bill because you're a lovable, squeez-able woman, and not a stuck-up, storybook doll," he teased her, as he covertly pinched her behind.

Poor Lorenzo, you truly did love me. You had a wonderful sense of humor, and your jokes always made me laugh until my eyes teared. Unyielding and distant, Rosa found the joke in poor taste and showed no interest at all in the book's illustrations. When father and daughter were finally done admiring them, Rosaura got up from her place and went to the kitchen to fetch the guava compote, which had been spreading its delightful perfume through the house all day. As she approached the table, however, she tripped and dropped the silver serving dish, spattering her stepmother's skirt.

I knew something had been bothering me for a while, and now I finally know what it is. The guava compote incident took place years ago, when we still lived in the country and Rosaura was almost a child. The small-town writer is lying again; he's shamelessly and knowingly altered the order of events. He gives the impression the scene he's retelling took place recently, that it actually took place only three months ago, but it's been almost six years since Lorenzo sold the farm. Anyone would think Rosaura was still a girl, when in fact she's a grown woman. She takes after her mother more and more; she fiddles away her time daydreaming, refuses to make herself useful, and lives off the honest sweat of those of us who work.

I remember the guava compote incident clearly. We were on our way to a cocktail party at the mayor's house because he'd finally made you an offer on the sale of the hacienda, which you had nostalgically named "The Sundowns," and the people of the town had rebaptized "Curly Cunt Downs," in revenge for your aristocratic airs. At first you were offended and turned him down, but when the mayor suggested he would restore the house as a historic landmark, where the mementos of the sugar-cane-growing aristocracy would be preserved for future generations, you promised to think about it. The decision finally came when I managed to persuade you, after hours of endless arguments under our bed's threadbare canopy, that we couldn't go on living in that huge house, with no electricity, no hot water, and no adequate toilet facilities; and where one had to move one's bowels on an antique French Provincial latrine, which had been a gift to your grandfather from King Alphonse XII. That's why I was wearing that awful dress the day of Rosaura's petty tantrum. I had managed to cut it from our brocade living-room curtains, just as Vivien Leigh had done in *Gone With the Wind*, and its gaudy frills and garish flounces were admittedly in the worst of taste. But I knew that was the only way to impress the mayor's high-flown wife and cater to her boorish, aristocratic longings. The mayor finally bought the house, with all the family antiques and *objets d'art*, but not to turn it into a museum, as you had so innocently believed, but to enjoy it himself as his opulent country house.

Rosa stood up horrified and stared at the blood-colored streaks of syrup that trickled slowly down her skirt, until they reached the silk embossed buckles of her shoes. She was trembling with rage, and at first couldn't get a single word out. When her soul finally came back to her body, she began calling Rosaura names, accusing her shrilly of living in a storybook world, while she, Rosa, worked her fingers to the bone in order to keep them all fed. Those damned books were to blame for the girl's shiftlessness, and as they were also undeniable proof of Don Lorenzo's preference for Rosaura, and of the fact that he held his daughter in higher esteem than his wife, she had no choice but to leave him. Unless, of course, Rosaura agreed to get rid of all her books, which should immediately be collected in a heap in the backyard, where they would be set on fire.

Maybe it's the smoking candles, maybe it's the heavy scent of all those myrtles Rosaura heaped on the coffin, but I'm feeling dizzier. I can't stop my hands from trembling and my palms are moist with sweat. The story has begun to fester in some remote corner of my mind, poisoning me with its dregs of resentment. As soon as she ended her speech, Rosa went deathly pale and fell forward to the floor in a heap. Terrified at his wife's fainting spell, Don Lorenzo knelt down beside her and begged her in a faltering voice not to leave him. He promised he'd do everything she'd asked for, if only she'd stay and forgive him. Pacified by his promises, Rosa opened her eyes and smiled at her husband. As a token of goodwill at their reconciliation, she allowed

Rosaura to keep her books and promised she wouldn't burn them.

That night Rosaura hid her birthday gift under her pillow and wept herself to sleep. She had an unusual dream. She dreamt that one of the tales in her book had been cursed with a mysterious power that would instantly destroy its first reader. The author had gone to great lengths to leave a sign, a definite clue in the story which would serve as a warning, but try as she might in her dream, Rosaura couldn't bring herself to remember what that sign had been. When she finally woke up she was in a cold sweat, but she was still in the dark as to whether the story worked its evil through the ear, the tongue, or the skin.

Don Lorenzo died peacefully in his bed a few months later, comforted by the cares and prayers of his loving wife and daughter. His body had been solemnly laid out in the parlor for all to see, bedecked with wreaths and surrounded by smoking candles, when Rosa came into the room, carrying in her hand a book elegantly bound in red and gold leather, Don Lorenzo's last gift to Rosaura. Friends and relatives all stopped talking when they saw her walk in. She nodded a distant hello to the mayor's wife and went to sit by herself in a corner of the room, as though in need of some peace and quiet to comfort her in her sadness. She opened the book at random and began to turn the pages slowly, pretending she was reading but really admiring the illustrations of the fashionably dressed ladies and queens. As she leafed through the pages, she couldn't help thinking that now that she was a woman of means, she could well afford one of those lavish robes for herself. Suddenly, she came to a story that caught her eye. Unlike the others, it had no drawings, and it had been printed in a thick, guava-colored ink she'd never seen before. The first sentence took her mildly by surprise, because the heroine's name was the same as her stepdaughter's. Her curiosity kindled, she read on quickly, moistening the pages with her index finger because the guava-colored ink made them stick to each other annoyingly. She went from wonder to amazement and from amazement to horror, but in spite of her growing panic, she couldn't make herself stop reading. The story began . . . "Rosaura lived in a house of many balconies, shadowed by a dense overgrowth of crimson bougainvillea vines . . . ," and how the story ended, Rosa never knew.

Translated by Rosario Ferré and Diana Vélez

Born in Santurce, Puerto Rico, in 1946, Magali García Ramis
started her professional life as a journalist. Her first collection of
short stories, La familia de todos nosotros, *appeared in 1976.*
Her novel Felices días, Tío Sergio *confirmed her reputation as*
one of Puerto Rico's best contemporary writers. She received a
Guggenheim Fellowship in 1989 to work on her second novel,
"Las horas del sur." García Ramis chronicles the world of the
Puerto Rican middle class and the marginalized classes through
a language that is at times poetic, ironic, colloquial, and evocative
as she recreates the last three decades of her island's history.

MAGALI GARCÍA RAMIS

Cocuyo Flower

Fuschia sweater, skin-tight white skirt, and flab quivering all
over—Clotilde was chubby, oh! how chubby Clotilde was! And
you would watch her get out of her husband's yellow wreck of
a car, and climb the steps of the Humanities building, briefcase
in hand, while everyone exchanged malicious glances because
they knew that when the car turned around with Clotilde's
husband in it, it would stop in front of the library and there the
thin, spinster librarian would get in (who would have thought
so!), she, the innocent one (still waters run deep), and they
wouldn't return until two hours later, at two o'clock, every
Monday, Wednesday, and Friday while Clotilde was teaching her
two morning classes, English 121 and English 315. Yes, you
watched her go by all those days of your fifth and sixth semes-
ters and you couldn't help comparing yourself to her, because
one day you too would be plump and pleasing like Clotilde, and
because in contrast to her you waited for the car that would take

you to study for two hours things for which you didn't receive university credit.

Luis appeared in your life without fanfare and you took his words as you would those of any professor; what he said made sense and you liked the ideas he sowed. The university is a house of learning where men and women prepare to become thinking human beings, shadows of Ortega y Gasset, an ivory tower and the tower of Clotilde! What's important is not to learn facts, but "to seed doubt," a powdered and fragrant Clotilde said to you when you took her humanities core course in your freshman year. And Luis made you doubt, made you tremble, and did to you two or three other things that you liked, and you found time in your semester for him.

"A history seminar and a language seminar, both without credit and beginning in the middle of September, how could that be?" your father asked with surprise when he noticed your changed schedule. And you explained to him, with that softness and precision you copied from your teachers, that they were special requirements, that they didn't represent an overload, that you would be better prepared when you graduated. "The University of Puerto Rico has changed so much!" your father said. You invented everything, just as those humanities professors invented themselves. Luis's bed was cold at eight o'clock in the morning. And the apartment was so near and lies flew so fleetingly, so harshly. Then you would return at eleven in the morning, on time for your nineteenth-century history class, and you would see Clotilde go down the steps to wait for her husband in front of her tower.

She puzzled you. She puzzled you, and he puzzled you the first time you heard him, because every Monday, Wednesday, and Friday you would go off campus to eat lunch with the group. Río Piedras's stinky curbs didn't bother you as they did at first, because now you liked the town with all its dirt, and its trinkets, and its jewelry stores packed with Arabs and Cubans. He saw you coming and he got ready. He dried the sweat from his palms on his thighs, he placed his right foot on the rail behind him; and he looked at you. You were last in the procession because all of you had to walk single file on the sidewalk, and he waited for you to go by to shout at you with a sibilant voice, "Goodbye, garlic flower"; you kept going, and he called out again, "and if you don't look at me you can go to hell," and you and your friends burst out laughing. You laughed aloud and so did he, and he walked behind you for a block, and from that very first time you knew that you shouldn't have laughed, that those characters are quite impertinent. And they follow young women. And they roam all over the university. And probably for that reason you laughed.

You laughed so hard that time when Luis brought a bottle of wine. "At nine o'clock, are you crazy?" Yes, he said, we're crazy, and you drank it naked on the fresh bed and you missed your eleven o'clock class because you were dizzy and you didn't see Clotilde that Friday because you were under Luis and the only thing you saw was the unlit bulb hanging from the ceiling.

The second semester (how well you learned) you invented an independent study in the Honors Program that you were allowed to attend by special permission. It was at eight o'clock in the morning so you didn't see Clotilde's arrival, just her departure at eleven. You always said hello to her and she smiled back and inside you would scream at her, "asshole Clotilde, how could you allow yourself to be used?" Your history seminar and your language seminar and your independent study became Luis 122, Luis 305, and Luis 465—the highest course number you knew—and you chose that number because that extra hour with Luis was out of this world. He would pick you up half asleep, without even having washed his face, and from the university to his apartment it was a matter of ten minutes, which left enough time for him to jump into bed and catch his last minutes of sleep, while you prepared coffee and did your math homework; no wonder you failed it that term, but how could you explain that to the teacher? They—male and female professors—demanded too much from you, and you, what the hell, were a humanities major and you were going to end up teaching there because you were promising, didn't you know it? You certainly were promising!

He waited for you, he waited every day and you realized that he knew your schedule. One day you broke your usual schedule and went to Río Piedras to buy fabric and a pattern. You found each other face to face, he and you, and he smiled right away. Low-class character. With greasy hair and pants so tight they fit like plastic. What did he say? You never told your friends because it hit you deep inside and you took a deep breath. So many years listening to characters like him telling you things, and now this one was impressing you. You decided, without deciding, to walk past him every Monday, Wednesday, and Friday. So did your friends, but they didn't realize that among the men standing in front of that snack bar on Ponce de León Avenue there was one, sort of skinny, who was always there. You knew he waited for you at lunch time. And you started to walk past him some Tuesdays and Thursdays, and then it was every day, to listen to the same words every day in a perfect and complete performance, as perfect and complete as your university life was, classes, questions, laughs, and habits . . . and Clotilde with her fuchsia sweaters and her eyes too big, too restless.

One day Clotilde's husband didn't return at eleven. Rumors mingled with instinctive malice and your schoolmates were saying that he had been shot in the English department. But it wasn't true. The wife of an American professor, one of those crazy guys, was the one who had run after her husband, gun in hand, through the department corridors the previous afternoon. That was to be expected in the English department, everyone knew it because oh boy! the crazy ones ran rampant there, and also, in that damp basement with low ceilings, spirits, as passions, were less dry, less clear. But Clotilde's husband didn't arrive that day because exactly at five to eleven his yellow car had crashed into a lamppost, a tall brown pine, and under the scalding sun on Barbosa Avenue flies were buzzing around Clotilde's husband's bleeding face, around Clotilde's husband's battered body, as he held fast to the steering wheel, his only means of escape from Clotilde. It was said (everything was always known at the university) that the librarian (who would have thought so!) ran from the car after the accident (nothing happened to her) and she walked back to the library, a little sweaty but that's all because an important book shipment was expected that afternoon and it had to be transferred to the natural sciences library. Important organic chemistry, physics, and biology books, and she sat down to catalogue them, a little nervous of course, the picture of spinsterhood innocence, with a dead lover.

From that day on Clotilde arrived and left by taxi, and she changed her hours: she arrived at eleven and left at one. She always called the company with the white and turquoise cars, and she got out of the back seat with a newly learned rhythmic movement, she who before had always gotten out from the front seat. At first she wore mourning clothes, but after a short time she showed mourning only on her hips, by the black skirts she wasn't going to discard and which she just threw on to compliment her fuchsia sweaters. And the only feeling you came up with when you heard about her husband was, how sad! university traditions shouldn't end; you felt sorry that your familiar world, habits, poses, and traditions were coming to an end and time beat more quickly each of your sweet and vain university years.

After spending almost two years in Luis's class you also began to tire of him. You were preregistering for your senior year and you wanted new classes, new doubts, new people. Luis and you had never argued, rather you dried up slowly like inferior brands of plastic glue, and the day arrived when nothing tied you together. One Monday you told him not to come for you on Wednesday and from the front of the tower you watched him leave in his small, olive-green car. Later you found out that he was picking up a fiery radical at the Social Sciences building around two o'clock in the afternoon and it felt OK to you, you were happy for him, or at least that's what you told your friends.

You took the final exam in your Spanish class early because the professor always left for Europe when the hot season arrived, and you took it, and copied all you wanted, and got an excellent grade. The professor congratulated you although he had his suspicions. Because in humanities, you and all of you told your half-truths, and all of you always wanted one more semester to learn the truth, and upon graduation (you already knew it) you would be one of them and you would remain forever waiting for another semester to learn even a little bit more and be a little closer to the truth; you had scheduled a full life ahead of you and you wouldn't be as stupid as Clotilde who now had to come to the university by taxi, her life disrupted and her old habits gone by the board. You would take refuge in your university life and you would learn so much in order to walk around with the certainty of THOSE WHO KNOW and you lied like all of them, as they lied to you and you lied and they all lied, all except him. That low-life character who waited for you every Monday, Tuesday, Wednesday, Thursday, and Friday, he was the only honest one and you came down to his reality. He would see you coming and he knew what you were coming for, both partners in crime, both looking at each other, and with his sticky voice as oily as saliva he would say as you passed in front of him in the daily game, "Goodbye, cocuyo flower"; he would wait for your imperceptible shudder and your deep breath and he would thrust his pelvis forward before completing his litany, "all that hangs between my legs is under your power." And you would feel a happy terror and you would go on walking. And you enjoyed thinking he didn't say that to anyone else, that you were his only cocuyo flower as his filthy voice was your only truth without any doubts and without Ortega y Gasset; and he would smile a viscous grimace because his truth controlled you. Then you would remember that you had to take advantage of your student years because you were going to be a great professional and you would run back to the Humanities building, University of Puerto Rico, Río Piedras Campus, around one o'clock, when Clotilde was leaving, her flab quivering as she went down the steps carrying her briefcase in one hand and in the rest of her body her truncated life.

Translated by Carmen C. Esteves

Ángela Hernández was born in Jarabacoa, Dominican Republic, in 1954. Although trained in chemical engineering, Hernández has worked primarily as a researcher and activist on women's issues. Known primarily as a poet and essayist—she has published two volumes of poetry and numerous essays and articles on feminism and women's rights—Hernández published her first collection of short stories, Alótropos, in 1989 to immediate and enthusiastic critical acclaim. "Cómo recoger la sombra de las flores" won the 1988 Casa del Teatro Prize. Her work is characterized by the poetic richness of her prose and by her blending of the vivid details of the external world with a poet's understanding of the fantastic world of the imagination.

ÁNGELA HERNÁNDEZ

How to Gather the Shadows of the Flowers

"Voyage of voyages with a hundred returns / capricious voyages / testimony of sighs / returns without turns / time in bouquets / and in my brow a sacred zeal to fade away / perhaps to return."

We found this text under the mattress and, like the rest of them, it seemed intended to provide us with clues to understand her. An impossible enterprise for us who had known her and loved her as a common girl, as the eldest sister, for whom our parents reserved certain privileges.

Faride was the only one of us to attend a private school (Papa got her a scholarship to an evangelical institute). The rest of us went to public school. When she finished high school she started working as a cashier in a supermarket; she remained in that job for six months. One day, surprisingly, she quit. Mama accused her of acting unconscionably, a judgment ratified by my father's recriminating glances. They both employed every possible means to extract from her the reason for her self-dismissal. She had not been laid off, nor had she had any difficulties in balancing the register every day, nor any trouble with any customer. It was not until after many weeks of siege that she said: "The supervisor kept pawing me." Nobody bothered her about it again. Two months later she began to work in a fabric shop. That's how she was, unaffected, serious, and reserved. I have brought you some photographs, but I must return them right away. My mother has forbidden us to touch her belongings.

From the very first glance the photographs captured my attention; I was intrigued above all by the well-defined combination of white and black features in one face: thick lips, very fine nose, long and kinky curls. In her eyes you caught a glimpse of an expression as dual and marked as the lines of her profile; there was in them a latent force: a vague expressiveness, a black blaze behind a deceiving curtain of void. From that day on, the image of her seductive gaze has been an obsessive burden in my brain. After that I would stay with José after class to hear more details.

The women of my family marry before they turn twenty. My grandmother married very young; my mother followed the tradition, and Faride got married a few months before turning eighteen. I don't think she had a good idea of what marriage meant; I'm not even sure whether she was happy or not, but I do remember her clearly, distressed and nervous, untiringly knitting tablecloths and bedcovers the year before Raúl left for the United States. Not that she had much choice. Faride supported the household. They had two children and had been married four years and he still had not found a steady job. When she returned to our house with the children, she seemed sad and somewhat relieved.

I have turned this information over and over in my mind, trying to understand the meaning of the events that took place in José's house. I haven't found anything that points to Faride having been subject to any special circumstances in her childhood and adolescence. There were nine siblings, who received the same upbringing and grew up in the same house. Three of them, including Faride, were born in the central mountains, but that doesn't make them different. The two eldest brothers seem to have nothing in common with her; José, the sixth child, whom I know best, is as normal a young man as they come.

Industrious and conscientious, when she moved back into the house Faride continued working in the shop and knitting tablecloths and bedcovers in the evenings and weekends. Her friends would say to her jokingly: "Aha! knitting while she awaits her husband, like Penelope," and she would reply with a smile: "I knit to eat, not to deceive myself."

In some ways, in some small things, my sister's behavior was different from that of other people. She showed no special interest in her physical appearance. She never wore lipstick or eye makeup. Her wardrobe was very simple; she made her own clothes of light fabrics and pastel colors; lemon yellow and lilac predominated in her apparel. I was the oldest of the siblings still living at home; I was then just past twelve; I don't remember ever seeing her angry at me; she never lectured me, nor did she offer advice on any subject. But these details of behavior don't make anyone special; least of all in our house, where chattering and long conversations between adults were extremely rare and where everyone preferred to keep to themselves; my mother listened to the radio; my father played dominoes; my older brothers cruised the streets; Faride knitted.

We got along very well with her and the children; life followed its natural course and none of us, not even our parents, had noticed the gradual transformation taking place within our sister; it was with great surprise that we witnessed the unexpected eruption of the world brewing within her. It happened at breakfast:

"He'll help me, this one will indeed help me, Mama. This man is really worth it. He is beautiful like a sun. He smells of May, he tastes like mint washed by a rain shower. He's not rich, nor young; he's not even heroic. But he's incomparably loving. He carries me to bed every day, and you should see what a bed, soft like a song filtered through water. He only needs a glance to understand me; he knows what I yearn for just from sensing it."

We couldn't quite understand her words. Not even Papa and Mama seemed to understand, since they were looking at her with puzzled expressions on their faces.

"The house has burst into flower in the few days we have spent together. Flowers assumed gigantic proportions with every minute of love. Violets and poppies growing deliriously; fennel and sunflowers and red-wine-colored hollyhocks like open umbrellas. It's like a jungle now. The orchids climb the walls, forming very elegant nosegays, they barely let you see anything through the glass. The whole house is made of transparent glass. At first I was embarrassed; someone could see us when we did things in bed. Then I realized that the house was alone in the world. Swarms of bees embroider honey hives around the stalks of the carnations, green crickets and fireflies gather pollen to build their homes. Ah, the hollyhocks fascinate me with the red-wine blood exquisitely retained in their corollas! Please advise me: What can one do with a garden gone out of control? What would we do if the flowers continue to climb to the ceiling and manage to conceal the sun? He could abandon me. He knows the garden grows only for me. What tragic pleasure! What sweet mortification!"

We remained silent. We couldn't understand her speech, but it fascinated us; Mama and Papa looked at her in astonishment. She got up, washed her hands, took her purse, and left.

The children delighted in our daughter's stories as if they were fairy tales. We got very agitated; we had never heard Faride talk about men, least of all in such insolent terms. We went over the details of the past week, and not finding anything extraordinary to justify her words, we decided to question her when she returned.

She didn't come back until eight o'clock that night, and didn't even allow us to approach her: "I'm dying to sleep," she said as she threw herself onto the bed between her children without changing clothes. She was snubbing us for the first time in her life, and the disrespect of her action poisoned our evening.

The correspondences between their description of Faride's words and her writings were remarkable. The papers she left in her own handwriting share a similar tone. In one and the other the central mystery derives from the comparison between her discourse and her slight intellectual training. Where did these figurations come from? Was it perhaps a peculiar type of schizophrenia? Sometimes her brother worries me; more than by vocation, he has chosen this career with the hope of solving her enigma, and perhaps he's only moving further and further away from the clues.

We had been watching for her when she came in and sat next to me at the table. She seemed peaceful, cheerful; there was a disconcerting clarity in her eyes; two drops of dew hung from her pupils. A serenity and happiness which I felt spreading through my body.

I shuddered, my hands shook, when I saw her approach. A presentiment oppressed my heart. I saw the six-year-old girl with a wide ribbon holding her hair, the lively girl who grabbed my legs and whom I pushed away with a slap; the angel of light who kissed me, licked my lips, hugged me, caressed my breasts, and whom I pushed away, annoyed because two younger children demanded my attention; the insistent girl that got under my skirt wanting to play, and whom I spanked because I had too much work and her moving bothered me; the little one who at dawn cuddled at my feet hoping to remain unnoticed, and whom I would put back to bed screaming at her to be quiet. The one who would take care of her little brothers and sisters so I would love her more, the one who asked me to let her suckle when I breast-fed her little brother, the one who exasperated me with her cajoling, when it was already too late. The same face, the same ribbon, the same laugh, the same eyes. I would have wanted to hug her, but too much time and distance had passed between the two of us.

"I gave him a shell of twelve colors. Uf! it was so hard to find. It was between rocks, in a big hollow. I placed a strong tree trunk across the hollow, hung from it and walked with my hands to where the treasure was. It is the size of a teacup. The colors spring from the outside and then spread to the inside. It is so curious, so many colors emerging from a dark little knot."

She lowered her voice, as if she were speaking to herself; then she continued, excitedly.

"He loved my gift. *C'est très joli, comme la vie,* he said to me."

My mother contained herself. Who is he? she asked her. Faride looked at her, puzzled, and replied naturally: "The director of the Oncology Institute."

"I never imagined he would be so beautiful. When he laughs, and he's almost always laughing, he leans back, chair and all. His laughter soars to the sky like bubbles of music coming out of a flute. I feel like sucking his mouth, I feel like eating him with lettuce and carnations. His teeth look moist. His laughter flows from inside, as if a glass of water flowered in his throat."

Mama blushed; Papa was uncomfortable in his chair; we were enjoying the story.

"He has requested me as his assistant in his operations, in the radioactive treatments and the laboratory. I tell him I know nothing of diseases and healing. He soothes me with his beautiful laughter; you'll learn, we'll teach you. We spent long dead hours, no, better still, living, gloriously living hours seated in two wooden chairs, on the rocks, by the sea. The others were far away. The rocks jutted out of the sea, we sailed on an indigo air several meters above the water."

Then, deep in thought, she commented to herself: "This special man makes me forget cancer." She devoured her breakfast and left hurriedly. We remained there talking about cancer. For some of us it was a bumblebee with horns, to others a plant with white spots. Unable to agree, we asked Mama. Anguished, she replied: "It's many things at the same time."

My husband and I were troubled. We had educated Faride as a good Christian and didn't recognize her in these daring speeches. We even came to suspect that she was keeping bad company, but anyway, people don't change just like that, from one moment to the next.

"They're dreams. Did you notice today? They're only dreams."

"She believes they're real. This is very unusual. She'll go telling those filthy stories around. They'll say she's a tramp. The husband working in New York and she living with other men."

"People who know us won't take her words seriously."

On Monday Mama woke us up early; she made us have breakfast and get ready for school in a hurry. Before we left, however, she couldn't prevent our overhearing our sister telling her in the kitchen:

"Mama, the young ones are darlings. His name is Andrés and Lucía introduced me to him at her party. Fire at first sight! One look and we were captivated. It's understandable: tender, passionate, soft, with his big green eyes, he's like a big son between my legs."

I found the piece of paper on the nightstand in her room; it was in her handwriting, and the contents seemed to refer to the story of the shell and the doctor. I woke her up very early, dawn had not yet broken. I took her to the kitchen, I wanted to speak to her without interruptions. Maybe the paper would clarify something, maybe her stories were nothing more than ideas copied from some disturbing book. What is this? I asked her.

"Can't you see? I wrote it night before last: I am a relative of the stones / of the delicate waves of the coast / of the fragile horizons / the ever winding and unwinding snails / rocking in the vigils of their chiaroscuro moves / with their easy melodies / with their sonority of distant sea / with their peaceful and oblivious song / with mother-of-pearl winding and unwinding around submarine lines / drinking them like wine, like salt, like elementary milk."

She had repeated from memory the words on the piece of paper; she half-closed her eyes and continued to recite, as if she were reading something written inside her lids:

"Wet and surprised / like a newborn / I can barely touch myself / I did not take the sun, there was no time / nor did I learn my tongue / nor did I detect the clues to my surroundings / I lie on myself / drowsy and timid / my textures are tender / in this my very embryo / sometimes I renew myself."

I felt a tingle down my spine. I didn't dare interrupt her, it wasn't my daughter talking.

"To exist and not to be / is a miracle / to be the frontier to the undecipherable / equidistant to acceptance / a wisdom on the margin of precepts / a lucid candor / a hidden golden vertebra / a lace made of spinning violets / forming a violet heart."

Almost voiceless, I said: Faride, my daughter, what is happening to you? I didn't even dare touch her, I sensed her distant and alien.

"Nothing is the matter, Mama."

"Where do you get these stories from?"

"What stories?"

"The ones you've just told me, the ones from breakfast on Saturday and Sunday."

"They're not stories. I wrote that poetry fifty years ago. It's mine. I don't tell stories, I never could learn any."

"Are you telling me that these are truths, reality?"

"What is the truth, Mama? What is reality?"

"The truth is the truth, the same truth you learned when you were a child. Reality is that you're twenty-three years old. You couldn't have written anything fifty years ago. Tell me the truth; you never lied."

"I'm not lying."

"Don't drive me to despair. Trust me; tell me what's happening in your life."

"I trust you. Nothing is happening to me; I am well."

"Tell me then, why are you inventing these extravagant stories so detrimental to your good name?"

"What extravagant stories?"

"These fantasies of men and love affairs so different from your reality as a serious woman."

"What is reality, Mama?"

"Reality is eating rice and plantains, giving birth to a child, working, seeing clearly what things are like!"

"And what are things like?"

I didn't insist anymore; this senseless conversation was driving me mad.

The next day, she sat at the table, giddy. The children had left for school. One of our older children was with us. I had asked him to be there, knowing that Faride respected him almost more than she did her father, she feared him more. From the time she was very young we entrusted her care to her brother. His presence, however, didn't inhibit her.

"It was a beautiful, but at the same time, boring trip; two months at sea, seeing sky, seeing blue and more blue, seeing the same people, the unseasonal birds hovering over our heads. But it was worth it. My mother's friends were waiting for me, with a bouquet of flowers and open arms. I went with Ferita to register at the university. I took only two courses: botany and history, because I first must grow used to the city and my new friends, before I throw myself completely into my studies. I get my teachers confused; they are so white, so similar. God made white people's skin with the same roll of fabric. Yesterday we went to see Unamuno's *Shadows of Dreams*. The theater is very elegant, and so are the people. After the performance we went to my apartment, we drank wine and beer, we danced, and rolled on the floor."

"Enough!" I said with anger and sadness. My oldest son only commented: "What is she talking about?" We had to practically push him out of the house by force, he was furious and wanted to beat her up. According to him, Faride had become a trollop and two or three good blows would straighten her out. She didn't seem surprised, and when we returned she even added:

"The trolley cars, the buildings, the beautiful paintings in the museums, the Graf Zeppelin, the romantic friends reciting verses in the parks."

The narratives at breakfast became routine. They sent us away from the table, they made us run out to school, they separated us from her and her belongings, managing thereby to sharpen our curiosity. We spied on conversations, searched her purse, and eluded Mama's and Papa's watchful eyes to be with her. Mama thought that Faride's ravings were a passing thing, attributing them to lack of news from Raúl. In effect, there had been no news from him since he had left. Mama had gone to the group that had organized the trip, but they said they weren't responsible for people after they took them over. Papa considered Raúl a scoundrel; he wasn't interested in his whereabouts, and even less in his fate. That Saturday, Faride came in to the kitchen, trembling: there was a somber expression on her face. Papa and Mama were alarmed.

"It was alive, the desiccated bird, the prehistoric desiccated bird sent to me by my friend from India was alive. It chased me into the rice bog, into the labyrinth of caves in San Juan, between my legs. It seemed dead when it arrived through the mail, but it was alive. An atrocious bird, sticky, with long legs and long sharp goads instead of feathers. It was humid and dead and moved. I don't know what to do with it. I tried throwing it out the window only to find it again under my bed. Ten times I took it out of my room and it would return to my side, like an amulet reeking of death, and it is in my room, and it holds its viscous skin to my face. Oh God, it has made me throw up my insides!"

Papa and Mama listened to her in consternation. Even we, spying through the gaps in the kitchen wall, were profoundly impressed. She suddenly changed her expression and laughed:

"Ah, but what a beautiful little house. He sent it to me as a gift. It came in the mail today. It's not taller than my legs, but it has a thousand little doors, all pink, all painted in a different pink. A thousand shades of pink on the façade. When you open a little door, you find a three-verse poem and a painting which explains that year's history. A thousand years of Indian history in a thousand paintings and a thousand poems. In the last little door, the one in a pink so intense it approaches the orange of red-tinted clouds, is the Salt March and the Peace Poem: Peace, salt, autumn splendor / they are within us and together they will sprout / like a water spring that blinds certain fires."

When we, intrigued, asked her about the little house, she told us that she would show it to us later. In India, she told us, children didn't use books to study history, but little houses like these. Through millennia, Hindus have learned the exceptional art of miniaturizing trees and history.

On Faride's birthday her colleagues at work organized a little party for her, to which they invited us. We went to the store in the afternoon, after the shop closed, feeling apprehensive. To our surprise, the celebration proceeded quite normally. The shop owner gave her a certificate commending her for her exceptional performance as a salesperson; he also gave her a small gold chain, exhorting her to keep up the good work with her usual cordiality and efficiency. Her co-workers loved and admired her, as we could attest to.

At home, however, the modifications in her conduct were marked. She knitted less and spent long periods of time in silence.

She didn't waste any chance to play. She would get lost in the ring around the rosie, pocket full of posies, look who's here Punchinella, Punchinella, Miss Mary Mack Mack with silver buttons all down her back back; she ran and jumped with boundless energy, and none of us could catch her when we played tag. Papa and Mama rested easy when they saw us like that. But a turn in the situation agitated the entire household, and from then on our parents didn't even bother to hide their anguish from us.

It was Sunday. Papa was playing dominoes with a group of friends, in front of the house. Faride, euphoric, started to turn around the playing table, jumping as she held the edges of her skirt, opening it like a fan. She sang out the words, heaping them onto each other in an easy flowing laughter.

"My lover returned from the crystal house. He has brought me his riddles once more. This time I will guess the answers. The glass house is celebrating tonight, all the windows have been opened and the rooms are bursting with full moons. We are going to Moscow to ride the Ferris wheel. He amuses himself with the trapeze artists. Together we built a sculpture to the tenderness of the panda bear / Providence shines like a firefly in the Caribbean Sea / with the fishermen on the golden beach / at dawn / we encircle its waters / with boreal ribbons / we wove a basket / that knows about Ithaca / through eternal ice / we go animatedly / on expeditions / silver camels / carry us on their rumps / through snowy peaks / so clear / so beautiful / that in their translucency / time melts / and the soul dissolves."

From that moment on, our household was in an upheaval. Faride would tell her rapturous stories to anyone who would listen. Some people would come to our house and incite her to talk so as to feed the rumors circulating around the neighborhood. Mama and Papa quickly gathered together some money and took her to a psychiatrist.

He examined her, and submitted her to different tests. He tested her reflexes, laid logical traps for her; they spoke for more than a hour. Faced with our bewilderment, he told us she was undoubtedly sane, and that he found her to be an intelligent and cooperative young woman. We narrated to him the events of Sunday and of the days before. He asked us to understand her youth and her ideas. The dreams of each generation differ, he insisted. I insisted on his hearing her in front of us, thinking that perhaps she had pulled the wool over his eyes. We called her in and I asked her to read one of her poems. She then proceeded to recite with great spontaneity, looking us in the eye:

"Populations of stars uninhabit the sky to hurl themselves at my heavens / matrixes of fresh bubbles / pay deaf ears to their original water springs / and make a watery bouquet in my sex / juice of virgin meadows / squeezed by sheer will / form the blood of my wanderings / I am with them / a game of love / a born traveler."

The doctor expressed that that poetry confirmed his diagnosis: Faride was intelligent and original, and advised us to let her be. We left his office even more baffled; no one said a word on our way back.

Her dreams gained ground as the days went by. It was hard to wake her up in the morning. Sometimes she would wash up, have breakfast in the kitchen, and return to bed. We would wake her up again shaking her roughly. She would then do two or three routine chores and then return to bed to continue her interrupted sleep. When we forced her to get up and kept her from returning to bed, as I lectured her on her lack of responsibility toward work and of the importance of her salary to the family's finances, she would walk through the house as if it were a stage and she the leading actress, playing a role known only to herself.

Sometimes, sitting upright in bed, she examined her surroundings as if she didn't recognize anything. She walked by inertia, repeating to us previous dialogues. Pensive and inexpressive, it would take her up to three-quarters of an hour to cross the line dividing her two realities.

We did all we could to isolate the neighbors from the atmosphere of our house. Our older children would entertain visitors in front of the house, taking chairs out to the sidewalk and engaging in conversation almost on the street. I abstained from going out. I went only to mass on Sunday and I tried to do so with the greatest discretion: I was terrified of questions. We forbade the children to enter Faride's bedroom. After repeated excuses, we had to admit that she wouldn't return to work, and so we informed the shop owner. But all our efforts did nothing more that unleash more rumors. The neighbors' assumptions were like knives in my heart. As far as they were concerned Faride was pregnant, Faride had had a botched abortion in a back-alley clinic, Faride had an unstoppable hemorrhage, Faride had gone mad and walked naked through the house making pornographic gestures, Faride was rotting with cancer, her face had been eaten up by maggots, and therefore we had locked her up.

Our friends asked us in school if it was true that our sister smelled bad, if we were having another little brother or sister, how many men had given her children; they asked us if we would get sick just like her. Faced with that rosary of rumors, Mama drastically changed policies. She opened doors and windows, invited the neighboring women to the house for coffee, canceled the orders that kept us away from our sister, allowed her children to sleep with her again, and no longer prevented her from going out into the yard.

The friends and neighbors saw her walk the sidewalk, water the eggplants planted in the yard, and frolic with her children. They took turns spying on her, since she would let herself be seen only once in a while. Some ended up attributing to her a passing illness or a harmless dementia. They also agreed, however, that her physique did not betray any ailment whatsoever. They saw her like she looked then: her profile more defined, her cheeks rosy and with a profound calm always peeking through her eyes.

Every once in a while I would sit down to watch her sleep. Certain discoveries had awakened in me hopes of a cure. Watching her fixedly, I noticed the movements of her eyelids and the slight stretching of her lips when the familiar voices of the market women offered their pigeon peas, coriander, and oregano for sale. She didn't seem disconnected from the prattle of children playing baseball in the neighborhood park. If my daughter was not completely rooted in this reality, neither was she in the other.

Mama's hopes soon began to fade. Faride's residence on this side of reality diminished progressively, until it was reduced to the narrow space of no more than an hour. Then she would awaken completely, drink a glass of water, bathe and perfume herself. She would talk briefly with Mama and Papa, and would romp with us for a while, demonstrating a complete command of her two diverse time frames. When she was asleep, she lay totally submerged in a deep tranquility; when she was awake, she was nimble and clear-sighted.

One day she awakened all of us with a frantic cry. It was a calm dawn in April, fresh and fragrant, I will never forget it. Standing around her bed, we heard her last words.

"I have found the solution!! Kiss me all of you!! Kiss me and hold me in your arms because I have found the solution!! Now I know how to irrigate a garden that won't stop growing, how to gather the shadows of the flowers, how to prevent their concealing the sun, and how to walk diagonally across the instants."

She went to sleep definitively. She slept for exactly six months. Pale, on her back, smiling: her heartbeats began to fade. At the end she looked like a beautiful dream dressed in pink, a dream that our parents refused to bury.

I don't know why the family opted for the diagnosis of madness. The notion that it was a singular form of dementia, still unexplored by psychiatry, is taking root in José; his career plans are driven by the desire to deepen the investigation of the case.

The one exception is the mother, for whom the daughter was possessed by a woman from the past; her eagerness leads her to think that José, sometimes, is possessed by Faride's spirit. They alone knew her intimately, having witnessed every detail of the most intense moments of her extraordinary behavior; but they could be mistaken, however, and it could perhaps be a mere matter of poetics.

Translated by Lizabeth Paravisini-Gebert

Jeanne Hyvrard is a prolific writer who has produced novels, poetry, and short prose pieces about a French Caribbean island which could be either Guadeloupe or Martinique. For a long time Hyvrard refused all interviews and public appearances, and seemed to encourage speculation as to her origins. She is, in fact, a white woman now living in Paris who spent her formative years in the Caribbean. Hyvrard's fiction is marked by her scathing critique of Western, patriarchal society. The extended metaphor of "woman as nigger" and her fragmented prose are used to explore the voicelessness imposed on women and blacks by male/colonial-oriented discourse.

JEANNE HYVRARD

Opéra Station. Six in the Evening. For Months...

The subway. The belly of the city. The womb of all new beginnings. Ovaries of new times. The tubes of what changes? The subway. Opéra Station. Six in the evening. For months. The suspended race of passersby. The mob. Sight. Hearing. Another people. Another time. Another story. Another world going back to the depths of memory. Caribbean musicians. *Bumidom.* Emigration. Deportation. Deportation is starting over again. Again and forever. Eternal exile. *Bois Lézard. Crève-Coeur. Mon Désir.* I can't forget. The river of words in the mangrove thicket of writing. The impossible return. *Trinité* through *Brin d'Amour.* Frizzy hair. Kinky hair. Curly hair. Perpetual deportation. Sing! Sing or you'll die. Get over it or perish. A woman in mauve. A woman in tears. A people in drama. A city in water. Deportation starting over again from one continent to another. Bundle of wrenching. Breaks of uprooting. The hold of repression. Caribbean musicians. The leopard beret comes from which improbable battle? The bloody beret, from what earthly sufferer? The ocher beret, from the memory of which cacao tree? More and more musicians. Green. Yellow. Red. The forbidden flag colors the calabashes. Contraband instruments pulled from a bag. A group. An orchestra. A people. More and more people Opéra. Auber. Havre-Caumartin. More and more. At each suffering. Each trampling. Each discharge. Endless deportation. From Africa to America. From America to Europe. From Europe to music. The dumb assembled around their misery. Their drums. Their calabashes. *Crève-Coeur. Mon Désir. Trou l'Enfer.* Memory. I can't forget. What man said: "Shut up, you're tearing me up." Shut up I can't hear you. Shut up. Will you shut up! You can't hear me. You don't want to listen to me. Weariness. Fatigue. Depression. The peaceful wailing of those who have no more speech. The revolt of the broken-down. The war of the defeated. You can't hear the protest of raped life. First one sound. Then two. Then so many. Then everything. It's hardly audible at first, this music of the underground belly. The orchestra of the other world. An entire people in revolt. People more numerous with each trampling. The Opéra River. Auber Hill. Caumartin Peak. The drums. The graters. The barrels. Carburetors. Odds and ends from an old motor. Out-of-date fragment from the Associated Scrap Metal Corporation. Aubervilliers. Levallois. Mairie d'Ivry. Garbage from mercantile production, recycled as protest. A sound. A noise. A music. The underground body entering into resonance. Explosion. Time in pieces. Place in shreds. Breaking the shackles of death. Separation no longer separates anything since they're here with me in the subway's night. People melting into a single population. The single earth becoming a single culture. The woman in mauve over there, leaning against the wall, her shoulderbag pulling out her shoulder. Homework for next week: "In the context of globalization and faced with Third World industrialization, does national interest exist?" To survive by outliving memory and forgetfulness. To survive through writing. Six o'clock. Opéra Subway. Deep breathing of the body

of things. Suspended suffering. Abandoned time. Ivry Cabin.
Opéra Hill. Aubervilliers Peak. At first a moan. Music. Words of
the voiceless. Slaves on the plantations. No. It's over. You can
sleep. They don't complain any longer. Their hands nonetheless
stronger and harder on the drums. You can sleep. Write no more.
Cane felled into tired hands. Children hold the binding rope.
Cows. Humps. Horns. Carriages. The mill. Unloaded bundles.
Blows. Turbans. Cabins between the bay and the mill. Coconut
palms in the distance. The bay, Anse Charpentier, in the wind.
The hands on the drums, harder and heavier. The mills of
stubbornness grinding our days and suffering to make the flour
of writing. Slaves' feet treading endlessly over the mills' blades.
Crushed hatches on the weir. Women's lives lost in sugar mills.
Words that make you deaf. The woman in mauve against the
subway wall. Shoulderbag on her arm. The story she can't
repress any longer. Marie Galion calling out your name on the
plantation roads. This story she can't write. Homework for next
week: "In the context of globalization and industrialization of the
Third World, what does Marie Galion's life become?" The plea of
women lost in the sugar mills. The juice of lost lives. The
bittersweet harvest between death and insanity. Your entire body
given in to the music. Open to the music. Pierced by the music.
Body turned belly in the plenitude of the living. Eyes shut but
not tired. Powerful, all of them. Every memory between bush
and savanna. Journey and laguna. Pirogue and mangrove thicket.
Marie Galion is walking on the plantation, calling out your name.
The bittersweet revolt. The plea of the drums that couldn't be
silenced. Crushed life's reproaching. The grindstones crushing
themselves. The juice of life drained. The mill of death from
exhaustion. From wear. From depletion. Anemic plants, sapless
but for the last drop of water. Depleted lives. The liquid chan-
neled to the refinery. I feel sick. Sick of beating on the drums of
equality. Sick of hearing the drum's beating. I feel sick. My life
hurts. My love hurts. "In the context of globalization and
industrialization of the Third World . . ." Slaves. Vats. Ladles.
Channels. These stories that get crossed. Caumartin Peak. Marie
Auber. Galion River. A thicker and thicker nectar. The trays

cooling down, crystallized sugar on top of the molasses. The woman against the wall. Marie Galion can't stand it any longer. Words above our heads. The molasses, in turn, transformed into rum. Alcohol of survival. Writing. The woman in mauve overwhelmed by the music. Opéra. Six o'clock. Opéra six o'clock for months. Going back in the world's memory. Why go back home when this is where it's happening? The face recognized among them all. Deserted by the body. What did that face say? A police day. A mercenary day. A day of the French army. A day of trampling. A day of silence. What did that assassinated man say? Down with . . . Down with . . . who was it? You can sleep and not write. He'll no longer come into town on days of rioting. Toward Aubervilliers. Levallois. Mairie d'Ivry. To dance. To dance for him. To dance again. Dance with my whole body. My story. Our story. History. To dance the transfigured city with my whole body. Opéra. Opéra. Every night. Six o'clock for months, Caribbean musicians. Emergency exit. Blocked passageway. To dance, nonetheless. To dance the lyrebird spreading its wings through music's grace. To dance the white body abandoned to black music. To dance collective misery. To dance the empire of the world in a single hand. To dance the broken voices reemerging from everywhere.

Translated by Thomas Spear

Born in 1949 in Antigua, Kincaid moved to the United States in 1966. She worked for some years as a staff writer for The New Yorker magazine, where her first prose pieces were published. Her first book of stories, At the Bottom of the River, made her an instant literary celebrity. Her first novel, Annie John (1983), a penetrating study of a young girl's passage into adolescence, was followed in 1990 by the critically acclaimed Lucy. Praised for her "unique, compelling voice" and ferocious integrity, Kincaid offers powerful evocations of the island of her birth and intense explorations of the mother-daughter relationship. She is among the best known and most highly regarded of contemporary Caribbean writers.

JAMAICA KINCAID

Girl

Wash the white clothes on Monday and put them on the stone heap; wash the color clothes on Tuesday and put them on the clothesline to dry; don't walk barehead in the hot sun; cook pumpkin fritters in very hot sweet oil; soak your little cloths right after you take them off; when buying cotton to make yourself a nice blouse, be sure that it doesn't have gum on it, because that way it won't hold up well after a wash; soak salt fish overnight before you cook it; is it true that you sing benna in Sunday school?; always eat your food in such a way that it won't turn someone else's stomach; on Sundays try to walk like a lady and not like the slut you are so bent on becoming; don't sing benna in Sunday school; you mustn't speak to wharf-rat boys, not even to give directions; don't eat fruits on the street— flies will follow you; *but I don't sing benna on Sundays at all and never in Sunday school*; this is how to sew on a button; this is how to make a buttonhole for the button you have just sewed on; this is how to hem a dress when you see the hem coming down and so to prevent yourself from looking like the slut I know you are so bent on becoming; this is how you iron your father's khaki shirt so that it doesn't have a crease; this is how you iron your father's khaki pants so that they don't have a crease; this is how you grow okra—far from the house, because okra tree harbors red ants; when you are growing dasheen, make sure it gets plenty of water or else it makes your throat itch when you are eating it; this is how you sweep a corner; this is how you sweep a whole house; this is how you sweep a yard; this is how you smile to someone you don't like too much; this is how you smile to someone you don't like at all; this is how you smile to someone you like completely; this is how you set a table for tea; this is how you set a table for dinner; this is how you set a table for dinner with an important guest; this is how you set a table for lunch; this is how you set a table for breakfast; this is how you behave in the presence of men who don't know you very well, and this way they won't recognize immediately the slut I have warned you against becoming; be sure to wash every day, even if it is with your own spit; don't squat down to play marbles— you are not a boy, you know; don't pick people's flowers—you might catch something; don't throw stones at blackbirds, because it may not be a blackbird at all; this is how to make a bread pudding; this is how to make doukona; this is how to make pepper pot; this is how to make a good medicine for a cold; this is how to make a good medicine to throw away a child before it even becomes a child; this is how to catch a fish; this is how to throw back a fish you don't like, and that way something bad won't fall on you; this is how to bully a man; this is how a man bullies you; this is how to love a man, and if it doesn't work there are other ways, and if they don't work don't feel too bad about giving up; this is how to spit up in the air if you feel like it, and this is how to move quick so that it doesn't fall on you; this is how to make ends meet; always squeeze bread to make sure it's fresh; *but what if the baker won't let me feel the bread?*; you mean to say that after all you are really going to be the kind of woman who the baker won't let near the bread?

Born in Puerto Rico in 1938, Olga Nolla started her literary career in Zona de carga y descarga, *an influential literary journal she edited with her cousin Rosario Ferré. The author of three acclaimed volumes of poetry, Nolla has written numerous short stories scattered in journals and newspapers in Puerto Rico. A handful of these appeared in her first collection,* Porque nos queremos tanto, *published in 1990. Her work is marked by its painstaking skill and its sensitive and evocative exploration of the seemingly flawless and idyllic Puerto Rican upper-class world, whose dark underside is dramatically, violently, laid bare.*

OLGA NOLLA

No Dust Is Allowed
in This House

[handwritten: Narrator – The Umbrella ↓ shelter from sun ↓ to keep from getting darker]

Every day at exactly nine thirty in the morning, they grab me by my wooden handle, painted black and worn out from many years of use, and they shake me mechanically, purely by habit since it's impossible to gather dust overnight, much less in a house like this, where they even sweep under the rugs and behind the furniture every day, each day of the week they dismantle a room to make sure there is no dust behind the bedposts, or around the legs of the armoires, Eusebio has the written instructions tacked to a wall in his room, in long and elegant letters on an already yellowed piece of paper that should have been removed from the wall a long time ago, the thumb-tacks are rusty but the paper still remains nailed there despite the fact that after so many years of following the same routine it's impossible to make the mistake of doing on Wednesday what should have been done on Tuesday, if it's Wednesday he knows that besides sweeping the entire house and polishing the floors—the back stairs at six before the master and mistress get up, the front stairs at seven, he was already sweeping the yard at five in the morning: that he does every day—but on Wednesdays he has to move the furniture in the living room and roll up the rugs to take them to the terrace where he hangs them from the balcony and beats them very hard with a stick to loosen the dust, then he leaves them out to air a bit since the morning sun does not hit that part of the house, the sun shouldn't shine directly on the rugs, it makes the colors fade, but at this time of the morning it doesn't matter, the sunlight is weak, and in the meantime Eusebio returns to the living room to inspect the legs of the armchairs, only the ones that are not mahogany, he does not have to worry about the rocking chairs because they are made of fine native wood, built right here by someone named Amechazurra, but the piano does have to be inspected from one end to the other because it comes from heaven knows where, big and black with a curved top they raise when they're going to sit down to play, it's a really beautiful hulk of a thing, and the eldest girl plays very well, more than well, in the evenings she plays waltzes and traditional Puerto Rican *danzas* while the others dance or recite poetry, a theater with music that really makes Doña Inés laugh and over which Don Abelardo presides bursting with pride for the beauty and talent of his daughters; then there is no dust in this house, I'm completely sure of that, Eusebio polishes the piano once a week, Eusebio is always extremely careful with the sendal and cotton draperies, the white cotton ones with the little flowers in drawnwork are washed once a month, every Thursday they polish the silver, every day Eusebio puts fresh flowers in the dining room, Eusebio paints the house inside and out every time Doña Inés notices that a wall is peeling or stained since sometimes they clean them with a brush, Eusebio wets the long-handled brush in a pail full of soapy water to scrub them when necessary, that's determined by Doña Inés who does not have written instructions for things like these,

Eusebio's daily schedule follows the same routine that Doña Inés set down for him in writing in her beautiful exclusive-*Colegio-de-las-Madres* penmanship on the first day he began service in this house, but there are additional duties, that was all seventeen years ago and the mistress has never had any complaints about Eusebio, no, Eusebio always follows her instructions to the letter. That's why there's no dust in this house and I don't understand why they shake me every morning as if there were, because Eusebio also cleans the tall wicker basket in which I rest, he places me on the table and turns the basket upside down to make sure that no tiny leaf is caught in my stays or trapped in the bottom of the basket, and he does this every day because the entrance hall is cleaned daily, it isn't carpeted, and from the screen door in the entrance to where I stand in the basket there are only the naked tiles with their beige and tomato-red geometric designs and a big mirror with a wide wooden frame hanging exactly in the center of the wall facing me, and underneath it one of those tables that stand against the wall, with long legs that bulge out like bellies and then curve inward until they almost reach the floor, then the legs dare venture outward to rest on the naked tiles; but the hall is filled mostly with photographs, all of them in silver frames, photographs of the entire family, the grandparents, the master and mistress of this house, all the children in pairs or by themselves, the girls wearing organza bows surrounding Don Abelardo's first automobile, a picnic at the beach, the aunt and uncle's *hacienda*, Don Abelardo as a slender adolescent on horseback, Don Abelardo as a child, sitting all alone on a chair in front of a flounced velvet curtain, the sugar mill in the middle of the canefields, Doña Inés as a young girl, the wedding photos, Doña Inés with her daughters and her four boys seated in the front row, Doña Inés with her hands resting on her daughters' shoulders, with her abundant black hair gathered in a bun and her forehead clear, the perfect straight nose and the mouth like a moist bud and the eyes black and deep like a moonless night, with stars sparkling from within, two drops of starry night suspended on the matchless whiteness of the forehead and the cheeks, and on the other parallel wall are the boys with their dogs and horses and the girls with their dolls, half-hidden between the shrubs in a garden or seated pigeon-toed on iron benches, the shoes made immaculate with white shoe-polish, sole against sole, with some toys before them, sometimes a tricycle. And there is nothing else between the entrance and the dining room, only I in my wicker basket by the kitchen door, a swinging yellow door that opens and closes hundreds of times every day, the upper half and the lower half, and between the dining room and my basket there's another marbled-topped table, with those same belly-like legs and always a deep bowl filled with fruit, Eusebio never fails to keep that bowl full of grapefruits and apple-flavored bananas, avocados, lemons and loquats. And on some days there are also fruit baskets for the relatives, Doña Inés goes out of her way if she knows they are coming and even if they haven't sent word she has one or two fruit baskets ready. I think she knows when her people from Cabo Rojo or San Germán will be coming. Doña Inés seems to know everything, she is the soul and order of this house, Doña Inés is the eye that guarantees that each day all the pieces of the puzzle will fall into place and remains watchful even as she sits on the porch to listen to the sea, even as she sleeps she knows everything that goes on in the house and I listen to her contented breathing from my basket since her bedroom is next to the dining room, between the dining room and the terrace, and even if it weren't so I would hear her, because in this house at night you can even hear the slow ripening of the fruit, I know when the zinc roof is enjoying the embraces of the moon and the crickets that enter the house cannot stifle the sighs of happiness of the sands every time the sea moistens them only to abandon them and return and leave again, and they become, in turn, dry and moist, dry and moist, at night you can hear them suck in the sea-water, as if dying of thirst.

But, dust? definitely no dust is allowed in this house, so every morning when Doña Inés shakes me I feel really annoyed even though she looks so pretty in her mauve cotton dress and the old black leather shoes that she wears only to go out into the yard and her hands so soft on my worn-out handle and so soft when she presses with her open palms my black fins while she gives instructions to Eusebio and to the nannies and opens the yellow door to make sure that Margarita is making the flan that Don Abelardo likes just like Don Abelardo likes it, with lots of eggs and caramel as dark as the molasses that they keep in the big drums at the sugar refinery. Sometimes Don Abelardo brings molasses in ten-liter bottles, molasses is so precious, they make a drink out of it that they serve to visitors between four and five in the afternoon, that is, during the time of the cane harvest, because otherwise they serve aromatic drinks, made from lemons, grapefruit, or bitter oranges with lots of sugar. These days they're serving grapefruit drinks, Eusebio brings in a silver tray with the glasses full of juice with bits of ice dancing inside them, the glasses sweat but Eusebio hands a small napkin of embroidered linen to each one of those gathered on the covered terrace. And since it is grapefruit season, I'm sure today I'll spend a lot of time in the grapefruit grove; once there, Doña Inés counts each and every one of the grapefruits in the thirty beautiful trees, one by one to make sure not one of her aromatic jewels has been stolen, she says that people break in at night to steal grapefruits, once already she ran into some thieves when we were going around the shacks at the end of the property, there were three men and she ordered them to leave, immediately, she said, she confronted them with a firmness that tensed my stays, and the thieves lost their nerve and fled climbing the wall, Doña Inés, when she gets really angry, can intimidate a mad dog. And that's because she's not afraid of them, she's not afraid of anything, and when her voice sounds really angry you feel like hiding; however, her hands are so soft when they grab me by the handle, and so soft when they shake that imaginary dust and so loving when they caress the grapefruits. Today we will surely return with the most beautiful ones in her own hands, held against her chest. That is why, as we go out into the hallway, through the screen door, and down the steps, I am already anticipating the delicious aroma the grapefruits give off when they're warmed up against Doña Inés's chest, and as we reach the last step and open the small white gate with delicately carved rails to go out into the yard, it seems to me that I can smell them already. Then she begins to open me slowly, and as I unfurl my folds I drown in sunshine and happiness because I enjoy the warmth like I enjoy keeping Doña Inés cool under my wings, and knowing that thanks to me her skin maintains that special paleness at which everyone marvels, knowing that the sun will never violate the purity of her complexion, and her eyes will continue to look like black pearls emerging from the foam of the sea.

The stroll through the garden is always the same. We go out through the laundry, to the right side of the garages over which the servants' quarters have been built, past where the chicken coops begin, followed by those of the geese and ducks. We climb three wooden steps to a small bridge, also made of wood, and then we can see the first grapefruit trees. We reach them through a well-worn brick path and Doña Inés wants to make sure the geese have enough water, we have to take good care of them because they are Don Abelardo's favorite animals, and Eusebio comes and gives them water and feeds them corn and they make a devilish racket running after the food that Eusebio scatters around. They don't bite Eusebio because they know him, and they don't bite Doña Inés either, but any stranger that shows his face around, even if accompanied by someone from the house, is risking losing a finger or, sometimes, a hand. The screams of the geese can be heard from miles away, my stays and my stretched-out rump tremble when I hear them scream at the top of their lungs, but that's precisely why Don Abelardo keeps them, it's an old custom in his family to have geese as guards; he explains that the Romans had geese in their villas and the tradition had its origin back then. Don Abelardo's gaggle of geese is now up to sixteen, some of them are ancient because in Puerto Rico geese are not eaten and least of all Don Abelardo's, so they grow old without being disturbed and they run in V-formation under the grapefruit trees, a white spearhead zigzagging between the trunks. And the earth is the color of dark ashes, a sand mixed with soil in the heat and smoke of millenarian volcanoes that is very good for growing citrus trees because it filters the water

Imperial Colonial Dictionary

splendidly, they say that that's why Doña Inés's grapefruits are famous for being the best in the world.

At the end of the brick path is Don Abelardo's old office, now boarded up and abandoned, a couple of wooden shacks crumbling bit by bit. At the beginning, Don Abelardo had his office under the house, next to the laundry and the guests' quarters, but the comings and goings of the employees and the clacking of the typewriters bothered Doña Inés, and that's why Don Abelardo, to please her, I think, had his offices moved to the grapefruit grove in the midst of which he had these shacks built. I have never seen them from the inside, but there is a balcony where the overseers used to wait to speak to Don Abelardo and it was painted white with windows that let in the breeze and the smell of the grapefruits. Doña Inés never went in during our walks, she greeted the employees from a distance and went on her way, quickening her steps, and very soon Don Abelardo had a new office built on a dairy farm he owns a mile away from the house. Then there were no more farm employees disturbing our walks. The groves have grown and the shacks look smaller, they are useless now but no one has taken the trouble of demolishing them; two crossed boards block the entrance to the porch. As always, Doña Inés ignores them and examines one by one the trunks and the number of grapefruits. She indicates to Eusebio which of them he must gather, and she brings the biggest and juiciest ones close to her cheeks to smell the perfume that emanates from their yellow rind when they have just been separated from the stem.

Doña Inés was opposed to the construction of the wall from the moment the idea sprang up in Don Abelardo's mind. During our daily stroll, we walked past the grapefruit trees until we reached a palm grove that extended the length of the right border of the property. A barbed-wire fence marked the boundary line and on that side there was a path under the centenary kennip trees and the luxuriant mangoes, the boulders on this path had been pulled up by their roots, something that amused Doña Inés. She

[handwritten marginalia: Doña Inés — Wall — doesn't want to acknowledge that there is such a huge separation — out of her friend; doesn't even want the place there; European Imperial Colonization Symbolism]

sometimes closed me to use me as a cane, to jump over the cracks, or to poke at the fissures in the cement with my tip. There are two semi-abandoned water fountains on this side of the property, one has been filled with soil and Doña Inés had Eusebio plant anthurium and Chinese parsley in it, the shadow of the kennip trees protects the plants from the strong sun and they have grown splendidly. It is true that Doña Inés would have preferred to freshen her hands and forehead in the crystalline waters when she reached this spot, that was her purpose when she had the fountains built, but her romantic notions had to cool off when the water turned into a breeding pool for mosquitoes. At the other extreme of the cracked pavement, the other fountain kept its water, but on condition of stocking it with mosquito-eating fish that required that algae be allowed to grow until the water was green and impenetrable.

It was just at this spot that Don Abelardo wanted to build the wall. Here the barbed-wire fence, concealed by a hedge of hibiscus, didn't quite hide the neighboring property, an extensive palm grove where a handful of very poor families lived as squatters. Their wood and zinc huts formed a diminutive settlement in the center of the palm grove, and the barefoot and ragged children often peered through the hedge of hibiscus; Doña Inés sometimes stopped to speak to them, to ask them about school, about their fishermen fathers or about a mother who had been ill. Her voice sounded motherly and affectionate, but I didn't know if she really felt sorry for them, I was content to breathe at my ease through my black skin taut in my stays so that Doña Inés's complexion would not be blemished by the sun. That was my job, and I didn't have to get involved in things that were none of my business even though I couldn't help but look at the dirty and snotty faces crowded behind the hedge of hibiscus.

When one of the daughters accompanied Doña Inés to the hedge of hibiscus, she would remain very quiet, glued to her mother's skirts, while Doña Inés spoke to the children of the fishermen. It was, of course, absolutely forbidden for the daughters of Don Abelardo to play with those children, and they

[handwritten marginalia, left margin: Wall — symbolized like the umbrella; as a shield; Wall — against poverty; umbrella — against darkening her skin]

would not have dared do so. However, one day I heard Eusebio comment to Margarita in the kitchen that Don Abelardo's girls loitered around the hedge of hibiscus and sometimes looked with curiosity toward the huts in the palm grove and I believe he said that on several occasions he had seen them talking to some of those people. One day one of them had been frightened when one of the boys had shown her a big blue crab he had just fished out of a cave and she had started to cry. But no one at the house heard anything about that, no one but Eusebio mentioned anything about it, or maybe thought about it, I cannot be sure. I often get confused. In my wicker basket at the end of the hallway I have even managed to hear thoughts, only on occasions, of course. A lot of things escape me when the perfume of the grapefruit grove grows very intense to the point of almost obliterating my understanding.) — *gaps just like human beings*

I never found out what Doña Inés thought of those miserable huts, or if they were something that had any particular importance for her. She acted as if they didn't displease her and to judge by her reaction when Don Abelardo brought up the issue of the wall, who knows if she sympathized with them, who knows. I will probably never know why she was so violently opposed to the building of a cement wall high enough to conceal the palm grove adjacent to the property and the little houses and the people that lived there. Don Abelardo wanted to obliterate the sight of those things, he didn't say so but that's what he wanted, to isolate his beautiful garden and his beautiful family from things they could not understand. He proposed it for the first time one day during lunch and Doña Inés shook her head in a gesture of denial, no, no, no, she didn't want workers stepping on the grass, she said. The topic surfaced again at the most unexpected occasions, when they were leaving for a picnic on the beach or in the middle of the amorous wrestling bouts celebrated every so often in the matrimonial bed. I had the feeling that Don Abelardo was trying to crack his wife's will gently, softly, with gifts and wooing, for example, but after her orgasms I would feel Doña Inés's heart freeze when she perceived the proximity of the question to her husband's lips.

Throughout many never-ending months and weeks Doña Inés withstood Don Abelardo's siege on her will, she withstood it until one day, right by my wicker basket, precisely in front of me! she stood squarely before him, and raising her voice, something unheard of in her, she declared she did not want to hear another word about it, that it had been settled and the answer was no, no, so there, over her dead body, staring defiantly at her husband, saying that she was in charge here, that he was not to interfere in household matters, couldn't he understand that? that she didn't want to know anything about his business affairs, wasn't that so? she did not understand a word about the percentage of glucose in the crop or the price of fertilizer, or the weekly payroll, but in her territory, the house, in this house I am in charge, she said, they would do what she determined and her disagreement was enough to put a stop once and for all to the question of the wall. Doña Inés's attitude made Don Abelardo retreat; abruptly, with acrobatic agility, he changed the topic, told her she looked very pretty, kissed her cheeks and embraced her body, rigid like a steel rod, he told her he adored her and that the girls were around calling her, wasn't it true that they were calling her from everywhere in the house and that the perfume of the grapefruit groves was soaked with salt that day? Wasn't it true that the washerwoman, the seamstress, the cook, the gardener, the chauffeur, the three nannies, and even Eusebio were demanding her presence and supervision? Wasn't it true that she had to have the lilies and the hydrangeas in the vases replaced and to make sure nothing was lacking in the larders? Didn't she want to order a *bien-me-sabe* for dessert? Didn't she want Eusebio to fix the leg of some piece of furniture or to have the plumber sent for in reference to that leaky pipe in the girls' bathroom? Didn't she think that the curtains in the living room needed replacing? Didn't she agree that the pillows in the terrace were already fading? Wouldn't she like to wear her diamond studs that evening, so he could admire her from the other end of the table, like an indisputable queen presiding over the children? And over Don Abelardo? I felt Doña Inés's breaths like leather lashes during the tense reconciliation that crowned that confrontation; she was nervous, inexplicably agitated despite her apparent serenity. Don Abelardo, cajoling, with that ability that had made him famous in his business dealings, skirted around the issue, little by little; it was a sneaky shrewdness sure of its aim and as untrappable as an electrical spark. Within the boundaries of the home, this aspect of Don Abelardo's personality surfaced very rarely, but that day I could catch it in its entirety, and I thought that if Doña Inés was the queen of the house, it was because he allowed her to be, because he had decided it would be so. Could she suspect that although he seemed to shower her with affection he had not yielded an inch in his determination to build the wall?

I don't know why, but I felt that Doña Inés had chosen to trust her husband's good will. Did she talk herself into it out of fatigue? In the weeks that followed the scene in front of my wicker basket the silent pitched battle between those two wills seemed to diminish. Doña Inés spent part of her days organizing her daughters' household chores when they returned from school, she set some down to mend socks, others to wash lingerie, to organize drawers and the older ones to learn pastry-making with Margarita. I watched from my basket the grimaces of displeasure of the girls, listened to their muffled laughter as they hid under the beds so their mother could not assign them any tasks, I listened to the days slipping by the hallway, marked by Eusebio's sweeping, by Eusebio's painstaking industriousness, his delicacy when he inspected my folds to make sure that there wasn't one single particle of dust in the house.

Toward the beginning of May, Don Abelardo suggested to Doña Inés that it would be convenient to take the four older girls to Europe. He couldn't accompany them because of his business commitments, but he wanted them to go ahead, it was time for them to get to know the world and learn about foreign customs. Yes, yes, the girls say, so excited by the news they forget to eat their chicken with rice, oh, yes, yes, Mamá, the boat-trip would be so nice and we would learn French. Doña Inés allows herself to be convinced without much of a struggle because I know she has always wanted to go to Europe, when we take walks by ourselves she sometimes sings softly in French and in her bedroom there are books by writers from there, I know she reads them when she can, in hiding, and her thoughts linger on verses and things like that when we walk down the path of the centenary kennip trees. Maybe she also thinks of some of those books when she talks to the children of the fishermen, and then, instead of pulling together the bushes to make them cover all the holes in the wire fence, it seems to me she separates them, that she would like to cut them down and open a breach through which they could walk freely into our yard while at the same time she could walk into the palm grove and approach the huts. It is not that she thought of these things, the truth is I cannot be certain of having understood that, I only spread over her, protecting her beautiful head from the sun. Her thoughts go through the taut threads on my rump but I am not convinced that that's what she thought, I rather doubt it, it was that . . . it was more like she felt it somehow, she had the feeling of wanting to cross the barbed-wire fence under her skin, it was as if that feeling burned my seams, but she would not have been able to understand it, no, possibly not. On the other hand, after the argument with Don Abelardo Doña Inés had acquired a special affection for that hedge of hibiscus and the fertilizer with which she fed the shrubs twice a month had them bursting with sprouts and delicate flowers with long pistils sprinkled with gold.

What happened? How to explain now what took place? I did not leave the house for three months, I did not spread at my ease under the sun, I remained abandoned and dormant in my basket next to the yellow door. But was it really three months? Maybe it was three centuries. The days and nights of the sea, the steps of Don Abelardo's boots, Eusebio's punctual and meticulous routine mingled in my folds, confusing me. I only know that not for one moment did I gather dust. During Doña Inés's absence Eusebio did not once miss dusting my fins and my handle or turning over my basket to make sure I was in impeccable shape even though I am faded and quite weak in some of my seams. Since I had so much time to think, I noticed that my hinges open with difficulty and that my skin is rotten. I think that if they were to open and strike me I would collapse right through the middle of my frame. After so many years of service they will throw me into the trash because I don't think there is a thread that can mend these frayed borders and my stays can't take much more. Does Doña Inés know? She doesn't seem to realize my condition. The truth is she doesn't seem to notice much, although the house, of course, continues to be impeccably kept, Eusebio could not fail in the fulfillment of his duties even if he tried, he couldn't even attempt it. When Doña Inés was away those three months he didn't need any supervision, every day he swept and cleaned carefully what was already clean, since the house without the four older girls seemed like a tomb and hardly anything got soiled, only the hallway got a bit filthy every time Don Abelardo returned from the farm with his boots covered with mud.

Nothing should have changed in this house, I say, but there's no doubt that things are different, because now when Doña Inés grabs me by the handle her soft hands tremble and I feel that she squeezes me with a drop of cruelty. She has little patience with the nannies and she sometimes rams me forcefully between the cracks in the path under the centenary kennip trees. Twice already I have remained nailed to the ground as if I were a spearhead, feeling the earthworms crawl around me down there with quite a bit of apprehension since I am not used to soil. Until Eusebio comes to rescue me; by then Doña Inés has already walked past the fountain with the green slimy water and the mosquito-eating fish and is striding quickly toward the house. She takes me again in her wet hands and I notice that her cheeks are also wet and her eyes are swollen.

There's no doubt that things are different. After that evening the walls in the house have not recovered the exuberance they used to have, that freshly-cut-flower aura that emanated from the woods and the draperies, no, even if Eusebio cleans as always the house is somehow different and on rainy nights the sea beats against it with so much fury that it seems as if it were going to enter the living room and it makes me feel very afraid. I've heard

Eusebio and Margarita comment that the sea is eating away at the beach, that they will have to build a sea wall so the road will not crumble.

That evening I thought the house was going to crumble. At two in the afternoon, Doña Inés had returned from her trip to Europe with the girls, looking so beautiful in their French dresses and so was she, wearing a silk dress that is the prettiest thing that has ever been seen around here, and a hat with a wide brim of the same color as the dress which we all marvelled at. They descended from the cars in a mad rush, two cars with two chauffeurs because Don Abelardo had gone to pick them up at the dock and they had mountains of luggage. The house at first was filled with laughter, embraces, greetings, Doña Inés happy to see the rest of her children, gifts of lace mantillas and fans for the nannies and Margarita, a Toledan leather wallet for Eusebio who turned it around and around without understanding what it was. Everything was laughter and tales to be told and we had hours of celebration, with visitors and everything, with cool drinks and cakes and the piano and French and Spanish songs. But when the excitement began to die down, Doña Inés left the gathering and began her reencounter with the house. She went room by room touching the walls and the bedposts, opening drawers and looking under the rugs. She walked through the hallways and the bathrooms, the front terrace, the closets, the kitchen and the larder, she scolded Margarita because the reserves of rice were low. Then she went down to the yard without bothering to take me with her or to wear the black leather shoes she wore for our walks, she went down quickly, agitated all of a sudden as if she suspected, she was biting her hands when she went past me and marched down the steps, in great strides, alone.

When she returned I saw her face before anyone else, I, alone in my basket, awaited her while the rest were having a great time in the living room. I alone saw that beautiful face by the door that Doña Inés had just crossed, walking heavily, with difficulty, the length of the hallway. Her eyes were dry but they threatened to leave their orbits, her mouth was half-open, with an expression of infinite stupor on her entire face and her lips trembled violently. With her delicate hands where I saw, horrified, that there was blood, she beat on her chest, her legs, and her head, as if wanting to spend on her own body a fury that was beyond her strength. I noticed a destructive will that froze my understanding. I thought she was going to take me in both her hands to charge at the house and at everyone in it, but she only looked at the photographs, slowly, at the whole gallery of photographs, one by one as if trying to understand, to see something she couldn't see, to see me, the floor-tiles, the fruits, the yellow door, her face in the mirror. Shaking her head from side to side she walked straight ahead past me, making a supreme effort to reach her bedroom in silence, locking the door behind her.

Half an hour later the children began to look for her throughout the house and finally crowded in front of her door. They called her loudly, shouting for her to come down, to come down with them to the party. They got no answer and Don Abelardo himself knocked loudly on the door, calling her. Silence. Eusebio and Margarita, next to me by the wall, observed the spectacle without moving. The guests, politely, said goodbye and left quietly. I did not understand a thing but those two, Eusebio and Margarita, they did seem to understand, heads bowed, that something grave had taken place. Their hands, rough and deformed by work, hung limply from their arms, on both sides of their bodies. Eusebio mumbled to himself some phrases that I couldn't catch. I looked in his eyes and saw a long sadness, long and dark like a caravan of ants in the forest. When at last Doña Inés unlocked the door, giving in to the frightened entreaties of her children, the first gaze she encountered was that of Eusebio, whose eyes had not left the door for a single second.

That evening Doña Inés did not sit at the table. She sipped only a few tablespoons of pumpkin soup that Eusebio took to her room on a tray. The children, exhausted by the novelty and the excitement, went to bed early and twisted and turned on their beds restlessly, whimpering in their dreams. When Don Abelardo went in to speak to his wife the screams unleashed by both of them resounded through every corner of the house and made the children suck their sheets in despair. They cuddled up with each other, frightened to death. The house will never forget that night even after it has been swallowed up by the sea. Doña Inés's fists against the walls and Don Abelardo's threats were worse than an earthquake. I heard, terrified, the words treason, coward, a wall, the wall! the wall built in her absence, behind her back, Doña Inés screamed, between sobs, beast, coward, he wouldn't have dared in front of her, he couldn't have done it facing her, coward, brute, and he, his voice breaking a bit but very firm, yes, withstanding like a rock that has not moved an inch from the beginning of the centuries. *CLASS* –

I have said that Doña Inés doesn't seem to notice that I am falling apart bit by bit. If we go out for our walk every morning I feel that I won't be able to stand it much longer. When the branches of the grapefruit trees graze me I get very achy. How can I protect Doña Inés if my weave is almost transparent? Now the sun, no doubt, will damage her skin. Doesn't she care anymore? She's acting very strangely lately. When we stand before the wall that Don Abelardo built against her will, Doña Inés orders Eusebio to weed in front of it carefully, to make sure no underbrush will grow there. The wall is painted white and looks heavy and ugly, completely out of proportion to the rest of the garden. It's strange that Doña Inés hasn't had it covered with a climbing vine, strange, very strange; she, who is so careful about the sense of harmony in all corners of the house. It's also strange that when we stand twenty steps from the wall and Doña Inés looks at it, it explodes without a sound, as if a gigantic flower had opened up, and the pieces fly several feet in the air, the petals open in points of cold flame, they climb, climb in a tremendous, silent explosion. And between the pieces of masonry that find themselves ejected with a heavy and lingering violence and fly slowly, slowly in the air, floating, particles of white paper floating in the atmosphere, we see the palm grove, the huts, and the children there in the center of the flower, there in the depth of the current of its vegetable veins. The explosion can last up to a minute more or less, I couldn't tell for sure because I am stunned every time it happens. Then the pieces of cement reverse their direction and return bit by bit to their place of origin, the folds of the petals closing and descending one by one and returning to their predestined place on the wall, the wall that defies us and binds each and every one of its molecules together even more strongly than before to remain closed. This takes place every morning and I don't know where this business will lead because I can't take it anymore. If ever the flower of masonry opens forever, if from within, from the roots that were crushed by the cement, the hibiscus bushes sprout again and crack the wall once and for all, and weaken it in such a way that the flower will never close again, I will not be here to tell about it.

Translated by Lizabeth Paravisini-Gebert

its so unlikely that this will happen (destroying of the wall) that I (the umbrella will not be here to tell about it)

*Opal Palmer Adisa was born in Jamaica in 1954 and presently
lives in San Francisco, where she teaches creative writing. A poet,
playwright, and short story writer, she has published two
collections of poetry,* traveling women *and* Market Woman; *a
children's book,* The Many-Eyed Fruit; *and a collection of short
stories,* Bake-Face and Other Guava Stories. *Her fiction
captures the magic hidden behind the everydayness of Jamaican
women's lives, and offers strong, marvelously nuanced female
characters.*

OPAL PALMER ADISA

Widow's Walk

She goes looking for Neville. This is obvious to all. Many times
she has to blink her eyes, which keep fooling her into believing
that she sees his boat out at sea. It is only a mirage. Another
wave swells up before breaking on the shore.

June-Plum was tense all week, even before Neville left, but she
never articulated her fears. Then, just before he left Sunday
morning, she broke a saucer—a sure sign of unpleasant news. She
didn't know then that it was connected to Neville, but she should
have. Several times within the last couple of weeks she was
visited in her dreams by a beautiful chocolate-colored woman
with thick, wild hair piled upon her head like a straw basket.
This shapely chocolate goddess with inviting hips and thighs
wore a cloud-white dress with several ruffles of blue cotton that
flounced with her every move. She taunted June-Plum that she
was the more desirable of the two, but June-Plum did not heed.
She stubbornly refused to believe that her dreams or the broken
saucer might have anything to do with the very contented life

she led with Neville. How foolish could she be? June-Plum bursts out with a big laugh of astonishment at her own foolishness.

June-Plum's deep belly laughter, so big that it scared people off because they couldn't imagine a pleasure as enormous as the one her voice suggested, used to delight her mother. "Yuh gi weh laugh fi pea soup," she would say. June-Plum recalls that her laughter was like pea soup in those days, in never-ending supply. Happy memories of her mother heighten June-Plum's sadness and she fixes her face like a funeral mask. She lingers on the boardwalk long after all the other women have turned into their houses and closed their windows to bar the mosquitoes' entrance. A handful of stars shines through the purple sky. To block out the wind, June-Plum folds her hands over her belly swollen with child. The waves are just ripples gliding calmly, and, at each fold, they glitter. There is almost no flow, only motion going nowhere. The effect is inviting, yet disturbing.

Neville should have returned yesterday. The smell of smoke and burning bush (to keep the mosquitoes at bay) swirls through the air like perfume—no, more like the pungent smell of the flamboyant tree's blossoms. June-Plum sighs and hugs herself more tightly, hearing the waves beginning to grumble.

She searches the expanse of water while waves splash against the boards, sending salty foam rising up like vapor into the night. Each time she thinks she sees something, someone. Who is this goddess Yemoja? As ruler of the sea and children, she is as generous in her gifts of children as she is ruthless in taking men. But June-Plum is not her enemy. She, too, is woman and mother, and she wants her man. This one Yemoja cannot have, and June-Plum means for her to know this, means to challenge and fight her if need be. As her thoughts take form, June-Plum takes in a deep breath and lets it out with a sigh. She takes several abortive steps before throwing off her slippers and descending into the water to wet her feet.

The waves rush in as if to meet her challenge. They chase her and she runs to and fro before standing her ground, lifting her dress until her thighs are bared, confronting her competitor with knowledge that she too has thighs, almond-stained and diaper-soft, which wrap themselves around her man's back when he enters her deeply, pleasing her to tears. But soon June-Plum is disarmed by the comforting touches of this woman. She eases in completely, and the salty water, cool, bathes her aching heart and massages her weary limbs so that she forgets herself and simply imagines Neville's hands about her body as the waves continue to recede.

Gasping for breath and swallowing water, June-Plum treads until her fingers touch the sandy bottom. She wipes salty water from her eyes, shakes her head and drags her drenched body to the shore, sighing and laughing. This woman is mistress indeed, and more powerful than she, June-Plum, could ever hope to be. Flopping on the damp sand, she wonders where the sea ends and the sky begins, as it all just seems a mass of blue and white foam. But it doesn't matter; she likes the unity of blues—only how can she and Neville become melted in unity like that? Then she remembers that Neville is already part of that unity. The woman has already taken him. He might be that very wave which is the same as the one before and no different from the one which follows it. June-Plum knows that she could not win if she fought Yemoja, so that all that is left is pleading, hoping that as a woman Yemoja will understand her need and giver her back her man. "De sea so pretty; yuh so free and easy. Ah ave fi gi Neville time wid yuh, but meba dat me need im."

June-Plum comes to the quay and strolls along the boardwalk, the sea mewling beneath. Her sense of destiny tells her nothing. What is today, anyway—Wednesday? Thursday? Friday? Yes, it's Thursday—Thursday is the only day the fishermen sell their fish to whoever comes to buy, not putting aside any for the higglers, the small vendors. Neville left early Sunday morning, when the sky was ashen white and the wind oblique.

"Im been gwane longer dan tree days before. Why me mus worry meself wid bad expectations?"

"Nite, Miss June-Plum, yuh out ere late by yuh-self."

"Bertram, ah didn't even ear yuh approach."

"Yuh nuh fi worry yuhself. Ah confident widin me body Neville gwane return safe."

June-Plum allows herself to hear what Bertram has said. He is confident Neville is safe and will return. She doesn't know if she should laugh at such consolation. She is doubtful . . . afraid . . . not able to eat anything. Not sure of what to say, she looks up at the sky. "De nite so pretty. No often de sky so purple wid stars. De sea calm. Look how de waves hardly move. De book people dem seh de world round, den somewhe at de hedge de sea an de sky lock fingers."

She looks out at the sea, forgetting that Bertram is with her. Her mind cannot hold any one image; it flits from Neville to the children, to last Sunday's sermon, to all the wash that still has to be done. Why is she here on this walk? Her children are home asleep and she should be in bed. And her husband is at sea or gone. June-Plum rubs her arms where cold-bumps have appeared, then turns, remembering Bertram.

"Bertram, wha yuh doin out ere? De nite wind cold. De sky an eberyone lie wrap warmly in bed. Yuh ave a good nite an seh howdy to Beverly."

She lingers longer on the boardwalk, raises her wet dress, and examines her thighs. Then, on impulse, she pulls off her dress and jumps into the sea, floating on her back like a piece of log washed to shore. She probably would have passed the night there, but she is suddenly aroused by a harsh voice and firm hands that drag her out of the water and roughly pull her dress over her head.

"Is fool-fool yuh fool or is nuh sense yuh ave. Ooman, yuh ave picknie in yuh belly an four at yuh house—is mad? Yuh mad? Way afta midnite yuh a wade in de sea. Seems like yuh nuh know de sea bad. She nuh joke; she is a funny ooman. Seems like yuh mus mad." And so Miss Country, the old woman who sells fried fish, roast fish, and bammy from a little shack by the seashore, reprimands June-Plum as if she were a disobedient child. At this, June-Plum laughs and allows herself to be pulled along and fussed over by Miss Country, who walks her directly to her house and makes sure she is safely inside.

At home, June-Plum makes herself a cup of cocoa and the radio provides company while she rambles around the kitchen wiping off clean counter tops and drying plates that are already stacked in the cabinet. Finally, she sits and folds her hands in her lap. A couple of times she catches herself nodding . . . "Who on de ladder? Neville, wha yuh doin up dere? Eberytin look so funny. De sea upside down! Whe all dis leaf come from on dis wata-wooden shack? Neville, min yuh drop! De ladder nah lean pan nutten! Wata can't hold yuh. Mek de sea so rough. Neville, come down, come down, de ladder a shake. De waves gwane cova yuh!"

June-Plum focuses her eyes and looks around the kitchen. Her cup is half full of cocoa and the only sound that comes from the radio is hissing. She didn't hear the national anthem but she knows it is after midnight, so she pulls herself up heavily from the chair. Four children have made her stout and motherly, and in another four months, there will be a fifth. She doesn't want any more children as times are too hard, but the pill is something new, unfamiliar, and Neville never will use rubbers. She sighs. The Bible did say be fruitful and multiply. She hangs her dress on the nail behind the door and opens her Bible:

Then the Lord said unto Moses, Now shalt thou
see what I will do to Pharaoh: for with a strong
hand shall he let them go, and with a strong
hand shall he drive them out of his land . . . .

Something bangs. June-Plum springs out of bed and runs to the back door, thinking Neville has returned. Mist and emptiness greet her. She goes outside into the yard, opens her back gate, and looks down the lane. She sees a figure. A smile rushes to her face, and her voice is a gong in the night: "Neville! Neville, yuh come home." She waits by the gate, suddenly aware that she's barefoot and in her nightie. The figure disappears and only the night remains. Again, her eyes have deceived her. No, she tricked herself—allowed herself to be fooled.

She closes her gate and looks out at the wailing sea that is sending big waves up to the sky. Then she sees her, the woman with whom she shares her man. Yemoja is riding the waves. A lacy turquoise and white turban is wound around her head, ascending to the sky like a cone. She wears strings of shells around her neck and arms and she is naked except for a satin blue cloth around her waist. This cloth blows in the wind like miniature wings. Yemoja's nails are blue on fingers and toes, and a diamond fills the gap between her front teeth. She is beautiful, more lovely than the moon, more lovely than an idea. June-Plum bows to her. Yemoja winks at her, then dives into the roaring waves.

June-Plum is suddenly very cold. Shivering, she runs into the house, bolting the door behind her. For several minutes she stands by the door afraid to move, trying desperately not to think of anything, not even Neville. After several deep breaths, she walks to her children's room and switches on the light. They are all there—safe. More or less. She shakes her head. The noise she heard was her youngest son Garfield fallen off the bed again. She looks at her children—two single beds, four children, a little dresser, and there is no place to turn in the room. June-Plum sighs, rubs her stomach and bends down—bending tears at her back—and picks up Garfield. She starts putting him back on the bed beside his brother Floyd, but then, she turns and takes him to sleep with her. June-Plum tosses. Garfield kicks her at every turn. A rooster crows one, two, three times. The sun rushes through the window like an unwanted fly. June-Plum pulls her dress over her nightie and heads straight for the kitchen, where she puts on water to boil. She burns herself.

"Jennifa, get up. Wake up yuh broda dem, an come grate de chocolate fi mek oonuh tea."

"Marnin, Mama, me a fi guh school today? Ah could help yuh wash an company yuh to de market."

"Jennifa, nuh boda ask stupidness: Yuh know yuh go to school wen it ran, wen yuh sick, an if school did open pan Saturday and Sunday, yuh would guh too. If me did only ave fi yuh chance."

"Daddy come home today, Mama?" Jennifer cuts off her mother, having heard her mother's lament numerous times about how she had to leave school in the fifth class after her mother took ill to help care for the house and the other children. June-

Plum sizes up Jennifer and reaches for the bottle of Solomon Gundy (smoked herring with pepper and escallion), her craving, along with guavas, since she became pregnant. She smiles, thinking if it's a boy she will name him Solomon and if it's a girl, Guava. After all, that was how she got her name, June-Plum. Her mother supposedly ate several of the green prickly plums daily during the last two months of her pregnancy.

"Mama!" It's Jennifer, interrupting her memories: "Daddy comin home today?" June-Plum regards her daughter and is angry at her question. She doesn't know when her husband will return, if he ever will. Since she has to make some response, she snaps, "Yes, Jennifa, maybe."

That early hour of the morning, the sun shining through the kitchen windows reminds June-Plum of a pack of fierce, charging dogs. She feels the heat very keenly, and her thighs are beginning to sweat and rub against each other. She raises her dress and examines her thighs, another of her habits since being pregnant, and gradually becomes aware of someone watching her. As she raises her head, her eyes meet Jennifer's, who acknowledges her look before turning to the stove. Jennifer's eyes are so like her missing father's that June-Plum kisses her teeth before emitting one of her deep belly laughs as she leaves the kitchen and walks to her backyard. From there she surveys the sea and the entire community. In another couple of months it would have been ten years since she and Neville began living here where the sea and its smell are always dominant.

Anton Bay is a fishing community. The sea is everywhere. The dock has been christened "Widow's Walk" because many wives, sweethearts, and mothers have paced the boardwalk awaiting their men, some of whom have returned from fishing trips while others have not. Women usually gather there in the evenings to exchange gossip, to throw kisses to their men already out at sea, and to stare and marvel at this beautiful/treacherous woman who feeds them, lulls their men, and soothes their bodies with her waters. Mostly, though, the women wait. June-Plum feels as if she's been waiting all her life like the rest of them for a man to bring happiness into her life.

This morning, the sea is a smooth blue blanket in sharp contrast to her backyard, which is a mixture of gravel and leaves. The guava tree is in bloom, but birds have picked at the green fleshy fruits. June-Plum runs her hand between her thighs, waves a nonchalant hello to someone passing by her gate, then goes and sits at the open kitchen door where swarms of flies compete, and where a few minutes later her children stumble past her, after kissing her on the cheeks, on their way to school.

June-Plum settles in the doorway, her back partially resting against the door frame. She pulls up her dress and absent-mindedly massages her thighs as she again succumbs to her memories.

Ten people were living in four small rooms and she was one of the ten, the older of two girls and the fourth of eight children. When she was eleven, her mother had a stroke, so she had to leave school to wash khaki pants, darn plaid shirts, clean wooden floors using a coconut husk, cook, and, on occasions, help dig yams and pick cocoa to sell at the market. The work was not as painful as not being able to go to school, and the Bible was the only book in the house to read. So each day, June-Plum would read to her mother. She began at Genesis: "In the beginning God created the heaven and the earth. And the earth was without form, and void; and darkness . . ."

Halfway through Revelations, her mother died. "And there was given me a reed like unto a rod; and the angel stood, saying, Rise and measure the temple of God . . ."

June-Plum didn't cry at ther mother's death. Nor at the funeral, and not even during the Ni-Night celebration, the feast for the dead nine days later. She was happy she didn't have to live each day with the painful look in her mother's eyes and so she grew, keeping things to herself and surviving without friends. She learned to be patient and to cup her sadness in her palms—to guard her feelings.

For ten long years, June-Plum washed clothes, cooked, and cared for the house of her father and brothers, while Jennifer, her sister, had been rescued to live with their maternal aunt and family. Jennifer had not come home to visit, but she always remembered to send June-Plum a card on her birthday. And that was why June-Plum named her first daughter Jennifer—in remembrance of her sister.

June-Plum rouses herself. The children's breakfast dishes are still on the table. She looks at them and frowns, moving off into the room where she and Neville have slept for the last nine years. She sees Neville curled up on the bed, covered from head to foot, regardless of the heat. She tugs at the sheets and he dissolves right in front of her eyes. . . . A wail rocks her body. Her lying eyes.

In a drawer to the back, hidden under some clothes, is a picture of a man and a woman. The woman is slim and tall, wearing a white dress that stops midway between her knees and ankles, a white hat, and white shoes. In her hand is a bunch of hibiscus flowers. The man is tall and muscular, wearing grey baggy pants, a white shirt, and plaid bow-tie. His face says his shoes are pinching his toes. The woman's smile does not conceal the uncertainty she feels about herself, but they look nice together, standing beside a bicycle which the man holds. June-Plum sees only the bond that exists between the two persons as she recalls how she met Neville.

On her way from the market she had stopped to buy fish, as her father insisted on having fish for dinner every Saturday. Neville had been riding his bicycle, shouting: "Fish! Fish! Fresh fish! Fish nice wid yam, fish nice wid rice, fish an bammy, fish an chocho, fish an pumpkin. Fresh fish! Buy some fish!"

She waved him down and watched as he jumped off his bicycle with ease, reached into his back pocket for a handkerchief and wiped the sweat from his face before looking at her and flashing her a mischievous smile.

"Wha de lady wan fi buy?"

"Leh me see yuh snapper."

"De finest snapper yuh gwane get, mam, de very finest. Catch dese meself early dis marnin."

"Yuh fisherman, too?"

"Yes, mam. Catch me own fish an do me own sellin."

June-Plum resented him calling her mam, especially since heat was prickling between her thighs. She barked at him, "Gi me five pound snapper."

"Yuh wan me clean dem, man?"

"Nuh worry, me'll clean dem meself."

"Yuh husband an chilren gwane enjoy dese fish."

"Me nuh ave no husban, nor chilren, sah."

"Such a pretty ooman like yuh."

"Yuh sell fish out ere ebery Saturday?"

"Yes, man."

"Good. If me like yuh fish, me will look out fi yuh." With that, June-Plum walked off, feeling the fish vendor's eyes following her. The thought made her stumble, so she was glad when she moved out of his vision and only his voice was heard trailing off in the distance: "Fish! Fish, fish, fresh fish. Fish nice wid yam, fish nice . . ."

June-Plum shakes her head at those memories and goes to sit under the guava tree. From there the sun moves from directly above at noontime to an angular slant indicating that the day is passing, but still June-Plum sits, the memories traveling through her head until she is startled when Blackie her dog barks and runs off to greet the children returning from school.

Floyd is the first to approach: "Mama, is true Daddy lost at sea?"

June-Plum's heart skips a beat and she makes laughter drown her fear. "Floyd, mek yuh mus ask stupidness, go inside and tek off yuh school clothes." The children all go in to be fed.

After dinner, the kitchen clean, June-Plum moves to her veranda to pass the evening in her cane rocker. Every so often, she is interrupted by a good evening or a howdy or by the children's bickering, but for the most part, her mind lingers in the past.

The next week when she went to the market after she hurriedly bought yams, tomatoes, and other produce, she sought the fishman. When she heard "fish, fish" behind her, she turned around with delight on her face, but only a toothless man with greying hair hopped off his bicycle, coming to stop in front of her. June-Plum looked at him, kissing her teeth before walking away. She had not run into the young fishman. Disappointed, she climbed into the bus and slumped down on the seat. There was no fish in her basket. A woman carrying two large baskets entered the bus and accidentally brushed against her, and June-Plum immediately flew into a rage: "Yuh did gi me dress put-down. Yuh tink me is wall fi push gainst!" All of her pent-up anger and frustration were released. Two older women sitting in the back of the bus commented quietly that John Crow must have spat in June-Plum's eyes, while another woman, looking pleased with herself, declared that all June-Plum needed was a good piece to keep her quiet. At this, the men in the bus chuckled and massaged their crotches, while the bus sped around corners at a dangerous speed, sending goats, chickens, and people scampering onto the bankings.

When June-Plum got home, her father greeted her: "Me did sit ere worry bout yuh. Yuh out late."

"Me a big ooman an can come an go as me please," she retorted.

"Chile, wha troublin yuh? Wha mek yuh vex wid de whole world?"

"Me just tired," complained June-Plum. "Me nuh clean an cook an keep house fi nobody but meself nuh more."

The next day, June-Plum quietly packed an old cardboard suitcase and left home, heading for an unknown destination with very little money. After numerous failed attempts at securing a job in several towns, June-Plum went to a bus stop to rest. The sideman of one of the buses bounced off his bus, picked up her suitcase, and secured it on the top carriage of the bus.

"Come, daughta, jump in; we ave fi keep movin."

She complied and the bus lurched off, sending her stumbling down its aisle. At the next town, Anton Bay, thirty-six miles away, she got off. The town was surrounded by the sea. The air smelled salty-sweet. Four fishermen with nets were gathered, talking. June-Plum walked past them, glancing at their faces, hoping to see the young fisherman. They nodded their heads and bid her good evening. Timidly, she reciprocated the head gesture. Her feet were tired, but she must find a job and somewhere to sleep. She came to a small grocery store and entered.

"Mam, could ah trouble yuh fah a little ice-wata?"

The woman behind the counter looked at June-Plum from head to toe before going to the back of the store from where she returned shortly, with a glass of water. June-Plum drank thirstily. Finishing, she wiped her mouth with the back of her hand.

"Tank yuh, mam. Me did well thirsty. God bless yuh." She moved off to go, and still the woman behind the counter had not said a word. June-Plum turned to her: "Excuse me, mam, ah new ere. Know anyone who wan help?"

"Yuh can count money?"

"Count money? Yes, mam."

"Yuh know how fi handle people?"

"Yes, mam, me had to deal wid me eight broda dem."

"Yuh start now?"

"Start, mam?"

"Yuh wan de work or not?"

"Yes, mam, but . . ."

"Yuh a fi live in, keep yuh room clean, help keep de shop clean an sell behine dis counter ere."

"Yes, mam."

"Yuh in de family way?"

"Oh, no, mam, me nuh sleep wid man yet."

And this was how June-Plum and Neville finally got together. Two weeks after June-Plum began working in the shop, the fish vendor rode up and parked his bicycle in front of the shop. A happy mood came with him.

"Pretty daughta, whe do ooman?"

June-Plum looked at him and was tongue-tied. He did not remember her, at least so she thought.

"Daughta," he began again, his eyes shining, "ah wan yuh fi tell de ooman dat de fishman out ere wid her favorite fish."

At that very moment, the woman walked in and the fish vendor turned to speak to her, leaving June-Plum to stare at him. The woman and the fishman were on good terms, joking with each other. When the woman took the fish and went to the back of the shop, the fishman turned to speak to June-Plum: "So how yuh like workin wid de old ooman? She nuh talk much, but she is a good soul."

He laughed as he spoke, but June-Plum just stood there. He ordered a soda which he took his time drinking, relishing each swallow. June-Plum turned her back and began straightening the jars of sweets, sweat forming on her brows and beneath her armpits.

The fishman watched her, remembering the first time he saw her.

June-Plum remained with her back to him, her heart racing.

"Daughta." It was the fishman. "A little youth wan buy sometin."

June-Plum turned and attended to the little boy while the fishman finished his soda. She then took his empty bottle and went to place it in the crate with the other bottles. When she turned back to face the counter, he was already on his bicycle, shouting, "Fish, fresh fish, fish nice wid yam. Fish nice fried, fish nice fi mek soup, fish . . ." His voice trailed away. For the remainder of the day, June-Plum pouted and was short and unfriendly with all the customers.

It was several weeks again before June-Plum saw the fishman and it was only then that she learned his name. He entered the shop and his presence was like a welcome afternoon breeze. "Wha happen, pretty daughta? Long time nuh see. People who know me call me Neville. De old ooman seh yuh call yuhself June-Plum. Me like de fruit well bad and me like the person who guh by de name, too."

Neville reached over as if to tickle her and she drew back, startled. "Who vex yuh suh? From dat first time yuh buy snapper from me, me did wonder who step pan yuh toe. Yuh fi laugh. It will do yuh good. Yuh name suit yuh: yuh fleshy an nice an prickly, too."

So June-Plum smiled because she felt happy and because Neville the fishman was jolly, and yes, her name told of her personality.

They became friends, and each week when he came, she had his favorite soda ready for him and they talked and laughed and he told her when he would be coming again. For four months, Neville and June-Plum only saw each other inside the shop, Then, on one of his visits, he asked her to go to the dance with him.

At the dance, Neville was popular. His friends shouted greetings and June-Plum, shy, did not know how to act. Neville sensed this, so he kept his arms around her. A pretty woman with pearly teeth came up to Neville and stroked his arm, and June-Plum felt her face get hot. She wanted to slap this woman, to stake claim. The music was loud and sensuous, but she did not feel confident enough to dance. Neville insisted, though, so they danced, June-Plum losing herself in the rhythm and heat of the crowd. After a while, Neville took her outside, where it was cool, and kissed her on the mouth. She felt hot and faint. It was her first kiss. She pulled away from him and ran ahead. Neville caught up with her and she abandoned herself to him, resting her head on his shoulder.

Six months later, during the hurricane season and the dark nights, June-Plum, two months pregnant, moved into Neville's one room and two months later one Saturday morning, they dressed up and went and got married. It was the first time June-Plum had had her picture taken.

"Mama, Mama!" It is Floyd, shaking her gently.

June-Plum wonders if she is dreaming. "Neville . . . Neville is yuh? Yuh come home?"

"Mama, is nite an Daddy nuh come yet. Time yuh guh bed." Floyd is embarrassed by his mother's tears. He helps her off the rocker, locks the door behind them and leads her like a blind person to her room. As he walks back to his room, he mumbles to himself: "Me hope Daddy come tomorrow. Im gwane longa dan im seh."

June-Plum tosses and wakes at every turn. She's afraid to sleep, visualizing herself swallowed up by the sea. She's angry at Neville for not coming home and not sending word to her. She hears her heart racing and tries to drown out the noise by covering her chest with Neville's pillow. This only adds to her agitation, as she smells Neville until his smell fills the room.

June-Plum pants for breath. Neville's smell and the sea's—his face and Yemoja's—merge, making her dizzy. The bed spins and June-Plum holds on for dear life. The splashing of the waves rises to a crescendo and all she can do to keep from going mad is to hold her head and plead, "Please, please, leave me alone. Yuh can keep Neville. Keep im." After a while all noises stop and June-Plum dozes, waking at 5:00 A.M. She gets up and heads for the beach, where the fishermen are drawing in their nets. The early morning air is cool and the grey of the night is almost gone. On the beach, she abandons her slippers and heads toward the group of fishermen. She makes out Tony, Bill, Bigger, and Nobel—no sign of Neville. Still, she approaches the men, whose muscles are taut from hauling in their nets. Bigger is the first to notice her.

"Marnin, June-Plum. Neville still out pan de sea?"

"Seems like it, Bigger. De sea is im true wife."

"Well, yuh know me men ave fi ave more dan one wife."

"Wha mek? Guess we oomen just ave fi catch who catch can."

The men turn back to their fish and nets. June-Plum stands looking at the fishermen, a forlorn look in her eyes. As the sun begins to peep over the horizon, she walks further down the beach where the rocks jut out forming a closure, and there, she undresses and, wading out into the water, submerges her body all the way to her neck. Her teeth chatter and she can feel cold-bumps all over her. By the time she comes out, the fishermen have gone off with their haul and only a tangled net and fish bones are on the beach. June-Plum bends down and scoops up a handful of sand which she sends swirling through the air, crying out Neville's name at the same time. She does this three times, then scoops up a handful of seawater and drinks it. She is beginning to understand Yemoja, more powerful than any person, including herself. She is a force in nature that prevails. Surrendering to her is not defeat; it's wisdom. June-Plum breathes more easily as she heads home.

Her children are already at the table eating breakfast. She is grateful for her very independent children. She kisses them all on the tops of their heads and sits where a place is already set for her.

"Mama." It is Garfield, her youngest. "Daddy come?"

"No."

"Wen im comin?"

"Soon."

"Mama," cuts in Jennifer, "how Daddy gone so long?"

Floyd comments, "Im seh im would be back Wednesday nite. Today Friday."

"Me know wha day it is, Floyd," June-Plum offers weakly.

"So wen Daddy comin?" insists Jennifer.

"Oonuh guh to school an stop de one million question."

"Mama, yuh tired?" As usual, Dawn, her very sensitive daughter, is concerned. June-Plum shakes her head in denial. Four pairs of eyes stare at her; she stares back at them, massages her thighs, sighs, and then declares, "Oonuh Daddy comin soon. Now guh to school fore oonuh late."

The children scramble out and June-Plum follows them outside, stopping by the guava tree where she squats for an inordinately long time before going back into the kitchen. She turns on the radio just as the announcer is saying, "It's 10:45 this beautiful Friday morning." The morning is passing. June-Plum looks around her kitchen. The dishes are still there from breakfast, there are clothes to be washed, the house has to be cleaned, and there is still much more to be done. She goes to fetch the dirty clothes. At the door, the sun blinds her and she shields her eyes. Blackie, by the fence, sees her and comes and rubs up against her leg. When she bends and pats his head, some of the dirty clothes fall to the ground. June-Plum looks at Blackie and smiles. He is her only company all day and she is in the habit of speaking to him.

"Blackie, whe Neville, deh? Ah time im come home. Me nuh like man who stay out longa dan dem seh."

Blackie whines in response and June-Plum rubs his back. She puts the clothes in the basin to soak, and goes inside to wash the dishes and to prepare lunch for Dawn and Garfield, her two younger children. She takes a long time doing everything, and by the time she finishes cleaning the kitchen, Dawn and Garfield are home and she has not made lunch for them. She sends Dawn to the shop to buy four patties and two cocoabread, which they have with mango nectar.

Afterwards, she walks her children back to school, all the while looking behind her, craning her neck out to sea, looking for a familiar sight. June-Plum stands by the school fence watching the children play. In all of their movements, she sees Neville with his strong arms pulling in his net full of fish. After a while, when the bell has rung and all the children have gone to their classes, June-Plum wonders why she is there. She does not want to go home and wash clothes or finish her cleaning. She resolves to wander until her feet decide where they will lead her. After all, genius is a capacity for withstanding trouble.

Finding herself at the seashore where some boys about ten years old are swimming and playing naked in the water, she looks at them, examining their small bodies, black and wet, glistening in the sun. She remembers, it seems like for the first time, how she used to swim naked in the river with her sister and friends before her mother died. But that seems like another life. Remembering that scares her. She had forgotten all the good times before her mother died. Could she so easily forget Neville? Since her marriage and four children, her body has become stout and, yes, ugly—something to be covered up. She throws off her slippers and pulls up her dress. The water is warm and the sea is very different today—not so blue, and seemingly satiated. The boys see her and cover their privates. June-Plum bursts out laughing and calls to them in a friendly voice.

"Nuh boda cova up. Me ave boys an see tings ebery day."

The boys giggle and continue to splash each other. The water feels so good June-Plum wades in further, wanting to go deeper until it reaches her shoulders and then covers her head. This woman, this Yemoja, is alluring with her blue waters. June-Plum pulls up her dress further, lapping it between her thighs. Two more steps forward and her dress will be up to her panties, but she cannot stop herself. She wades further. Perhaps if she shows Yemoja how capable she is of holding up despite the loss of her man, if she stops competing in a game that she does not understand therefore must lose, then maybe Yemoja will leave her alone to bring forth another life and to enjoy the four she has already been given. Clearly Neville is out of her hands now, completely in Yemoja's power.

"Sista June-Plum, come si down wid an ole ooman an remine er of tings." It is Miss Country, as old as spit. No one in the community knows Miss Country's age, but she seems older than the trees. Everyone who comes to the village sees her, and she knows everyone: children, cousins, aunts, uncles, and grandparents, and even great-great-grandparents. Miss Country spanks any children she sees misbehaving and sends them home to their mothers, who come to thank her for caring. Children are almost perfectly behaved when Miss Country is around. She is nutmeg color with a face as lined as the Sahara Desert. Toothless, she seldom smiles. Her arms are strong like a man's and she never wears shoes, her soles rubbery-tough like a tire. She says when she dies they can sell her feet to Bata, the shoe-store chain. June-Plum loves Miss Country and is not put off by her roughness. "Come, Sista June-Plum, yuh moda neba tell yuh fi min ole people?" Miss Country walks off, erect, a large basin of fish on her head, her stool in her right hand and a large knife in her left.

June-Plum pulls herself out of the sea and runs to catch up with this living history. Her legs are wet and her dress clings to her thighs, her firm and shapely thighs that she loves. People meeting June-Plum salute her with "Peace" and "God-bless," but no one mentions Neville, though everyone knows. Everyone in the village knows even the most intimate details about everyone else, down to how many times a week a woman "does it" with her man. So June-Plum knows that they know. She feels like a naughty child caught in the act with everyone whispering behind her back.

She sits on an empty crate and helps Miss Country gut her fish and wash them off with lime. Only their eyes and hand movements speak. Two pretty grey-turquoise ground lizards play nearby. Miss Country is smoking a cigarette with the lit part inside her mouth. June-Plum has always wanted to ask Miss Country how she smokes with the fire inside her mouth, but she has never had the nerve. It was the same way she felt around

Neville. There was so much she wanted to ask him, especially Sunday morning before he left when they lay awake in each other's arms. She had wanted to ask him how he felt about their having another child, but refrained, fearful of what he might have said. She couldn't bring herself to tell him how much she loved him either, how she wanted them to do something because she didn't want any more children. But her heart was in her mouth and she didn't want to spoil the peace, the beauty of the moment, because she knew—sensed—that Neville would not be returning as he said. How could she have known and not said anything, not done anything, to prevent him from leaving? June-Plum was too accustomed to acquiescing, to waiting patiently like a good woman for her man. Well, those days were over with, she decided. From now on, others would wait for her. Neville's going freed her of the cyclic burden handed to her from her mother, who took it from her mother before her. Women forever waiting for something to happen. June-Plum sees Miss Country observing her. "Betta late dan neba," she mumbles to herself and pushes out her chest. She will ask Miss Country about the fire inside her mouth.

"Miss Country, yuh eat de ashes dat fall from de cigarette inside yuh mout?"

Miss Country looks at June-Plum and frowns. "Wha mek a big ooman like yuh mus guh lif up yuh frock, expose yuhself to boy picknie? Neville nuh guh like it wen im come back an people tell im how yuh act foolish."

June-Plum spits. Silence surrounds them like a mosquito net. "Miss Country, yuh tink Neville comin back?"

"Me look like de sea to yuh? Me an dat sea-ooman nuh bosom-buddy, she nuh tell me nuttin."

At this, June-Plum knits her brow but says nothing.

"Wen de baby due? Yuh mus tek advantage of some a de new ways. Yuh an Neville a sensible people. Picknie expensive. Galang a yuh yard, guh cook fah yuh picknie dem."

June-Plum wipes her hands and heads home, feeling admonished. She looks back, and Miss Country is still gutting and cleaning fish with smoke coming through her nose and the lit part of the cigarette hidden inside her mouth. She still does not know how Miss Country is able to smoke without burning her mouth, but she shakes her head and moves on. Just before turning inside her gate, she looks out at the sea and sees Yemoja standing in the center of Neville's boat, combing her hair with a long wooden pick. June-Plum kisses her teeth and turns her back on her rival.

Her children are sitting around the kitchen table, a sad lot, looking like wet puppies. The suhsuh from their friends at school, who, in turn, heard it eavesdropping on their parents, has it that their father is lost at sea. Floyd and Jennifer are upset by this rumor. They remember that last year one friend's father and uncle drowned during the hurricane season when their boat capsized. Their father was a good swimmer, it wasn't hurricane season, and he had painted his boat blue and white in honor of the sea goddess Yemoja, but there were no guarantees. The sad faces of her children assail June-Plum. She silently warms up yesterday's fried fish and rice and puts the food in front of them. Her stern look warns them not to ask any questions. Blackie is fed most of the evening meal. She sends the children to play, but the girls, Jennifer and Dawn, choose to remain with her. They sit on the veranda but all are restless, so June-Plum decides they should go for a walk. They stop every so often to exchange greetings and a few words with people on the street and to clap at the mosquitoes that buzz around them. They end up at Widow's Walk.

June-Plum stops and stares out to sea until the shades of blue make her dizzy. Unsteadily, she holds on to the railing. Miss Country can be seen seated by her tray of fried fish. Jennifer and Dawn are playing closely by the seashore; they have abandoned their shoes and are wetting their feet. June-Plum sees them, but they seem far away. She calls to them, but no sound comes from her mouth. The waves are full. A trail of blackbirds is flying home. The sun is lost in a cloud. She looks at the waves. They dazzle and pull. Her head spins. Her thighs feel like logs. Suddenly she is going down, down. The salty water plays around her face and gets in her ears. She can feel the damp sand beneath her and hears the gentle cry of the waves. This woman means to take her, too, so she succumbs giggling, her mother's words echoing "yuh gi weh laugh fi pea soup . . ."

June-Plum finds herself lying in bed. Her head swirls like the waves. "Whe Jennifa and Dawn? She tek dem too? Neville seh de sea is im most beautiful ooman; dat why im love er. Im love er more dan me."

Miss Country, hearing June-Plum's chatter, enters the room and proceeds to rub her face and neck with bay rum. June-Plum smiles, still thinking she is a part of the sea, and remembers her earlier jealousy—how she wanted to master this woman, this sea which surrounds their lives and is woven into the beauty of the landscape. She is everywhere one looks and her song is the consistent noise lulling one to sleep. Almost all of the men of the community belong to her and sometimes in her greed, she takes one or two of them to live with her permanently.

Neville spent two weeks fixing his boat. He painted it dark blue with light blue oars, and he and Bertram and some of the other fishermen bought a large bottle of white rum to offer to the gods for protection and good luck. In addition, he had Basil, the local artist, draw a stately black woman with big legs and nappy hair like a mane surrounded by foliage at the stern. She was as June-Plum had seen her in her dreams—beautiful, enticing. Neville was so proud of himself he invited the entire community out on the beach for a feast and Miss Country prepared the fish and had everyone licking their fingers and smacking their mouths for days after. With this larger boat Neville could get a bigger haul on each trip. June-Plum was happy for him, but she was never able to say this to him, as each time she felt a lump in her throat.

His net is heavy. The waves are furious and sudden. He smiles, his white teeth the only light in the dark night, his laughter drowned by the wailing of the waves. Neville relaxes and surveys the sea. "Ooman, yuh wild tonite. Yuh mus need more rum." For a moment there is calm. Neville reaches out to pull in his net, but just then, a big wave tosses the boat. He lets go, losing his net. "Wha vex yuh, ooman? Relax—mek we talk nuh." Another wave comes, and still others. Neville wrestles with his boat, but the waves have pushed it into a current and he is unable to take control. "Now look ere, ooman, me ave wife a yard. She nah guh undastan." Neville is pulled along and the waves cave in on him, creating a valley. He sees no way out. He surrenders to his mistress, Yemoja, who leads him further, taking him into her depths until he goes under, smiling . . .

"Nooooooo!" June-Plum screams, her voice echoing through Miss Country's house and out the window, stopping passers-by in their tracks. Miss Country, in her kitchen listening to the news on her transistor radio sent to her by her great-grandson in New York, hears that a fisherman was found at sea.

Miss Country enters the room again and faces June-Plum, who is sitting up straight as a board, perspiration covering her face. Miss Country chews on her gum and shakes her head at June-Plum. "Radio man seh dem fine a fishman. Yuh should kill dat big ole roosta yuh ave an mark yuhself wid de blood."

June-Plum stares at Miss Country, who apologetically mumbles, "Me neba did hear nuh name. De radioman neba seh nuh name," she ends, staring at June-Plum, who slumps back on the pillow, the child kicking in her stomach. After what seems like an eternity, the thought comes to June-Plum like a whisper: "De beautiful ooman tek him!" Tears fill up her eyes, but she quickly wipes them dry, ashamed of her weakness. Miss Country's eyes relate an understanding of her grief as she hands her a cup of tea. June-Plum drinks the pumpkin leaf tea, then slowly gets out of the bed, Neville's words playing in her head, "bet yuh ah tickle yuh." She hugs herself and bursts into a laugh, an attempt to drown the sob rising in her bosom. The sound is hollow, disconnected, joyless, stopping Miss Country from leaving the room.

Miss Country looks at her: "Chile, yuh a loose yuh head?"

June-Plum shakes her head, her face shining like a full moon. Yemoja was always more woman than her. The sun is bright—

splendid, in fact. June-Plum parts the curtains and looks out. Seeing people dressed in their Sunday best, she is confused. It was Friday evening when she went walking with Dawn and Jennifer. Miss Country anticipates her question: "Yes, yuh did sleep an toss an act fool-fool fah a whole day an nite. De picknie dem alrite. Wen yuh faint, Dawn run come get me. Big ooman like yuh should know fi eat wen yuh a carry chile."

Suddenly, there is a great commotion. "Miss Country! June-Plum! June-Plum! Neville alive an comin home, Neville alive!" It is Beverly, Bertram's wife, running and panting with the news. June-Plum sticks her head through the window, her eyes large. Beverly grips her hand. People on their way to church wave to her. June-Plum is immobile for a while. Then, with great haste, she pulls on her dress, leaving her hair wild. Her slippers clap as she hastens to her house, thinking of all she has to do before Neville comes home: wash dishes and clothes, clean, bathe herself, and kill that rooster. Beverly says she will help. Neville is alive after all.

As she hurries along, June-Plum feels young again. She remembers that first evening she and Neville went to the dance, his mouth wet and hot on her neck, his arms firm around her waist. People greet her, but her smile is not for them, it is for Neville.

Velma Pollard, sister of novelist Erna Brodber, was born in Jamaica in 1937. A poet and short story writer whose work has appeared in Jamaica Journal, Bim, *and* Caribbean Quarterly, *Pollard has also published various articles on Caribbean language and literature. Her first collection of poetry,* Crown Point and Other Poems, *appeared in 1988, followed quickly by* Considering Woman *(1989), her first collection of short stories. Pollard's short stories, some written in Jamaican patwah, are alive with the vibrant voices of Caribbean women, whose warmth and humanity linger on the mind long after the reading of the texts.*

VELMA POLLARD

Parable II

My miserable Auntie, the one who always look like she dreaming, used to walk with her right hand cup halfway as if she constantly holding something; and since we always say, "Cho, she mad," I never ask her what she was carrying till the day after she come back from two months with Aunt B and I notice her hand keeping straight straight at her side like everybody else.

"Aunt May, what happen to you hand?" I ask her.

"How you mean, what happen to mi han?"

"You hand look straight. Not that same right hand you used to cup all the time since we small?"

She said, "Shhh. Listen, but don't laugh." And she look round to see if anybody hearing. Then she start talk to me sofly and say:

"You see, is a little child I was carrying right in my hand middle; small you know. One little beeny pickny; like one of dem jumping frogs; only plenty smaller; and every now and then if a take me eye off it, when I look again it shrink; and if I walking in the house I feel it going drop out of my hand and into one of those little cracks in the floor and disappear. So that's how I was walking with it cup in my hand and all the time I fretting that it sure to fall out. You notice how when a go to town where they have tile floor a still cup it but a never look down so much? . . ."

"So what happen now? You stop holding it?"

"Girl, is a long story. Suddenly one day the child change into one good-looking little boy with a square face and smooth smooth black skin . . . so bout two weeks a watching at my side to make sure he following me everywhere. Till one evening about three o'clock, I must be gazing, for you know B place strange, a just look round in time to see the little boy jump down inside a sink-hole . . . my heart leap, but you know, a didn't cry, is like I know that sink-hole didn't go to the sea. I follow my mind. Just as if somebody was guiding me. And a walk clear cross the town to where I think the sink-hole come out . . . I find the spot but not a sign of the child. Now you know how many years I been walking with that little one in my hand and a never had a mishap; and now this one, so much bigger, go lost from mi now. I sit down at the street side with me hand at mi chin. Then I walk back to where the sink-hole start, to see if it have another place where it come out again. But a find myself back to the same spot and a sit down again. This time I ready to cry. Dusk come, night start to fall. I sit down at the street side with my hand on my chin and somebody come up and pat me . . . who you think? No the boy! Not a word . . . but with the matinee ticket in his hand . . . now show the boy go; and reach back safe and sound . . . I said "Jeezas Christ" and I look up to heaven but not a word mi no seh to him for afta we no talk.

"But from dat, I don't even look down to see if anybody nex to me and as you notice, is months now since I stop walk wid me han cup."

Paulette Poujol-Oriol was born in Port-au-Prince, Haiti, in 1926. A member of the National Society of Dramatic Art, she has been actively involved in theater, radio, and television. In 1980 she received the Henri Deschamps Award for her social novel Le Creuset. *She has contributed to many journals, newspapers, and magazines and is the president of the Feminine League for Social Action. Poujol-Oriol's fiction,* Le Creuset *in particular, focuses on moral choices and social commitment, and explores Haiti's myriad socio-economic problems, offering possible, albeit perhaps sentimental, solutions.*

PAULETTE POUJOL-ORIOL

Red Flower

N'Gaou stretched out on his bed of woven straw. The spring night had been mild, and as morning approached, the mat was fresh as dew. He could feel his wife's lukewarm body next to his. Aloka slept, breathing calmly and evenly. Her pouty lips still retained the fullness of childhood. Sixteen times after her birth the palm tree planted by her father had dropped a dry yellowed leaf. In the round hut pierced by one single window, the air was mellow, and the hut seemed to gather upon itself to conserve the coolness of the night.

Aloka turned in her sleep. She was so beautiful, his wife! A body of polished ebony, hips like the contours of a shady valley. One of her young breasts was flattened artlessly against the mat, she slept so heartily after their night of love.

However, that night, he had been very gentle to her, to his Aloka. They had been joined for five moons. Five moons. And since then, every night, they had taken each other violently, almost with rage, and N'Gaou let burst from him all the ardor of a love whose intensity overwhelmed him.

He had known Aloka since she was a little girl, when she used to come from the neighboring village. He had watched her as a young woman, barely past puberty, dancing with her companions around the big tree. He had heard her laugh by the riverbank, when the women from the two villages went for water or to wash the linen. And she had invaded his heart and his flesh, with her lips of violet and her clear laughter which rippled like raindrops dripping from the big baobab after a refreshing shower.

When his father told him, "Son, it is time for you to choose a wife," he had bowed his head without replying. His father was chief of the tribe and he, N'Gaou, could have had his pick of the girls from the clan, he who was so big, so strong, the most handsome warrior in the village. He felt a profound devotion for his father, but his heart had dropped to his feet when the chief proposed three or four young women as possible wives. From the time he was a child he had obeyed his father's commands blindly, but this time he had felt something knotting inside him, like a big hard rock, right in his chest, and he had felt that, if need be, he would defend his love against all. He had held fast for three years, refusing all alliances proposed to him, and the old chief had finally relented and consented to his union with Aloka, the pretty young woman from the neighboring tribe.

They had been joined for five moons. Five months of heady love, of the dream becoming flesh every night. At first timid and hesitating, Aloka had become an ardent lover whose desire sometimes surpassed his. But yesterday evening she had timidly confessed a secret: she had not flowered for two months. For two months now the tender hope of a future birth slept within her. She would soon have a son. A son, he was sure of that, a son who would prolong his lineage, a son he would take hunting as soon as the child had left the women's circle, a son he would prepare for the initiation rites of his tribe, a son who would in turn give him other sons who would later honor his white hair.

And it was she, his beloved Aloka, who carried his seed, who would be the honored mother of his children, she who would manage his home and whom he would find when, weighed down with the spoils of the hunt, he would return home in the evening, exhausted from chasing fugitive game through the forest.

Those were the thoughts of N'Gaou, the big hunter, the valiant warrior, that morning. He felt himself melt watching his wife as she slept, trying to detect signs of that new life.

That was why, last night, their embraces had acquired a different nuance. They had loved each other, she with restraint, he with an anxious sweetness and a tenderness of which he would not have believed himself capable. He had been very tender to her, and had imposed upon himself a slower, less ardent rhythm, he had been afraid of hurting her, or wounding her. He had caressed her tenderly for a long time after making love, and she had fallen asleep in his arms, her head on his chest, and much later in the night, he had set her down by his side before falling asleep himself, heady and happy.

Thus daydreamed N'Gaou, the great warrior, that morning. He wanted to give Aloka a present, a present that would tell her of his joy, his pride, his gratitude. But she had received so many gifts at the time of their marriage that the jars were overflowing still with the thousand offerings that had marked the wedding of the chief's son. But this morning he, N'Gaou, would go far into the forest to look for a certain red orchid to give her, an orchid as red as blood, a flower for which she longed to adorn her hair, and which grew only in the deep forest, far away from their hut. And N'Gaou got up and placed a long deep kiss on the lips of violet from which emanated a fresh and even breath.

"Till this evening, my beloved."

N'Gaou left his hut and was suddenly dazzled by the dawn. He vigorously splashed some water on his face, and took his bow, his arrows, and his hunting spear. Since he was going into the forest in search of a flower, he may as well take his weapons and bring back a good hunter's bounty.

He walked for a long, long time before reaching the laughing stream which marked the hamlet's boundary. As he walked through, the village awakened to a new day. The air was buzzing with morning chants and the laughter of children just waking up.

"Soon," N'Gaou told himself, "I will hear my son laugh in my wife's arms." And he smiled to himself. N'Gaou felt good, permeated by an intense sense of goodwill which made his step lighter and more supple.

Hence, when he arrived at the riverbank, he lacked the heart to fish. The spear remained motionless in his courageous hand. The fish played at chasing each other in the water spangled with sunshine. N'Gaou smiled and told himself:

"Brother Fish, you can swim without fear this morning. I don't have the heart to kill."

And the great warrior continued on his way under the exuberant foliage. Upon entering a clearing, the sound of his footsteps roused a flock of birds who suddenly filled the sky like a big white cloud. The sudden puffs of wind created by their flapping wings brushed against N'Gaou's face, who shook his head and said:

"Brother Bird, you can fly in peace, my heart is too full of happiness this morning to wish to harm one single feather of yours."

And he entered the swamp area which separated him from the forest. There reigned an old crocodile, so covered with brown scales that it looked like an old dead tree stump. As he passed the pond, its waters shimmering with gold and green, N'Gaou shuddered. More than one valiant hunter had left an arm here, a leg there, between the jaws of Sir Crocodile, master of the waters. A tapir suddenly dashed past N'Gaou's legs. He made a half-hearted gesture toward his bow, but let his arm drop.

"Brother Tapir," the hunter said, "go in peace, for this morning N'Gaou, the warrior, has the heart of a child."

The sun was directly over the trees, and N'Gaou's shadow had gathered itself at his feet, when he reached the undergrowth which abounded with red orchids, the blood-red flowers with which that evening Aloka would adorn her hair, black like her eyes of fire. N'Gaou pulled out his knife and proceeded to gather the most beautiful orchids, those in full bloom. He made a necklace out of liana, threaded the flowers on it, and left with a light step.

The great warrior ran under the trees, he ran through the forest, he ran past the swamp, he ran across the clearing, he ran across the encompassing plain, he ran with broad and even strides; he wanted to bring his red prize as quickly as possible to the sweet child who by now had been awake for a long time, the child-flower who awaited him down in the cool hut.

And N'Gaou crossed the gold and diamond laughing river where the water is now warm like a human skin.

But what has become of the village which just this morning laughed with the dawn? The huts ransacked, burnt, or knocked down, the clothing strewn about, the implements broken. The corpse of the grand chief, his father, lies under the midday sun with one of his wives, her throat slit, stretched across his body. The sorcerer's hut is nothing more than debris, the sacred cult objects scattered on the ground, and the old wise man's head is speared on a lance, a grimace of horror on his face. N'Gaou's house is empty, as are the rest of the ravaged huts.

And N'Gaou runs now toward the river, toward the sea which is the source of this misfortune. The sea which brings big white vessels with huge sails which transport blacks torn from their land toward a faraway country where they are enslaved. There is no doubt in N'Gaou's heart that it has been the slave traders who have taken away his tribe, his family, his wife. The thought makes N'Gaou's heart mad with rage and grief. Slaves! Ah, no, never! And the mute cry breaks into a sob.

N'Gaou, distraught, reaches the dune which dominates the landscape. From there he overlooks the riverbank. A long procession of men, women, and children, roped to each other, walks toward the boats floating near the bank. The hunter's piercing eyes puncture the air vibrant with heat. Near the end of the second row he sees her, his Aloka. They have seized her, she's going to be pushed into a canoe, she . . .

A cry pierces the blazing space: ALOKA!

And the imprisoned woman stretches her arms toward the man she loves, toward the tall dark silhouette framed against the sunlight and the blue-gray sky. And the arrow shoots out. Piercing the silence, it strikes the woman right in the heart; a star-shaped red flower stains the delicate chest. A body crumples, and the golden sand slowly drinks the vermillion floodtide.

N'Gaou withdraws toward the forest. He is calm, strangely appeased: Aloka is free forever. His own son will never be a white man's slave.

The great black warrior walks toward the putrid swamp lapping in the setting sun. The brackish water closes upon him with a greedy click of its wet tongue.

A red flower floats on the surface for an instant, and then slowly folds into itself and disappears.

Translated by Lizabeth Paravisini-Gebert

*Rhys was born in Dominica in 1894 but lived in England from 1910 until her death in 1979. Having written most of her fiction—*The Left Bank, Quartet, After Leaving Mr. Mackenzie, Voyage to the Dark, *and* Good Morning, Midnight—*between 1928 and 1939, Rhys slipped out of sight and was generally thought to be dead. In 1966 she made a dramatic comeback with* Wide Sargasso Sea, *which won the W. H. Smith Literary Award, the Heinemann Award, and the Royal Society of Literature Prize. Almost obsessively concerned with women's alienation in a patriarchal world, Rhys explores in her fiction the psychological disintegration of her poignant characters.*

JEAN RHYS

The Day They Burned the Books

My friend Eddie was a small, thin boy. You could see the blue veins in his wrists and temples. People said that he had consumption and wasn't long for this world. I loved, but sometimes despised him.

His father, Mr. Sawyer, was a strange man. Nobody could make out what he was doing in our part of the world at all. He was not a planter or a doctor or a lawyer or a banker. He didn't keep a store. He wasn't a schoolmaster or a government official. He wasn't—that was the point—a gentleman. We had several resident romantics who had fallen in love with the moon on the Caribbees—they were all gentlemen and quite unlike Mr. Sawyer who hadn't an "h" in his composition. Besides, he detested the moon and everything else about the Caribbean and he didn't mind telling you so.

He was agent for a small steamship line which in those days

linked up Venezuela and Trinidad with the smaller islands, but he couldn't make much out of that. He must have a private income, people decided, but they never decided why he had chosen to settle in a place he didn't like and to marry a colored woman. Though a decent, respectable, nicely educated colored woman, mind you.

Mrs. Sawyer must have been very pretty once but, what with one thing and another, that was in days gone by.

When Mr. Sawyer was drunk—this often happened—he used to be very rude to her. She never answered him.

"Look at the nigger showing off," he would say; and she would smile as if she knew she ought to see the joke but couldn't. "You damned, long-eyed, gloomy half-caste, you don't smell right," he would say; and she never answered, not even to whisper, "You don't smell right to me either."

The story went that once they had ventured to give a dinner party and that when the servant, Mildred, was bringing in coffee, he had pulled Mrs. Sawyer's hair. "Not a wig, you see," he bawled. Even then, if you can believe it, Mrs. Sawyer had laughed and tried to pretend that it was all part of a joke, this mysterious, obscure, sacred English joke.

But Mildred told the other servants in the town that her eyes had gone wicked, like a soucriant's eyes, and that afterwards she had picked up some of the hair he pulled out and put it in an envelope, and that Mr. Sawyer ought to look out (hair is obeah as well as hands).

Of course, Mrs. Sawyer had her compensations. They lived in a very pleasant house in Hill Street. The garden was large and they had a fine mango tree, which bore prolifically. The fruit was small, round, very sweet and juicy—a lovely, red-and-yellow colour when it was ripe. Perhaps it was one of the compensations, I used to think.

Mr. Sawyer built a room on the back of his house. It was unpainted inside and the wood smelt very sweet. Bookshelves lined the walls. Every time the Royal Mail steamer came in it brought a package for him, and gradually the empty shelves filled.

Once I went there with Eddie to borrow *The Arabian Nights*.
That was on a Saturday afternoon, one of those hot, still afternoons when you felt that everything had gone to sleep, even the
water in the gutters. But Mrs. Sawyer was not asleep. She put her
head in at the door and looked at us, and I knew that she hated
the room and hated the books.

It was Eddie with the pale blue eyes and straw-coloured
hair—the living image of his father, though often as silent as his
mother—who first infected me with doubts about "home,"
meaning England. He would be so quiet when others who had
never seen it—none of us had ever seen it—were talking about its
delights, gesticulating freely as we talked—London, the beautiful,
rosy-cheeked ladies, the theatres, the shops, the fog, the blazing
coal fires in winter, the exotic food (whitebait eaten to the sound
of violins), strawberry and cream—the word "strawberries" always
spoken with a guttural and throaty sound which we imagined to
be the proper English pronunciation.

"I don't like strawberries," Eddie said on one occasion.

"You *don't like* strawberries?"

"No, and I don't like daffodils either. Dad's always going on
about them. He says they lick the flowers here into a cocked hat
and I bet that's a lie."

We were all too shocked to say, "You don't know a thing
about it." We were so shocked that nobody spoke to him for the
rest of the day. But I for one admired him. I also was tired of
learning and reciting poems in praise of daffodils, and my
relations with the few "real" English boys and girls I had met
were awkward. I had discovered that if I called myself English
they would snub me haughtily: "You're not English; you're a
horrid colonial." "Well, I don't much want to be English," I would
say. "It's much more fun to be French or Spanish or something
like that—and, as a matter of fact, I am a bit." Then I was too
killingly funny, quite ridiculous. Not only a horrid colonial, but
also ridiculous. Heads I win, tails you lose—that was the English.
I had thought about all this, and thought hard, but I had never
dared to tell anybody what I thought and I realized that Eddie
had been very bold.

But he was bold, and stronger than you would think. For one thing, he never felt the heat; some coldness in his fair skin resisted it. He didn't burn red or brown, he didn't freckle much.

Hot days seemed to make him feel especially energetic. "Now we'll run twice round the lawn and then you can pretend you're dying of thirst in the desert and that I'm an Arab chieftain bringing you water."

"You must drink slowly," he would say, "for if you're very thirsty and you drink quickly you die."

So I learnt the voluptuousness of drinking slowly when you are very thirsty—small mouthful by small mouthful, until the glass of pink, iced Coca-Cola was empty.

Just after my twelfth birthday Mr. Sawyer died suddenly, and as Eddie's special friend I went to the funeral, wearing a new white dress. My straight hair was damped with sugar and water the night before and plaited into tight little plaits, so that it should be fluffy for the occasion.

When it was all over everybody said how nice Mrs. Sawyer had looked, walking like a queen behind the coffin and crying her eyeballs out at the right moment, and wasn't Eddie a funny boy? He hadn't cried at all.

After this Eddie and I took possession of the room with the books. No one else ever entered it, except Mildred to sweep and dust in the mornings, and gradually the ghost of Mr. Sawyer pulling Mrs. Sawyer's hair faded though this took a little time. The blinds were always halfway down and going in out of the sun was like stepping into a pool of brown-green water. It was empty except for the bookshelves, a desk with a green baize top and a wicker rocking-chair.

"My room," Eddie called it. "My books," he would say, "my books."

I don't know how long this lasted. I don't know whether it was weeks after Mr. Sawyer's death or months after, that I see myself and Eddie in the room. But there we are and there, unexpectedly, are Mrs. Sawyer and Mildred. Mrs. Sawyer's mouth tight, her eyes pleased. She is pulling all the books out of the shelves and piling them into two heaps. The big, fat glossy ones—the good-looking ones, Mildred explains in a whisper—lie in one heap. The *Encyclopaedia Britannica, British Flowers, Birds and Beasts,* various histories, books with maps, Froude's *English in the West Indies* and so on—they are going to be sold. The unimportant books, with paper covers or damaged covers or torn pages, lie in another heap. They are going to be burnt—yes, burnt.

Mildred's expression was extraordinary as she said that—half hugely delighted, half-shocked, even frightened. And as for Mrs. Sawyer's—well, I knew bad temper (I had often seen it), I knew rage, but this was hate. I recognized the difference at once and stared at her curiously. I edged closer to her so that I could see the titles of the books she was handling.

It was the poetry shelf. *Poems,* Lord Byron, *Poetical Works,* Milton, and so on. Vlung, vlung, vlung—all thrown into the heap that were to be sold. But a book by Christina Rossetti, though also bound in leather, went into the heap that was to be burnt, and by a flicker in Mrs. Sawyer's eyes I knew that worse than men who wrote books were women who wrote books—infinitely worse. Men could be mercifully shot; women must be tortured.

Mrs. Sawyer did not seem to notice that we were there, but she was breathing free and easy and her hands had got the rhythm of tearing and pitching. She looked beautiful, too—beautiful as the sky outside which was a very dark blue, or the mango tree, long sprays of brown and gold.

When Eddie said "No," she did not even glance at him.

"No," he said again in a high voice. "Not that one. I was reading that one."

She laughed and he rushed at her, his eyes starting out of his head, shrieking, "Now I've got to hate you too. Now I hate you too."

He snatched the book out of her hand and gave her a violent push. She fell into the rocking-chair.

Well, I wasn't going to be left out of all this, so I grabbed a book from the condemned pile and dived under Mildred's outstretched arm.

Then we were both in the garden. We ran along the path, bordered with crotons. We pelted down the path, though they did not follow us and we could hear Mildred laughing—kyah, kyah, kyah, kyah. As I ran I put the book I had taken into the loose front of my brown holland dress. It felt warm and alive.

When we got into the street we walked sedately, for we feared the black children's ridicule. I felt very happy, because I had saved this book and it was my book and I would read it from the beginning to the triumphant words "The End". But I was uneasy when I thought of Mrs. Sawyer.

"What will she do?" I said.

"Nothing," Eddie said. "Not to me."

He was white as a ghost in his sailor suit, a blue-white even in the setting sun, and his father's sneer was clamped on his face.

"But she'll tell your mother all sorts of lies about you," he said. "She's an awful liar. She can't make up a story to save her life, but she makes up lies about people all right."

"My mother won't take any notice of her." I said. Though I was not at all sure.

"Why not? Because she's . . . because she isn't white?"

Well, I knew the answer to that one. Whenever the subject was brought up—people's relations and whether they had a drop of colored blood or whether they hadn't—my father would grow impatient and interrupt. "Who's white?" he would say. "Damned few."

So I said, "Who's white? Damned few."

"You can go to the devil," Eddie said. "She's prettier than your mother. When she's asleep her mouth smiles and she has curling eyelashes and quantities and quantities and *quantities* of hair."

"Yes," I said truthfully. "She's prettier than my mother."

It was a red sunset that evening, a huge, sad, frightening sunset.

"Look, let's go back," I said. "If you're sure she won't be vexed with you, let's go back. It'll be dark soon."

At his gate he asked me not to go. "Don't go yet, don't go yet."

We sat under the mango tree and I was holding his hand when he began to cry. Drops fell on my hand like the water from the dripstone in the filter in our yard. Then I began to cry too and when I felt my own tears on my hand I thought, "Now perhaps we're married."

"Yes, certainly, now we're married," I thought. But I didn't say anything. I didn't say a thing until I was sure he had stopped. Then I asked, "What's your book?"

"It's *Kim*," he said. "But it got torn. It starts at page twenty now. What's the one you took?"

"I don't know; it's too dark to see," I said.

When I got home I rushed into my bedroom and locked the door because I knew that this book was the most important thing that had ever happened to me and I did not want anybody to be there when I looked at it.

But I was very disappointed, because it was in French and seemed dull. *Fort Comme La Mort*, it was called. . . .

Astrid Roemer was born in 1947 in Surinam, but now lives in The Hague. Her published work includes Sasa, *a volume of poetry; several novels, among them* Neem mijn terug, Suriname *(Take me back, Surinam),* Over de gekte van een vrouw *(About a woman's madness), and* Negrens, ergens *(Nowhere, somewhere); and a musical drama,* Parimaribo, Parimaribo. *Her writing breaks away from the exploration of racial and cultural issues that characterizes most Surinamese literature to examine women's search for their personal and sexual selves.*

ASTRID ROEMER

Lola or the Song of Spring

Her eyes turn to the clock which hangs directly above the end of her bed. She takes the time and the Bible verse of the day out of the bedroom with her. She does not think the quotation through. It is clear the way it is and just as inescapable as the fact that it is eight o'clock.

While she dusts the square table with the side of her hand, she admits the face of her visitor: the head of a woman, oval and made up with cosmetics on the expected places. Even though she has stared at hundreds of different kinds of faces in the course of forty years, she can remember quite well which problem belongs to which face. The woman scheduled for two o'clock has a conflict with her son concerning an identity problem—according to her family doctor. With the flat of her hand she smoothes out the cloth over the table. It is spotlessly white and ironed stiff as a linen napkin. From the drawer of a high wall cabinet she pulls out a dust cloth. She shakes it out roughly, as if shaking off the thoughts that overcome her, and, without making a sound, she dusts the woodwork, the glass doors, and the bric-a-brac that people have given her out of gratitude for services rendered. She has given away most of these knickknacks to friends on their birthdays; otherwise, her house would have become a warehouse.

When she approaches the windows with her dust cloth, she opens the drapes—they are dark red and made of thick velvet. Light falls on her furniture and through the gauze curtain in front of the glass panes, the windows look like paintings. She loves to look outside at any hour of the day; the light changes constantly, but she knows the fragments of buildings, trees, and sky which fall within the frames by heart. She shakes out the dust cloth again: that child playing the whore to show her family how many men she can get—she sees that face when she thinks of her afternoon appointment.

The telephone—she hesitates and decides to answer it anyway. Too late. They had already hung up. She holds the receiver in her hand for a moment; deep in thought, she wipes it with her cloth. As soon as she puts the receiver down, the telephone tinkles through the living room—she is startled and answers immediately.

Her eyes closed, she listens to the voice of a man trying to explain that he needs help desperately—she can hear the panic in his voice. That he is not a native of her country is apparent from the hesitation with which he tries to hint at his problem. She opens her appointment book and gives him a date and time. She writes down his name and his work number. That apparently reassures him because he no longer stumbles over his words and hangs up with what sounds like a greeting.

With another glance at her desk and at the rest of the interior—and with a completely meaningless sigh—she goes to the kitchen. She sets water on to boil. She arranges a few cups and saucers on a copper serving tray. She hangs a tea bag of a well-known brand in the square pot made of clear glass. Then she leans back against the cupboard and waits until the kettle whistles.

She had told her son that she wanted to stop working—in case he was interested. After all, he has directed an institute for years and in that capacity has solved real problems for a lot of compatriots. But Armand let her talk herself out, and when she stopped talking, he shook his head; no argument, no apologies. Nothing but the grim shaking of the head on which she had wanted to bestow her knowledge and her skill. An entire year passed during which he made not even one reference to that talk. And when she made plans to travel to Surinam, so that she could at least finish off her business there, he immediately offered to pay the airfare.

She sympathizes with his attitude; her profession was not always a source of satisfaction, especially in the periods when she was overpowered almost daily by the *Winti* to whom she owed her talents.

She would blank out at the most inconvenient moments, and it was up to others to tell her what had happened during these moments of unconsciousness.

She had found this terribly embarrassing. Incredible. Horrible. And she had begged her too-early and too-tragically deceased husband to keep the *yorka*-spirit away from her. But. One night. After she had finished her supper. He appeared in her dream.

He was standing on the bridge by the gangplank in a sparkling white starched suit, smiling warmly at her. But. When she wanted to run to him, she heard heart-rendering cries from the shore. Her deceased husband had not spoken to her. He forced her with his eyes to take care of the people who were calling her. And. In the moment of doubt, the bridge crumbled under her feet—and he disappeared into the river mist with a smile which convinced her of the union that death cannot disconnect. Then she admitted the *Winti*.

Of course, she did not want to burden her children with something for which she could hardly find words: a power which was wrapped around her spine like an electric wire and which connected her to areas which are beyond the reach of our senses. Sometimes she resisted—like a woman can refuse to release her inner warmth. Then she did not give in to the pressure to isolate herself. To the contrary: she called her children and their friends to her and read them fairy tales until her jaws hurt from the strain. That often helped—and, although she felt the atmosphere of the hidden world burning in her nostrils, she stayed where she was: in the trust of the innocent. But there were also days of defenselessness. Moments of powerlessness. Defeats.

The children learned to live with a mother who sometimes changed into another person, and the older the children became the more able they were to see the connection between their mother's livelihood and her changes of identity.

They learned to live with the other who was hidden in their mother—they knew exactly when she would appear; and in addition to their mother, there was a guest to whom they were given, as if handed over to the state. The guest had imposed rules and offered protection. And they were free to withdraw from this but never without a gnawing feeling of guilt.

Had they burst into their mother's bedroom with unwashed feet, hands, and faces because the ice cream cart was on their street?! Or, had they let in friends who were menstruating while their mother was in consultation? And, are you sure there was no pig meat in the Javanese man's *sambal* sandwich? Or, how does the boy who is always wandering through the city know on which corners he may absolutely not hang around?

Above all, how do you hide your mother and that other voice inside her from others your whole life? Therefore, when the children still believed that, behind their hedge, they kept hidden a family secret, their neighborhood friends already knew why all kinds of people knocked on door number seventeen every day. But they were scared to death to talk even to each other about that, because powers such as those of a medicine woman could reach beyond the pills, salves, potions, and injections medical doctors got out of books.

Moreover, the woman at number seventeen had taken care of her neighbors so often that the adults too feared her as intensely as did their children, as they feared the fate in store for them. She was loved—and she was hated, preferably avoided as fate itself because she carried all the painful secrets of others behind her black, shining cheekbones. It had taken years—and in the end she had developed with her calling into a woman of awe.

Dreams would be left with her—longings for which there would not be any satisfaction—thoughts too shameless for words—and pain: incurable and too far gone.

The soul of an adult lies hidden behind a railroad system of memories through which no one travels without perishing.

She knows this because, through her hundreds of consultations, she has suffered more than a thousand human lives. Therefore she wants to stop her work—she's ready for it.

In her bedroom she spreads out the quilted blanket carefully over her bed. She pulls the ends tight. In the closet before her hang all the dresses from the trips she has made to the pantheon of the gods to beseech them for a proper way to end her profession. In the circles of the *bonu-sma* her intention had caused excitement, for who in good health wants to break away from such a powerful medium of Mother Earth as the *apuku*-spirit!

Determinedly, she had prepared the ceremony, avoiding every demonstration of exuberance; every ritual was precisely established.

In robes without ribbons, bows, or curls, she displayed herself for seven days and seven nights, danced, laughed, sang, cried, and screamed.

And the more than one hundred people who accepted her invitation to come to Lebanon Road for the ritual festivity were able to witness how the high gods of Light, Water, and Earth used her tongue to demonstrate their approval of her decision. It was more than the body of a sixty-two-year-old woman who weighed more than eighty kilos could withstand—but according to those present it happened: the most fascinating and unforgettable spectacle of all time.

She opens the closet and sees the clothes: historical costumes for her great-great-great grandchildren's carnival somewhere in the Netherlands—she shudders and grabs the white cloth which she put around her shoulders when the medium was finally ready to make itself known. First had come the spirits of those deceased to whom she had been of service while alive and then—.

She wraps the cloth around her and sits down on her bed. She looks at herself in the mirror on the closet door. She knows that she looks like her patron—the brothers, sisters, and other people who knew the woman have all told her that—but the fact that this patron had to anchor herself in her navel later drove her through waves of grief.

After the exhaustion of the retirement ceremony, she immediately took the next morning's bus to Parimaribo. First she visited the grave of her spouse—but the marble was even more deadly than the memory of his death; after all, what kind of surveyor drowns in a pond which he himself put on the map—. Her parents had been absolutely against the relationship from the very beginning. Families that remained on Lebanon Road have a history that goes back deep into the time of slavery and often even further.

But it was precisely their close bonds of race and kinship with families outside the capital that had initially attracted her to him; it is a sure guarantee of happiness in social circles that keep getting smaller and smaller. She too became a part of that chain of kinship, thanks to him, who, relishing the differences between them, had taught her that they were fated to meet. And it had been their destiny to be happy—for they met each other in church and no scrutiny from parents can stand up to such an alibi. She was sitting in that same Saron church—on the very last bench—and had fallen asleep. Had she dreamed this on that Monday morning on Slangehoutstraat or just now as she fell asleep on her quilted blanket in her second-floor apartment in Amsterdam-South? She did not sleep long, but deep enough to have dug up that memory.

He had not turned up for weeks, and it had begun to gnaw on her. Every morning, as she got off the Number 12 bus, her eyes had looked into the four streets searching for a glimpse of him. But for months now none of the men in smooth-ironed shirts and closely cut frizzy hair had approached her as he had done. Always with the same shy story that he, by coincidence, had to be at C.H.M. and he thought he could surprise her by standing on the square as if at a terminal. The first days she waited and openly looked for him. After that she walked to work a little slower. And not once did he appear in the store. Men, women, children, they came and they went. Some would be greeted by her and led past the boxes and bins of underwear. And for the first time her lips became stiff with the smile that she gave to every customer.

As soon as things would quiet down in the lingerie department, the longing for him overcame her. Then her eyes searched the windows, and she focused all her thoughts through its panels. Maybe his face would appear in the dullish glass if she just kept looking and kept thinking only of him—heavens, she had fallen in love with him during his absence.

She did not leave the underwear department anymore. Even during the lunch hour her fingers kept adjusting and readjusting things, as if the panties, bras, corsets, and slips reflected her own intimacy. Moreover it was far too busy in the cafeteria and elsewhere for her to make the kind of leaps to which her thoughts pushed her.

She does not answer the telephone in order to let the memory feel its way through to its conclusion: on a Friday morning she had asked her supervisor for the afternoon off. And because her diligence had not escaped him, he allowed her to go to Lebanon Road that same afternoon. Her heart throbbing in her throat, she was sitting in the bus heading in the direction of that Surinam district as if she were taking a trip into her very self.

When she made clear which family she wanted to visit, the driver looked at her from top to toe as if her white shirt and her straight dark blue skirt would confirm something. In any case, she was even allowed to sit next to him on the best seat with her back to the other passengers.

Only later did she understand why he had turned off the music and why he took her right to the country house and why everyone in the bus had stared, rubbernecking, out of the bus: there are one, two, three, four, five, six cars by the entry. Four motorbikes lie by the roadside. Bicycles lean against the fence close to the gate. Along the path, yellow flowers grow in the grass. On both sides, the widespread land is too overgrown to be called a meadow—there are cows, horses; chickens walk around.

A dog begins to bark in alarm—she hears a chain hit stone; a child begins to cry, and, finally, she hears voices in the home that rises high above her.

"Who are you!" a man's voice.

"I am looking for Armand."

"Who are you!" another head out of the window.

Then a door opens and he is there—in the clothes in which she had dreamed him morning after morning. He looks older or tired and he barely smiles. He reaches his arm to her and pulls her inside—there are too many people in the front hall and from behind a folding door more come to look at her.

"Who is that?" the same man.

"My girlfriend—she works at Kirpalani's, that is why she is dressed like this."

"Who is her father?"

She gives her name, and for the first time she looks at the person who has addressed her.

"My son has never talked about you," he says with an even voice, and "it is not convenient, we are in family council." Then to his son who rubs the whisker stubble on his chin with his index finger and thumb: "Take that girl back to the bus and excuse us."

After such precision a heavy atmosphere hangs in the room. Although no one makes a remark, she feels that not everyone agrees with this order. Moreover, the son stands stiff as a board, his chin frozen between index finger and thumb. A woman by the folding door to the kitchen asked her if she first wants to drink something. Shy but determined, she nods.

At that moment he puts his arm around her and says: "Do not mind Dad; we are in mourning—my twin sister is possibly dead."

"Over my dead body!" yells his father.

"Take her to the kitchen, Armand," requests the woman who later appears to be his oldest sister. First she begins to tremble terribly and then to cry, to cry—.

She has to wait, to wait—for every day the one who shall succeed her could be at her door. The *apuku* spirit made that very clear: be vigilant, for any hour can be the moment of transfer.

And her patience was sorely tried. Since she had returned from Surinam, more than two months had passed. She lets the verse of the day fall out of her mouth: "Behold, I stand at the door and knock—."

She thinks again about the dinner that her son and his children, her two daughters and their families shared with her in Scheveningen. Because nothing—nothing should be in any way connected to the very ancient customs of ritual dining. However, from experience they all knew that they should appear at her celebration completely bathed, clean, and neatly dressed—and without a heavy heart. And they all showed up; they even took along the youngest ones.

For hours, the waiters and waitresses did not have enough hands and feet to fulfill every wish to perfection—that had been her order and she had paid them very well.

Seven pink candles stood in the candleholders—and in the invocation she noted that pink commemorates the joy of life, gentleness, and friendship; therefore, it stands for charity or for the relationship between an individual as a human being and the earth.

She was not allowed to go any further, for already they had started to exchange meaningful glances when the waiters in uniform appeared with copper trays with wet napkins: "to clean your hands, if you please." Only the incense was missing because the management had rightly remarked that it could take days before the sandalwood, the myrrh, the cinnamon, the orrisroot, and the permeating smell of the ether oil would have left the upholstery of the restaurant. Therefore, instead, a box of small but extremely fine Havana cigars was passed around. And that was what floated around the candelabra by the time they finished the appetizer: the bittersweet aroma of the tobacco plant.

Ah, she allowed her glance to glide once more along the faces of her relatives.

Armand with his golden eyetooth. Mama, let's go live in the Netherlands, for I am so embarrassed about your practice—people use that against me. One half year later they got on board. Via a freighter to the harbor of Rotterdam. He was not even fifteen—her mirror image and even now her refuge.

Magda—and Peter and their two children who were named after Dutch birds; they were twittering comfortably to each other; yet there is little she has to share with her.

Carla—and Jan, the new father of her children; her stomach, filled with another halfbreed, bumped against the table; her face looked even heavier and her eyes finally had a contented look.

Sometimes she felt that there was a break in her family line. As if the daughters wanted to be removed and unreachable because of the ghosts of their heritage. As if they needed their mother more when they themselves became mothers—as if they could no longer listen to the voice which, according to the initiated, could only be that of their natural mother.

They took more and more after their father, who had blamed the disappearance of the children's natural mother many years before on the family's *Winti*-tradition—he is happy, his daughters tell her holding their breath, remarried years ago to an Indian woman from Colombia.

But back then, when, after a year, there was still no trace of their disappeared mother, and when no one had had a sign of life from her, the Republic of Surinam declared her to be deceased. And she and her twin brother decided immediately to raise the girls as their own. She, at that moment, was blessed with the expectation of Armand Kepler senior.

And the folk saying turned out to be right; after seven years, a deceased individual who had had no funeral shows up alive. Just at the moment when she was sitting with her head in her hands, wondering how to raise three children without a father—a new sound rang out in the silence of her raw sorrow.

First she thought that she was slowly going crazy, and she hid it like an undesired pregnancy. But like an irrepressible foetus, the character forced itself on her surroundings.

It was the oldest sister of her deceased husband who cried in horror when she witnessed it: Give her water out of a clean glass; it is my little sister who has walked too far and who is thirsty.

And then the whole family was called together, and they tried everything and anything—with her, on their plantation on

Lebanon Road. That was definitely the cause of the break with her own parents—a conflict she carried for years inside herself as a fishbone in her blood vessels.

Therefore, go ahead, talk about pain—I have that feeling constantly somewhere in my body. It streamed constantly from her eyes; even when she looked down when a client was talking.

The dinner rolled along like the North Sea which she could see through the window—calm, calm.

Only her son appeared to have understood why the dinner party did not take place as expected in Amsterdam, for when she asked him to accompany her on a walk along the beach he shook his head in a curt refusal.

He had even watched them, annoyed when they all sauntered toward the beach—even though she carried his own twin and had a basket on her arm with an offering to the water.

A cake—indeed, she will devote the whole afternoon to baking the *fiado*; a small one for the son, Armand, and a good-sized one for Carla who has just gotten up from childbirth. A little son—completely caramel-colored but with the head of his father and pleasantly plump. In a hurry, cheered up a bit, she smoothes the bed and organizes her closet—but what should she wear? It is the middle of April and the sun breaks through only slightly.

Her eyes flash along her clothes, excitedly. She smiles and says aloud: "As soon as this business is closed, this lady will take wonderful bus trips with the ladies' Bingo club: Brussels, Paris, London, Barcelona." She had picked up and leafed through piles of brochures at travel bureaus. Because what do you think she told her son when he came at her with his "Mama-what-have-you-got-to-do-when-your-work-is-over"!?

She started to laugh, laugh, and even in the mirror she could see that it was genuine.

"I will become carefree when my work is over, young man. Your mother has never been without worries since she was twenty-one." Of course, she had made quite a bit of money with it; but there is a time to cry and a time to laugh—therefore, there will be a carefree period for me now. She nodded at herself in the mirror. She put on a yellow coatlike dress with twenty-four copperplated buttons. And the rest goes in very quickly: makeup, brushing her hair once more and pinning it up, hat on, changing shoes, spring coat, and, with a last glance in the hall mirror, she steps outside onto the small porch.

She takes a deep breath as soon as she smells the fresh air. She carefully descends the fifteen granite steps. She bursts with desire to dance through life—a senior citizen set adrift; she almost laughs, from the heart. She is content with the image of her reflected in the shop windows.

Boldly she tilts her head backward and takes a deep breath; a lukewarm air from the South blows over Amsterdam; migrating birds are fluttering back from the warm continent of her ancestors. Everything is in motion—and she wants to be part of this spring; click-clack and click-clack and click-clack, her heels on the sidewalks set the rhythm.

Of course it is lively on the Ceintuurbaan. The streetcars with Marte R. designs shoot forth from everywhere; bicyclists with open shirts race past each other, and then there are the pedestrians who, together with the automobile drivers, keep the view of the street off balance; like the heart of a top athlete, the neighborhood pumps fresh blood to all its parts—she feels how it even finds an escape through her nipples.

She accepts the compliments of the flower vendor, and she lets a few young mothers get ahead of her in the line at the grocery store.

If she had not had such a feeling for rituals, she would have walked on to the Albert Cuyp market to enjoy all the people there to her heart's content. But her obligation presses, gently but perceptibly—and she slowly walks back to her corner house; shopping bags in her right hand and a fist full of long-stemmed roses given free by the flower vendor. As soon as her business is finished, he will be one of the first she will invite for coffee. She started to laugh uncontrollably as she climbed the stairs: Ai, goodness gracious, the heavy-heavy flower man with his wild hair and she—hahaha.

A woman stands ringing her bell. She recognizes her even though the visitor has her back to her. She coughs hard and the woman shyly turns forty-five degrees; not far enough to look into her face. The woman of the house puts down her groceries and stands close to the other.

"Listen," she whispers sincerely, "my practice is always closed to robbery, drugs, and prostitution—did you forget that, girl?"

But the one addressed does not respond; at last she smiles a little and turns languidly. That alarms the woman; she quickly reconsiders and decides to open the door with the words "no scoundrels, no junkies, no whores." It sounds rough and painful, even to her. Paying attention but seemingly nonchalant, she carries her groceries into the hall, and since the other one keeps her back to her she pulls the door shut behind her. She has not yet reached the kitchen when the bell rings—urgent and continuous. She reaches the door with a few steps and swings it open. "What do you want, Lola?" But the eyes that look up at her do not reveal anything of the Lola she knows—another character stands in front of her. She is chilled to the bone, as if captured by the northeastern wind.

She steps aside—and her visitor walks past her into the house, straight to the square table, where she remains standing.

Hesitantly, she closes the door. She walks to the table, lights the candles: how could such a well-kept spirit place itself into a body in which so many sad things have happened?

The grounding of reality begins with a bowl full of water which she places on the woman's open hand. An egg trembles in the liquid and she murmurs the formulas and sprinkles some water around the woman.

None of this has any effect because Lola keeps staring and smiling at her and does not reveal anything of her deepest self.

The woman goes to her bedroom and returns fifteen minutes later in her role of medicine woman; she has wrapped a batik cloth around her naked body and asks the other woman to follow her to the bathroom.

An earthenware tub covered with a red cloth is set on a sort of footstool.

Without shyness, Lola lets herself be freed from her clothing. Even though half of Amsterdam has waltzed on her body, it looks unspoiled. Her pubic area has been shaven, making her pelvis somewhat childlike.

The woman ties the red cloth around her own hair and the beer smell of the liquid in the tub fills the bathroom. As soon as she pours the prepared bathwater out of a wooden bowl over Lola's face, they both begin to move, slowly but forcefully. First Lola unwraps her batik cover. Then she scoops some water out of the basin with her hand and rubs it on the medicine woman's face.

At the same time she utters sounds understood only by lovers. And the possessed woman finally gives up: all her dignity, her prestige, her resistance.

She rolls together with the person she so often rejected, over the floor of the living room; she crawls with her to the bedroom; she turns back the cover with the evil-spirit-rejecting design— they disappear between the sheets; the bed begins to move.

The woman does not respond to her two o'clock appointment.

She is no one now.

She is al-one.

Lola heals.

From now on.

Translated by Hilda van Neck-Yoder

Olive Senior was born in 1941 and grew up in rural Jamaica and Canada. She has had an outstanding career as a journalist, researcher, writer, editor, and publisher, and was for many years editor of Jamaica Journal. She has won numerous awards for her poetry and short stories, most recently the Commonwealth Writers' Prize in 1987 for her first collection of short stories, Summer Lightning. *She has recently published a new collection,* Arrival of the Snake Woman (1989). *Senior's fiction brilliantly captures the beauty and anguish of common people's lives in Jamaica. She had an unerring sense for the dramatic which surfaces in the often surprising endings of her tales. Senior is presently living in England.*

OLIVE SENIOR

Bright Thursdays

Thursday was the worst day. While she had no expectations of any other day of the week, every Thursday turned out to be either very good or very bad, and she had no way of knowing in advance which one it would be. Sometimes there would be so many bad Thursdays in a row that she wanted to write home to her mother, "Please please take me home for I cannot stand the clouds." But then she would remember her mother saying, "Laura, this is a new life for you. This is opportunity. Now dont let yu mama down. Chile, swallow yu tongue before yu talk lest yu say the wrong thing and dont mek yu eye big for everything yu see. Dont give Miss Christie no cause for complain and most of all, let them know you have broughtuptcy."

Miss Christie was the lady she now lived with, her father's mother. She didn't know her father except for a photograph of him on Miss Christie's bureau where he was almost lost in a forest of photographs of all her children and grandchildren all brown-skinned with straight hair and confident smiles on their faces. When she saw these photograph she understood why Miss Christie couldn't put hers there. Every week as she dusted the bureau, Laura looked at herself in the mirror and tried to smile with the confidence of those in the photographs, but all she saw was a being so strange, so far removed from those in the pictures, that she knew that she could never be like them. To smile so at a camera one had to be born to certain things—a big house with heavy mahogany furniture and many rooms, fixed mealtimes, a mother and father who were married to each other and lived together in the same house, who would chastise and praise, who would send you to school with the proper clothes so you would look like, be like everyone else, fit neatly into the space Life had created for you.

But even though others kept pushing her, and she tried to ease, to work her way into that space too, she sometimes felt that Life had played her tricks, and there was, after all, no space allotted for her. For how else could she explain this discomfort, this pain it caused her in this her father's house to confront even the slightest event. Such as sitting at table and eating a meal.

In her mother's house she simply came in from school or wherever and sat on a stool in a corner of the lean-to kitchen or on the steps while Mama dished up a plate of food which one ate with whatever implement happened to be handy. Mama herself would more often than not stand to eat, sometimes out of the pot, and the boys too would sit wherever their fancy took them. Everything would be black from the soot from the fireside which hung now like grotesque torn ribbons from the roof. After the meal, Laura would wash the plates and pots in an enamel basin outside and sweep out the ashes from the fireside. A meal was something as natural as breathing.

But here in this house of her father's parents a meal was a ritual, something for which you prepared yourself by washing your hands and combing your hair and straightening your dress before approaching the Table. The Table was in the Dining Room and at least twelve could have comfortably sat around it. Now Laura and the grandparents huddled together at one end and in the somber shadows of the room, Laura sometimes imagined that they so unbalanced the table that it would come toppling over onto them. At other times, when she polished the mahogany she placed each of the children of the household at a place around this table, along with their mother and father and their be-whiskered and beribboned grandparents who looked down from oval picture frames. When they were all seated, they fitted in so neatly in their slots that there was now no place left for her. Sometimes she didn't mind.

But now at the real mealtimes, the ghosts were no longer there and she sat with the old people in this empty echoing space. Each time she sat down with dread in her heart, for mealtime was not a time to eat so much as a time for lessons in Table Manners.

First Mirie the cook would tinkle a little silver bell that would summon them to the dining room, and the house would stir with soft footsteps scurrying like mice and the swish of water in the basin. All the inhabitants of the house were washing and combing and straightening themselves in preparation for the Meal. She tried not to be the last one to the table for that was an occasion for chastisement. Then she had to remember to take the stiffly starched white napkin from its silver ring and place it in her lap.

"Now sit up straight, child. Don't slump so," Miss Christie would say as she lifted the covers off tureens. Miss Christie sat at the table uncovering dishes of food, but by the time Laura was served, her throat was already full and she got so confused that she would forget the knife and start to eat with her fork.

"Now dear, please use your knife. And don't cut your meat into little pieces all at once."

At the sulky look which came over Laura's face, Miss Christie would say, "You'll thank me for this one day you know, Laura. If you are going to get anywhere, you must learn how to do things properly. I just can't imagine what your mother has been doing with you all this time. How a child your age can be so ignorant of the most elementary things is beyond me."

The first time Miss Christie had mentioned her mother in this way, Laura had burst into tears and fled from the room. But now, remembering her mother's words, she refused to cry.

Laura's father had never married her mother. The question never came up for, said Myrtle without even a hint of malice in her voice, "Mr. Bertram was a young man of high estate. Very high estate." She was fond of telling this to everyone who came to her house and did not know the story of Laura's father. How Mr. Bertram had come visiting the Wheelers where Myrtle was a young servant. They had had what she liked to call "a romance" but which was hardly even imprinted on Mr. Bertram's mind, and Laura was the result. The fact that Mr. Bertram was a man of "high estate" had in itself elevated Miss Myrtle so far in her own eyes that no one else could understand how she could have managed to bear her sons afterward for two undoubtedly humble fathers.

Laura had come out with dark skin but almost straight hair which Miss Myrtle did her best to improve by rubbing it with coconut oil and brushing it every day, at the same time rubbing cocoa butter into her skin to keep it soft and make it "clear." Miss Myrtle made the child wear a broad straw hat to keep off the sun, assuring her that her skin was "too delicate."

Miss Myrtle had no regrets about her encounter with Mr. Bertram even though his only acknowledgment of the birth was a ten-dollar note sent to her at the time. But then he had been shipped off to the United States by his angry parents and nothing further had been heard from him.

Miss Myrtle was unfortunate in her choice of fathers for her children for none of them gave her any support. She single-handedly raised them in a little house on family land and took in sewing to augment what she got from her cultivation of food for the pot and ginger for the market. She did not worry about the fate of her sons for they were, after all, boys, and well able to fend for themselves when the time came. But her daughter was a constant source of concern to her, for a child with such long curly hair, with such a straight nose, with such soft skin (too bad it was so dark) was surely destined for a life of ease and comfort. For years, Miss Myrtle sustained herself with the fantasy that one day Laura's father would miraculously appear and take her off to live up to the station in life to which she was born. In the meantime she groomed her daughter for the role she felt she would play in life, squeezing things here and there in order to have enough to make her pretty clothes so that she was the best-dressed little girl for miles around. For the time being, it was the only gift of her heritage that she could make her.

Then after so many years passed that it was apparent even to Myrtle that Mr. Bertram had no intention of helping the child, she screwed up her courage, aided and abetted by the entire village it seemed, and wrote to Mr. Bertram's parents. She knew them well, for Mr. Bertram's mother was Mrs. Wheeler's sister and in fact came from a family that had roots in the area.

Dear Miss Kristie

Greetings to you in Jesus Holy Name I trust that this letter will find that you an Mister Dolfy ar enjoin the best of helth. Wel Miss Kristie I write you this letter in fear and trimblin for I am the Little One and you are the Big One but I hope you will not take me too forrard but mr. Bertram little girl now nine year old and bright as a button wel my dear Mam wish you could see her a good little girl and lern her lesson wel she would go far in Life if she could have some Help but I am a Poor Woman! With Nothing! To Help I am in the filds morning til night. I can tel you that in looks she take after her Father but I am no Asking Mr. Bertram for anything I know. He have his Life to live for but if you can fine it in You Power to do Anything for the little girl God Richest Blessing wil come down on You May the Good Lord Bles and Keep you Miss Kristie also Mas Dolfy. And give you a long Life until you find Eternal Rest Safe in the arms of the Savor

Your Humble Servant

Myrtle Johnstone.

The letter caused consternation when it was received by the old people for they had almost forgotten about what the family referred to as "Bertram's Mistake" and they thought that the woman had forgotten about it too. Although Myrtle was only seventeen at the time and their son was twenty-eight, they had never forgiven what Miss Christie called the uppity black gal for seducing their son. "Dying to raise their color all of them," Miss Christie had cried, "dying to raise their color. That's why you can't be too careful with them." Now like a ghost suddenly materializing they could see this old scandal coming back to haunt them.

At first the two old people were angry, then as they talked about the subject for days on end, they soon dismissed their first decision which was to ignore the letter, for the little girl, no matter how common and scheming her mother was, was nevertheless family and something would have to be done about her. Eventually they decided on limited help—enough to salve their consciences but not too much so that Myrtle would get the idea that they were a limitless source of wealth. Miss Christie composed the first of her brief and cool letters to the child's mother.

Dear Myrtle,
    In response to your call for help we are sending a little money for the child, also a parcel which should soon arrive. But please don't think that we can do this all the time as we ourselves are finding it hard to make ends meet. Besides, people who have children should worry about how they are going to support them before they have them.
    Yours truly,
    Mrs. C. Watson

They made, of course, no reference to the child's father who was now married and living in New Jersey.

Myrtle was overjoyed to get the letter and the parcel for they were the tangible indications that the child's family would indeed rescue her from a life of poverty in the mountains. Now she devoted even more care and attention to the little girl, taking pains to remind her of the fineness of her hair, the straightness of her nose, and the high estate of her father. While she allowed the child to continue to help with the chores around the house, she was no longer sent on errands. When all the other children were busy minding goats, fetching water or firewood, all of these chores in her household now fell on Laura's brothers. Myrtle was busy grooming Laura for a golden future.

Because of her mother's strictures, the child soon felt alienated from others. If she played with other children, her mother warned her not to get her clothes too dirty. Not to get too burnt in the sun. Not to talk so broad. Instead of making her filled with pride as her mother intended, these attentions made the child supremely conscious of being different from the children around her, and she soon became withdrawn and lacking in spontaneity.

Myrtle approved of the child's new quietness as a sign of "quality" in her. She sent a flood of letters to Miss Christie, although the answers she got were meager and few. She kept her constantly informed of the child's progress in school, of her ability to read so well, and occasionally made the child write a few sentences in the letter to her grandmother to show off her fine handwriting. Finally, one Christmas, to flesh out the image of the child she had been building up over the years, she took most of the rat-cut coffee money and took the child to the nearest big town to have her photograph taken in a professional studio.

It was a posed, stilted photograph in a style that went out of fashion thirty years before. The child was dressed in a frilly white dress trimmed with ribbons, much too long for her age. She wore long white nylon socks and white T-strap shoes. Her hair was done in perfect drop curls, with a part to the side and two front curls caught up with a large white bow. In the photograph she stood quite straight with her feet together and her right hand stiffly bent to touch an artificial rose in a vase on a rattan table beside her. She did not smile.

Her grandparents who were the recipients of a large framed print on matte paper saw a dark-skinned child with long dark hair, a straight nose, and enormous, very serious eyes. Despite the fancy clothes, everything about her had a countrified air except for the penetrating eyes which had none of the softness and shyness of country children. Miss Christie was a little embarrassed by this gift, and hid the picture in her bureau drawer for it had none of the gloss of the photos of her children and grandchildren which stood on her bureau. But she could not put the picture away entirely; something about the child haunted her and she constantly looked at it to see what in this child was of her flesh and blood. The child had her father's weak mouth, it seemed, though the defiant chin and the bold eyes undoubtedly came from her mother. Maybe it was the serious, steady, unchildlike gaze that caused Miss Christie sometimes to look at the picture for minutes at a time as if it mesmerized her. Then she would get hold of herself again and angrily put the picture back into the drawer.

Despite her better judgment, Miss Christie found herself intensely curious about this child whose mother made her into such a little paragon and whose eyes gazed out at the world so directly.

Soon, she broached the subject obliquely to her husband. One evening at dusk as the two of them sat on the veranda, she said, "Well, just look at the two of us. Look how many children and grandchildren we have, and not a one to keep our company."

"Hm. So life stay. Once your children go to town, country too lonely for them after that."

"I suppose so. But it really would be nice to have a young person about the house again." They dropped the subject then, but she kept bringing it up from time to time.

Finally she said, as if thinking about it for the first time, "But Dolphie, why don't we get Myrtle's little girl here?"

"What! And rake up that old thing again? You must be mad."

"But nobody has to know who she is."

"Then you dont know how ol' nayga fas'. They bound to find out."

"Well, they can't prove anything. She doesn't have our name. She bears her mother's name."

They argued about it on and off for weeks, then finally they decided to invite the child to stay for a week or two.

When Laura came, she was overawed by the big house, the patrician old couple who were always so clean and sweet-smelling as if perpetually laundered each day anew by Mirie the cook. She fell even more silent, speaking only when spoken to, and then in a low voice which could hardly be heard.

Miss Christie was gratified that she was so much lighter than the photograph (indeed, Myrtle had quarrelled with the photographer for just this reason) and although she was exactly like a country mouse, she did fill the house with her presence. Already Miss Christie was busy planning the child's future, getting her into decent clothes, correcting her speech, erasing her country accent, teaching her table manners, getting her to take a complete bath every day—a fact which was so novel to the child who came from a place where everyone bathed in a bath pan once a week since the water had to be carried on their heads one mile uphill from the spring.

In the child Miss Christie saw a lump of clay which held every promise of being molded into something satisfactory. The same energy with which Miss Christie entered into a "good" marriage, successfully raised six children and saw that they made good marriages themselves, that impelled her to organize the Mothers Union and the School Board—that energy was now to be expended on this latest product which relatives in the know referred to as "Bertram's stray shot."

Although her husband fussed and fumed, he too liked the idea of having a child in the house once more though he thought her a funny little thing who hardly made a sound all day, unlike the boisterous family they had reared. And so, as if in a dream, the child found herself permanently transported from her mother's two-room house to this mansion of her father's.

Of course her father was never mentioned and she only knew it was him from the photograph because he had signed it. She gazed often at this photograph, trying to transmute it into a being of flesh and blood from which she had been created, but failed utterly. In fact, she was quite unable to deduce even the smallest facet of his character from the picture. All that she saw was a smiling face that in some indefinable way looked like all the faces in the other photographs. All were bland and sweet. In none of these faces were there lines, or frowns, or blemishes, or marks of ugliness such as a squint eye, or a broken nose, or kinky hair, or big ears, or broken teeth which afflicted all the other people she had known. Faced with such perfection, she ceased to look at herself in the mirror.

She had gone to live there during the summer holidays and Miss Christie took every opportunity to add polish to her protegé whom she introduced everywhere as "my little adopted." As part of the child's education, Miss Christie taught her to polish mahogany furniture and to bake cakes, to polish silver and clean panes of glass, all of which objects had been foreign to the child's former upbringing.

The child liked to remain inside the house which was cool and dark and shaded, for outside, with its huge treeless lawn and beyond, the endless pastures, frightened her.

She had grown up in a part of the mountain cockpits where a gravel road was the only thing that broke the monotony of the humpbacked hills and endless hills everywhere. There were so many hills that for half of the day their house and yard were damp and dark and moss grew on the sides of the clay path. It was only at midday when the sun was directly overhead that they received light. The houses were perched precariously up the hillsides with slippery paths leading to them from the road, and if anyone bothered to climb to the tops of the hills, all they would see was more mountains. Because it was so hilly the area seemed constantly to be in a dark blue haze, broken only by the occasional hibiscus or croton and the streams of brightly colored birds dashing through the foliage. They were hemmed in by the mountains on all sides and Laura liked it, because all her life was spent in space that was enclosed and finite, protecting her from what dangers she did not even know.

And then, from the moment she had journeyed to the railway station some ten miles away and got on to the train and it had begun to travel through the endless canefields, she had begun to feel afraid. For suddenly the skies had opened up so wide all around her; the sun beat down and there was the endless noisy clacking of the train wheels. She felt naked and anxious, as if suddenly exposed, and there was nowhere to hide.

When she got off the train at the other end, there were no canefields there, but the land was still flat and open, for this was all rolling pastureland. Her curiosity about the herds of cattle she saw grazing in the shade of an occasional tree could not diminish the fear she felt at being so exposed.

Her father's parents' house was set on the top of a hill from where they could see for miles in all directions. Whenever she went outside she felt dizzy for the sky was so wide it was like being enclosed within a huge blue bowl. The summer was cloudless. And the hills were so far away they were lost in blue. But then summer came to an end and it was time for her to go to school. The nearest school was three miles away. Her grand-mother, deciding that this was too far for her to walk—though walking greater distances had meant nothing in her former life—had arranged for her to travel to and from school on the bus which went by at the right time each day. This single fact impressed her most as showing the power and might of her grandmother.

She was glad of the bus for she did not want to walk alone to school. Now the clear summer days were ending, the clouds had begun to gather in the sky, fat cumulus clouds that traveled in packs and in this strange and empty country became ugly and menacing. They reminded her of the pictures she used to get in Sunday School showing Jesus coming to earth again, floating down on one of these fat white clouds. And because the Jesus of their church was a man who had come to judge and punish sinners, these pictures only served to remind her that she was a sinner and that God would one day soon appear out of the sky flashing fire and brimstone to judge and condemn her. And until he came, the clouds were there to watch her. For why else did they move, change themselves, assume shapes of creatures awesome and frightful, if not to torment her with her unworthi-ness? Sometimes when she stood on the barbecue and looked back at the house outlined against the sky, the house itself seemed to move and she would feel a wave of dizziness as if the whole earth was moving away off course and leaving her standing there alone in the emptiness.

She would run quickly inside and find Miss Christie or Mirie or somebody. As long as it was another human being to share the world with.

While all day long she would feel a vague longing for her mother and brothers and all the people she had known since childhood, she never felt lonely, for if her mother had given her nothing else, in taking her out of one life without guaranteeing her placement in the next, she had unwittingly raised her for a life of solitude. Here in this big house she wandered from room to room and said nothing all day, for now her lips were sealed from shyness. To her newly sensitized ears, her words came out flat and unmusical and she would look with guilt at the photographs and silently beg pardon for being there.

There were no other children around the house and she was now so physically removed from others that she had no chance to meet anyone. Sometimes she would walk down the driveway to the tall black gate hoping that some child would pass along and talk so that they could be friends, but whenever anyone happened by, her shyness would cause her to hide behind the stone pillar so they would not see her. And although her grandmother said nothing on the subject, she instinctively knew after a while that she would never in this place find anyone good enough to bring into Miss Christie's house.

Although she liked the feeling of importance it gave her to get on and off the bus at the school gate—the only child to do so—most times she watched with envy the other children walking home from school, playing, yelling, and rolling in the road. They wore no shoes and she envied them this freedom, for her feet, once free like theirs except for Sundays, were now encased in socks and patent leather shoes handed down from one or the other of the rightful grandchildren who lived in Kingston or New York.

Most days the bus was on time. Every morning she would wait by the tall black gate for the bus to arrive. The bus would arrive on time every day. Except Thursday. Sometimes on Thursdays the bus wouldn't arrive until late evening. She would nevertheless every Thursday go to the gates and wait, knowing in her heart that the bus would not come. Miss Christie would sometimes walk out and stand by the gate and look the road up and down.

Sometimes Mass Dolphie passing on his way from one pasture to the next would rein in his horse and would also stand by the gate and look up the road. All three would stand silently. The road swayed white in an empty world. The silence hummed like telegraph wires. Her life hung in the air waiting on a word from Miss Christie. Her chest began to swell like a balloon getting bigger and bigger. "The bus isn't coming. You'll have to walk," Miss Christie pronounced with finality.

"Oh Miss Christie, just a few minutes more," she begged. It was the only thing she begged for. But she knew that the bus wouldn't come, and now, at this terribly late hour, she would have to walk alone the three miles to school in a world that was empty of people. She would walk very fast, the dust of the marl road swirling round her ankles, along this lonely road that curved past the graveyard. Above, following every step of the way, the fat clouds sat smirking and smug in the pale blue sky. She hated them for all they knew about her. Her clumsiness, her awkwardness, the fact that she did not belong in this light and splendid place. They sat there in judgment on her every Thursday. Thursday, the day before market day. The day of her Armageddon.

Thursdays the old bus would sit on the road miles above, packed with higglers and their crocus bags, bankras and chickens. The bus would start right enough: somewhere on the road above the bus would start in the dawn hours, full and happy. And then, a few miles after, the bus would gently shudder and like a torn metal bird would ease to a halt with a cough and a sigh and settle down on the road, too tired and worn out to move. It would remain there until evening, the market women sitting in the shade and fanning the flies away with the men importantly gathered around the machine, arguing and cursing until evening when the earth was cool again and the driver would go slowly, everything patched up till next Thursday when the higglers descended with their crocus bags and their bankras, their laughter and their girth and their quarrelling and their ferocious energy which would prove too much for the old bus. Then with a sigh it would again lie still on the road above her. Every Thursday.

Sometimes, though, if she managed to dawdle long enough Miss Christie would say, "Heavens, it's 10 o'clock. You can't go to school again."

"O Miss Christie," she would cry silently, "thank you, thank you."

Sometimes when she didn't go to school Mass Dolphie would let her dig around in his Irish potato patch collecting the tiny potatoes for herself.

Digging potatoes was safe. She could not see the sky. And she never knew when a really big potato would turn up among all the tiny ones.

"Like catching fish, eh?" Mass Dolphie said and she agreed though she didn't know how that was, having never seen the sea. But she would laugh too.

II

One day they got a letter from the child's father. He was coming home with his wife on a visit. It wasn't long after their initial joy at hearing the news that the grandparents realized that difficulties were bound to arise with the child. For one thing, they hadn't told their son about her, being a little ashamed that they had not consulted him at all before coming to the decision to take her. Besides, it was a little awkward to write to him about such matters at his home, since from all they had heard of American women they believed that there was a strong possibility that his wife would open his letters.

Their immediate decision was to send the child home, but that too presented certain problems since it was still during the school term and they couldn't quite make up their minds what they would tell her mother to explain a change of heart. They certainly couldn't tell her the truth for even to them the truth seemed absurd: that they wanted to return the little girl because her father was coming. For once, Miss Christie was at a loss. It was Mr. Dolphie who took a firm line. "Write and ask him what to do," he instructed his wife, "after all, it's his child. If he doesn't want her here when he comes then he can tell us what we should do with her."

They were surprised but not overly so when their son wrote that they should do nothing about the child as he would be greatly amused to see her.

Mr. Dolphie didn't see any cause for amusement in the situation and thought that it was just like his youngest son to take a serious thing and make a joke of it and all in all act in a reckless and irresponsible manner. He had certainly hoped that Bertram had finally settled down to the seriousness of life.

Long before they told the child the news of her father's coming, she knew, for without deliberately listening to their conversations, she seemed to absorb and intuitively understand everything that happened in the house.

Since hearing the news there had been a joy in her heart, for her mother had told her so often that one day this mysterious father of hers would come and claim her as his own that she had grown to believe it. She knew that he would come and rescue her from fears as tenuous as clouds and provide her with nothing but bright Thursdays.

But when she searched out the photograph from the ones on the bureau, his face held that unreadable, bland smile and his eyes gave off nothing that would show her just how he intended to present his love for her.

One day Miss Christie said to her, "Laura, our son is coming on a visit. Mr. Bertram." She said it as if the child and the man bore no relationship to each other. "He is coming with his wife. We haven't seen him for so many years."

Yes. Since I was born, Laura thought.

"Now Laura, I expect you to be on your best behavior when they are here."

"Yes, mam."

Laura showed no emotion at all as Miss Christie continued to chat on the subject. How does one behave with a father? Laura thought. She had no experience of this. There were so few fathers among all the people she knew.

Miss Christie turned the house upside down in a frenzy of preparation for her son's visit. Without being told so, Laura understood that such preparation was not so much for the son as for his white wife. She was quite right, for as Miss Christie told Mirie, "These foreign women are really too fresh, you know. Half of them don't really come from anywhere but they believe that everybody from Jamaica is a monkey and lives in trees. I am really glad my son is bringing her here so that she can see how we live." Laura silently assented to that, for who in the wide world could keep up a life that was as spotless and well-ordered as Miss Christie's?

Laura longed to talk to somebody about her father. To find out what he was really like. But she did not want to ask Miss Christie. She thought of writing secretly to her mother and telling her that Mr. Bertram was coming, asking what he was really like, but she was too timid to do anything behind Miss Christie's back for Miss Christie was so all-knowing she was bound to find out. Sometimes she wanted to ask Mirie the cook who had been working with the family for nearly forty years. But although she got into the habit of dropping into the roomy kitchen and sitting at the table there for hours, she never got up the nerve to address Mirie, and Mirie, a silent and morose woman, never addressed her at all. She believed, though, that Mirie liked her, for frequently, without saying a word, she would give her some tidbit from the pot, or a sample of the cookies, or bread and guava jelly, though she knew that Miss Christie did not approve of eating between meals. But apart from grunting every now and then as she went about her tasks, Mirie said nothing at all on the subject of Mr. Bertram or any other being. Laura wished that Mirie would talk to her, for she found the kitchen the most comforting part of the house.

Her father and his wife arrived one day when she was at

school. When she got home, she was too shy to go in, and was hanging around trying to hide behind a post when Miss Christie spotted her.

"Oh Laura, come and meet my son," said Miss Christie and swept her into the living room. "Mina," she said to a yellow-haired woman sitting there, "this is Laura, the little adopted I was telling you about." Laura first vaguely made out the woman, then Mass Dolphie, then a strange man in the shadows, but she was too shy to give him more than a covert glance. He did not address her but gave a smile which barely moved his lips. In days to come she would get accustomed to that smile, which was not as bland as in the photograph. To his daughter, he paid no more attention. It was his wife who fussed over the little girl, asking questions and exclaiming over her curls. Laura could hardly understand anything the woman said, but was impressed at how trim and neat she was, at the endless fascination of her clothes, her jewelry, her laughter, her accent, her perfume, her assurance. Looking at her long polished nails, Laura had a picture of her mother's hands, the nails cracked and broken like a man's from her work in the fields; of her mother's dark face, her coarse shrill voice. And she was bitterly ashamed. Knowing the mother she had come from, it was no wonder, she thought, that her father could not acknowledge her.

She was extremely uneasy with the guests in the house. Their presence strained to the fullest the new social graces that Miss Christie had inculcated in her. Now she had a two-fold anxiety: not to let her mother down to Miss Christie, and not to let Miss Christie down in front of this white woman from the United States of America.

For all the woman's attentions, it was the man that she wanted to attend her, acknowledge her, love her. But he never did. She contrived at all times to be near him, to sit in his line of vision, to "accidentally" appear on the path when he went walking through the pastures. The man did not see her. He loved to talk, his voice going on and on in a low rumble like the waves of the sea she had never seen, the ash on his cigarette getting longer till it fell on his clothes or Miss Christie's highly polished floor. But he never talked to her. This caused her even greater anxiety than Miss Christie's efforts at "polishing" her, for while she felt that Miss Christie was trying, however painful it was, to build her up, she could not help feeling that her father's indifference did nothing so much as to reduce her, nullify her. Laura would have wondered if he knew who she was if she hadn't known that Miss Christie had written to him on the subject. She decided then that all his indifference was merely part of a play, that he wanted to surprise her when he did claim her, and was working up to one magical moment of recognition that would thereafter illuminate both their lives forever and ever. In the daytime that is how she consoled herself but at nights she cried in the little room where she slept alone in the fearful shadow of the breadfruit tree against the window pane.

Then Thursday came round again and in this anxiety she even forgot about her father. As usual the bus was late and Laura hung around the gate hoping that Miss Christie would forget she was there until it was too late to walk to school. The road curved white and lonely in the empty morning, silent save for the humming of bees and the beating of her own heart. Then Miss Christie and Mina appeared on the veranda and obviously saw her. Talking together, they started to walk slowly toward the gate where she stood, trapped by several impulses. Laura's heart beat faster then almost stopped as her father appeared from the orange grove and approached the two women. Now the three of them were walking toward her. They were now near enough for Laura to hear what they were saying but her eyes were only on her father.

"Oh dear, that old bus. Laura is going to be late again," Miss Christie said.

"Oh, for chrissake. Why don't you stop fussing so much about the bloody little bastard," her son shouted.

Laura heard no more for after one long moment when her heart somersaulted once there was no time for hearing anything else for her feet of their own volition had set off at a run down the road and by the time she got to the school gates she had made herself an orphan and there were no more clouds.

Ana Lydia Vega was born in Puerto Rico in 1946. She has published three collections of short stories: Vírgenes y mártires, *written with Carmen Lugo-Filippi;* Encancaranublado y otros cuentos de naufragio, *which won the Casa de las Américas Award, and* Pasión de historia y otras historias de pasión. *Vega's fiction is characterized by its innovative and liberating use of language, by its preoccupation with the struggle for women's rights, and its denunciation of exploitation and oppression.*

ANA LYDIA VEGA

ADJ, Inc.

Hate oppression; fear the oppressed.
V. S. Naipaul

I

On the second of December, 1990, Her Excellency the Magistrate blew a fuse. The rage she had been trying so hard to contain finally exploded. Pressing down hard on the intercom button, she had her secretary cancel all appointments and come in right away to take a letter. She then dictated the following urgent missive:

Honorable Supreme Benefactress:

Your letter of 27th November has more than chagrined us, it has unsettled us. But it gives me great pleasure to remind you that in seven years of uninterrupted operation under my leadership, the Agency has established an enviable record: 5,999 cases satisfactorily resolved. Our carefully monitored dossiers and the effusive letters of appreciation we receive almost daily from our clients attest to the fact that we aim to please and succeed admirably in doing so.

Statistics don't lie: 3,995 husbands rehabilitated and 1,994 corrected or neutralized. The Censor's Board was forced to recommend Final Solution in only ten cases, a tiny percentage considering the overwhelming success of our rehabilitation drive.

This brings me to the difficult subject of this letter, dear Benefactress, the purpose of which is to rid you of any doubts regarding the competence of either ADJ, Inc., or myself, its humble director. Case #6000 has monopolized our professional activity for the last four months. Due to its complexity and unique character, we are now undergoing a technical recycling of our operative personnel. In light of the surfacing of this case, which may well be the harbinger of a new social reality, we have considered setting up an Unresolved Questions Bureau to deal with this and similar cases.

I trust this initiative will go some way toward restoring your confidence and that of the other members of the Social Benefactresses' Club so that we may once again enjoy a climate of mutual trust. This will allow your members to continue to provide us with generous and anonymous financial support as they have done in the past during our brief but efficient existence.

As per your request, we enclose photocopies of documents related to Case #6000. We sincerely appreciate the interest you have shown in the resolution of this most complex of cases, and we ask that you call on us for any additional information you might need in your deliberations.

Awaiting your wise decree, and on behalf of our entire team, I send you my best sisterly regards.

Cordially,
Bárbara Z.
Magistrate
ADJ, Inc.

APPENDIX A: Case #6000
Client's Sworn Affidavit

I, Porcia M., duly sworn notary and complaint recorder of ADJ, Inc., hereinafter referred to as the Agency, declare that on September 15, 1990, there appeared before me a married woman, a housewife and resident of San Juan, Puerto Rico, whom, in the interest of privacy, we shall hereafter refer to as the Client. Client testified to us under oath that:

Whereas she has no cause for complaint regarding her husband, whose behavior to date has been exemplary; and

Whereas she thinks the vast majority of the nation's wives would envy her exceptional marital position since she is the unhappy owner of what she insists on calling the Ideal Husband; and

Whereas said Ideal Husband, hereafter referred to as the Accused, shares housework, is a good provider, is considerate, responsible, sweet, courteous, affectionate, serious, and faithful, as well as an efficient executor of all physical husbandly duties, lacking any defect other than his absolute perfection in every respect; and

Whereas the Accused's said perfection is an assault on the Client's self-image as it thereby calls attention implacably to her own imperfection; and

Whereas in the interest of her mental well-being the Client feels an urgent need to file for divorce; said Client, lacking even the faintest cause to justify such action, turns to the Agency in the hope that it will provide requisite pretext so that official rupture of the matrimonial bond may be initiated without further delay and with the celerity merited by the circumstances.

Sworn before me on this 15th day of September, year of our Lord, 1990.

Porcia M.
Principal Notary
Complaint Registry
ADJ, Inc.

APPENDIX B: Case #6000
Assessment and Training Division Report
Re: Operation Assault

A preliminary screening revealed that the Client had behaved in exemplary fashion during her ten years of marriage. Our conclusion was obvious: systematic subversion of this model behavior was necessary if the couple's stability was to be undermined. Client therefore attended our Exasperation Techniques Workshops I and II. Our Division offers these workshops free of charge as a service to the community. Client passed with a grade of "A+" and subsequently launched into a four-week "Operation Assault" program custom-designed for her by our expert programmers.

There were four phases to the operation, each methodically designed to bring about a crisis in the domestic system. Outlined below are the Client's evaluative statements on each phase:

Domestic Sabotage

I took the opportunity afforded by my husband's business trip to cease and desist from all household cleaning. I let dirty dishes pile up in the sink. The bathtub had more than twelve rings in it. Bedsheets were rank with sweat and Vicks Vaporub. I piled dirty clothes everywhere. I disconnected the fridge, so that meat would thaw and the freezer would fill with maggots. I spread leftovers over the kitchen counters. The oven became a luxury condo for cruising roaches. . . .

Physiological Terrorism

Just as I expected, my husband returned and, before I could bat an eyelash, he had donned his plaid bermudas and pulled on a pair of rubber gloves. He put everything in order in a flash. But since forewarned is forearmed, I had already gotten into bed faking dizzy spells and other symptoms, complaining about phony aches and pains and refusing to see a doctor. The poor slob thought I was pregnant. The joy on his face was almost more than I could stomach. It gave me a special delight to show him my stained underwear the following week.

What followed constituted an enormous sacrifice on my part, meticulous as I am about personal hygiene. I stopped bathing, despite the unbearable September heat. I gave up brushing my teeth even after eating mangoes. I let my legs, thighs, and underarms grow Amazonic. I threw into the garbage all brushes and combs so as to not succumb to the temptation of taming the tangled and greasy mess I had for hair. Since my skin and scalp are naturally dry, it wasn't long before I was scaly as an iguana. I had never been so wonderfully frightful; it turned my own stomach; I don't know how he was able to put up with it.

Psychological Offensive

My husband's understanding and tenderness almost drove me insane during this phase. The phony tics which had been recommended came naturally. My eyes began to twitch, my nose jerked, and my mouth contracted into spasms. What's worse, for that long month of Operation Assault I couldn't even count on the Agency's moral support, as we had decided to cut off all communication to avoid any suspicion on his part.

By this time I found it relatively effortless to yell obscenities at him and subject him to all sorts of verbal abuse whenever he spoke a kind word to me. Whenever he tried to talk on any subject, I would yawn obviously and act annoyed. I would refuse to go out with him anywhere. And if he asked me why, I would let loose with all the verbal violence I could muster. Insults and curses were the order of the day. . . .

Sexual Strike

I've never much enjoyed the pleasures of the flesh, anyway.

My main erogenous zone is definitely my brain. That's why the final phase was not as much of an effort as the others. I simply denied him any intimate contact, turning away from him as soon as my head hit the pillow. This strategy, which would have been misinterpreted and exploited by any other Puerto Rican husband, was actually my safest approach: his democratic principles kept him from taking rearguard action without my consent.

No king-sized bed had ever seemed so small to me before. In my overwrought state the sound of his regular breathing, his most discreet movement, his very heartbeat seemed like deafening drumming that wouldn't let me sleep a wink. After a month of this, he was looking younger and more handsome than ever. I, on the other hand, was on the verge of anorexia nervosa.

The Division's Recommendation

Urgent transfer of Case #6000 to Dirty Tricks Division.
  Medea H.
  Head Trainer II
  Assessment and Training Division

APPENDIX C: Case #6000
Dirty Tricks Division
Re: Operation No Holds Barred

Transcription of tape recorded by Olga the Vamp, *Agente Provocateur*

MAGISTRATE'S NOTE: The agency claims no solidarity *with*, and accepts no responsibility *for* the linguistic unruliness and the concomitant loose style that characterizes the jargon of the agents of this division.

I was having me a delicious and well-earned vacation in Boquerón after having had to screw about ten Accuseds in a row, each one a bigger mother than the one before him, when Dirty Tricks sent for me. Since I always put business before pleasure if

I can't manage to combine the two, I gathered my duds and in a blink found myself getting a briefing from the girls in the Assessment and Training office. The Boss Lady gave me twenty-four hours to pull a workplan together. That didn't make me lose no sleep since I can check out any dude and tell you what makes him tick in two hours flat. After reading the statements and laying in some good brain time on it like I do, I checked out the photographs of the Accused in question. Especially the full-length shot. No two ways about it. No problem dealing with this one: nice graying sideburns and temples, cute face, firm body for someone his age. But definitely *not* my type.

My first thought was: "piece of cake." These tall, light-skinned types, kind of cute, you know, Clark Kent glasses, the whole bit—they're usually a cinch. Nine out of ten, it's a case of they've been stirring it up since they were fourteen and by the time they've been married a few years, they can't wait to let it all hang out. That's where I come in. The only thing that didn't fit in with this dude's image were the three large onyx rings on the three fingers of his right hand. I say three because the other two were missing. Vietnam vet, I figured. But since that detail wasn't in the records I'd been given, I filed it away for future reference.

One of the chicks in Corporal Sanctions followed him for me for a few days, so as to catch his moves, you know, so I wouldn't get screwed in the process. The guy was a case. He went from home to work, from work, home; no stops on the way. No bar, no pool hall, no health club, no liquor store, no chicks, no chums, no nothing. Straight. According to the file, he only traveled once a year and that was on bona fide business. Maybe he fooled around while he was in New York, but as far as the island goes, nothing. No two ways about it, if we were to catch him in the act it would have to be staged right here and that's that. I figured the best place for it was his office.

One of our informers who worked in the Office of Economic Development gave me the break I needed. As head of the unit, she figured out how to get me into his office by firing their receptionist and putting me in her place. I blew quite a wad on fine threads and makeup, and Assessment made me take a crash course in office protocol and a mini-finishing school-type program. But by November 1st there was yours truly at her post behind the reception desk with a low-cut skin-tight dress slit up almost to my belly button. Then I grabbed me one of those Bette Davis cigarette holders and was off and running. They don't call me Olga the Vamp for nothing.

About a week after I started, I swear on my mother each and every one of the dudes working there was after me to go out—even the janitor. But mostly they were after me to go *in*, you know. Everyone but the one I was after, the damned Accused. And it wasn't that he hadn't noticed me; it was impossible not to notice me. Besides, he had to go past my desk every morning after punching in. I would about split a lip smiling at him, batting my false lashes, and leaning forward so he could practically see my navel. Then I'd say "Good morning" to him in a voice that would make even a battalion of eunuchs get a hard-on. No dice. The only thing left for me to do was to hoist my ass on the desk to exhibit the rest of the merchandise made in Puerto Rico. Modesty aside, nature has been good to me, as those who know know. At work they all know there's nobody who can beat me at getting, processing, and dispensing with the male element. But the son of a bitch was something else. All I could get out of him were polite hellos and toothpaste commercial smiles.

Since I don't have a stupid bone in my body, I wouldn't miss a chance to sashay by his office, ass swinging and tits erect, during coffee breaks and on my way to the ladies' room. I tell you, I would swing that thing. None of the other guys could get any work done watching me take my swinging strolls. A broken pencil point, a few photocopies to be done, any little thing was an excuse to end up by his desk. Sometimes I'd wait as long as an hour just to ride down the crowded elevator with him, then I'd seize the time to establish some breast-to-back physical rapport. But none of it made a dent.

Then to top it all off, his secretary started giving me a hard time. She was one of those ambulatory antiques who'd noticed the moves I'd put on her boss and looked at me as if she had just bit into a sour mango every time she'd intercept my vibes. Every morning she would greet me with the scowl that launched a thousand shipwrecks, and one fine day she subjected me to an atomic barrage in the copying room: her boss was a decent family man and I'd better lay off, this, that and the other, including a few uncalled-for remarks about the morals of your truly. I blew my stack and told her in no uncertain terms that what she really needed was a good macho to check her oil, and I knew just the guy who could do it for her. All hell broke loose. She turned purple, stammered, her jaw started quivering, and she threatened to slap me silly, to which I replied with "You and what fucking army?" which calmed her down some since she was a midget if I ever saw one. Good thing she didn't try anything because, though the Agency's policy is never to hit broads no matter how bitchy they get, that particular historical monument held all the numbers for the solid whack in the head I was raffling. . . .

They'd given me a deadline at the Agency and this mess with his secretary was slowing me down, so I had to take the bull by the horns and make my move. I went straight to the Accused and, in my huskiest voice, told him I needed to see him urgently when he was through with work. I licked my lips in slow motion so there would be no mistake about my meaning. He said, no problem, to wait for him at five, that he'd be there as soon as he finished "verifying some overdue accounts . . ."

I was still pacing around at quarter past six, waiting for that half-wit to finish putting x's and circles in his godforsaken columns. I was surprised at my own patience. But the best part was, the hag kept hanging around trying to see what I was up to in the interest of protecting her beloved boss's good name. Finally he says to her, "That's fine, Ms. Thelma, you can go home now. Good night," and she had no choice but to take off with steam blowing out her ears. I gave her my best smirk and a look that said, "Chalk one up for the Vamp."

To make a long story short, I exhausted all my tricks and hints, all my winks and leg crossings, and you know that when it comes to that, I'm the best there is. . . . Zilch. I probably could have taken a little longer with it, but when he asked me in that polite tone of his "what it was I wanted to ask him," I lost it. I pounced on him and started messing with his fly, panting into his ear, to see if at the moment of truth, he'd respond, if only to show he'd been put together right at the factory, shit. But before I could get more deeply into things he pushed me away, shifted into reverse, and took off carrying that silly attaché case of his, and with such a shit-eating grin on his face that I wanted to rip off his glasses, grind them into a fine dust with my heels, and paint his graying moustache red. And I would have done it, too, if it hadn't been that I was still figuring I could get him to play ball.

Next day I was fired. That son of a bitch reported me to the personnel office for "sexual harassment." Never in all my years as *Agente Provocateur* Level III have I ever come across a specimen like this one. There's just no way to lay your hands on him!

As far as the Client is concerned, in my book she's either a moron or one of those types that gets off on being punished. Why don't they send this hot potato over to Corporal Sanctions? Let Chiqui the Fist handle him. She likes nothing better than to give a well-earned smack in the head to any jerk who deserves it.

APPENDIX D: Case #6000
Sexual Rehabilitation Division
Re: Operation Motel

At her age and considering the social costs involved in such an action, the idea of going to a motel with a strange man was not exactly to the Client's liking. But the impasse which had been reached, combined with her desperation, made her accept the plan. With the little that remained in the budget for this case we contracted the services of a well-known gigolo who was very popular in the resort areas. We hoped this would be the first and last time we would be forced to resort to the services of a member of the male gender in solving a case. We gave him money for clothes and rented him a car. We reserved a room in a motel on the Caguas Expressway, a motel famous as a place for illicit trysts. Assessment decided on a place called "Swing Butt Low," their reasoning being that the lower the class of the establishment chosen, the bigger the insult to marital honor.

On the 20th of November at three o'clock sharp, the contracted gigolo, one Sly Stick by name, drove up to the Client's house with the radio blaring. He proceeded to honk boisterously and raised the volume of his radio as instructed, so the neighbors would have no choice but to peep through the blinds of their respective windows. The Client made Sly wait a few moments in order to create some suspense. When she finally came out she was wearing a skin-tight, most revealing crepe dress and mounted on stilt-like spike heels. She walked over to the door Sly was holding open and the two of them French-kissed for a full sixty seconds.

They then screeched out of the neighborhood and made their way to the aforementioned motel. While participating in joint action at the motel, they were guarded by Chiqui the Fist in case any violence ensued.

The Agency had sent several anonymous notes to the Accused before the date of the meeting. On the day itself, Chiqui the Fist made the necessary phone call from a pay phone. She disguised her voice with her chewing gum as she does on these occasions. She very politely asked to speak to the Accused. She covered herself by faking a heavy Cuban accent and using an alias. When he got on the line, she breathed hoarsely into the phone (verbatim quote): "Listen, jerk, your wife's getting it on with some pimp in Caguas. She's screaming so loud you can hear her three miles down the road."

Chiqui asserts that just when she was about to give him the name and address of the motel, she heard a sudden click. This report was subsequently confirmed. Not only didn't the expected action take place as a result of the call, but the Client reports that, upon her return home, looking as disheveled, disarrayed, and distraught as if she'd just spent the night performing sadomasochistic rituals with a band of banshees, she found the table set with their best silver candelabra and their finest china and stemware. He didn't even ask her where she'd been all afternoon as he was too busy with the supergourmet meal he was preparing for their tenth wedding anniversary.

We have been forced to come to the conclusion that results have been inversely proportional to the effort expended on this case by our division. The infallibility of our operations has been checkmated. I fear that Case #6000 has set an inauspicious precedent in the glorious history of ADJ, Inc.

Circe F.
Rehab Counselor IV
Sexual Rehab Division
ADJ, Inc.

II

The Honorable Supreme Benefactress shuffled through the documents one last time before putting them into a manila envelope marked in red with the number 6000. A thoughtful stroking of the salt and pepper mustache. A quick tap on the glasses to set them straight on the bridge of the nose. Plastic gloves slipped elegantly, expertly on the hands after depositing the three black rings on top of the desk.

The sheet of paper with its official letterhead carefully centered on the typewriter, he smiled with vague tenderness. Then his eight virtuoso fingers rested delicately on the keyboard to write, very carefully, on the very center of the sheet:

BURN FILE.
SILENCE CLIENT.
ASSIGN #6000 TO NEXT CASE.

Translated by Diana Vélez

Bea Vianen was born in Parimaribo, Surinam, in 1935. She began her career as a writer with the publication of a collection of poems, Cautal, *in 1965, and has since published several volumes of poetry and five novels, among them* Sarnami, hai *(Surinam, I am),* Strafhok *(Punishment coop), and* Ik eet, ik eet, tot ik niet meer kan *(I eat, I eat, until I am full). Vianen's works center on vulnerable individuals who resist social injustice and individual cruelty. Her later work is deeply pessimistic, centering on a multiracial nightmare where integrity can only be preserved by escaping into mental and physical illness or by creating a fictional world in one's imagination.*

BEA VIANEN

Of Nuns and Punishments

A dream woke me up. I dreamed that I was in boarding school and was walking in a line. Next to Norine. A rosary in my hand. I heard the voice of the Mother Superior. She was mumbling. Ahead of me, the girls jostled each other, mocking the sister's prayer. I was eight. My mother was in the hospital. She would be there for years. Hand in hand with my father, I climbed the broad, high steps of the convent on Gravenstraat. The sun was going down. I think it was four o'clock. I was crying. The silence in the lobby of the convent overwhelmed me. I felt imprisoned, far from the games I so enjoyed: catching earthworms with long blades of grass, made wet with our saliva to attract the *soekroeboes*, as we called the little worms. I felt far from the *hangalampoe* hedges, whose leaves I used to pierce with the hard thorns of the baby grape. And then my *tadja* made of sand, decorated with the yellow flowers I used to pick along the gutter in front of our house. The buzzing honeybees, caught with a piece of paper.

Well, I was eight when I was introduced to long prayer services, punishments, corridors, lobbies, dining rooms, laundry rooms, coops, halls, confessionals.

The boarding school of the Order of the Franciscans was a microcosm centered on the power of Christian colonialism. A small world where all races of our society suffered the same punishments, confessed the same sins, and spoke the same language. Dutch. The medium of communication. The language of the civilized. Spoken by Chinese girls from the Nickerie district and from Morowijne. Spoken by Indian girls, the brazen daughters of the Caribs and the Arawaks from Donderskamp and Corneliskondre at the lower course of the Coppenameriver. Spoken by so many others whom I remember so very well. Especially the rebels, just as brazen as the Indian girls whom I deeply admired: Stella, Wilma, Joosje, with their surname of "Indian." I got along well with them, even though they were much older. Yet I never dared ask if it was true that three-fingered Indians wandered about at night in the darkness of the palm garden.

The boarding school was a part of the convent, connected to the chapel by a path covered by a corrugated zinc roof shored up on both sides by white painted wooden poles. The house was also painted white, with green windows and doors that looked out on the bleaching field: lawns where the white laundry was put out to bleach. The lawns were separated from each other by paths made of crushed shells. Short orange trees dropped their leaves on the soft grass. Once a year, when their fruits were ripe, they gave the impression of orange bouquets. Orange bouquets for orphans, half-orphans, girls whose parents had taken them to the city to attend high school or to learn a trade. Orange bouquets for the punishments in the darkness of the bleaching field, the darkness of the coops. The darkness of the attic. In the attic the laundry would be hung to dry: wide dresses with pleated skirts that reached far below the knee. Pants with buttons on the back of the yoke and long legs, connected to the bodice by buttons or by cords. Even during the day the attic was dark and terribly quiet. Peeping bats behind the rafters. In a corner a coffin. Covered by a black cloth with white skulls sewn onto it. The sister, dragging you by the hair upstairs, would say "a devil will come out of each corner" and would leave you there with your bedding. The best you could do was to wrap the sheet around you so that only your nose stuck out. He will come out of every corner. Our clothes hanging outside in the convent gardens looked like scarecrows. Like ghosts.

Our ages ranged from three to twenty-five. The dormitory was divided into three sections. One for the little ones. One for the in-betweens, and one for the big girls. Our dormitory, that of the in-betweens, was notorious for its chamber-pot closet. A low space under the stairs that led to the attic. It smelled of the creosote and Lysol used to wash the little one's chamber pots. There were also other closets, coops, in which they would lock us up to ponder our sins. The Clemens closet in the lobby with the broad staircase to our dormitories. Next to the stairway stood the life-size statue of holy Joseph on a pedestal. The statue was as white as a sheet, hollow on the inside, and had a large hole in its head. One day, when I returned from school, I saw the statue of Saint Joseph outside on the bleaching field to be cleaned. The orange and plantain peelings thrown into the hole in his head had drawn the Mother Superior's attention. To the right of the lobby with the marble statue of the holy Joseph were the dining halls, then the brick part with the lavatories and the bathrooms. One of the bathrooms at the end of the brick hall was called the broom closet. We could be locked up there too.

You could also relax if you were lucky. All around the convent were beautiful gardens with the sweet smell of sunflowers, Saint Joseph lilies, and roses. You could stare at them and dream of bees, butterflies, or dragonflies. You could also romp about. The schools connected to the convent had enough playgrounds and recreation areas for us to enjoy ourselves. Our intimate play-ground was next to the lavatories and the bathrooms. We would get there by going down a wooden staircase with black oily banisters. One part of it was bricked in, covered with a corrugated roof and closed off on one side by a wall. At shoulder height were cubicles for our notebooks and tin boxes filled with fluff, dolls, and other toys. Below the cubicles a long wooden bench with narrow dowels. Across from this bench were tables with heavy, functional school benches. We would sit there reading or chattering with each other when it was raining. We would sit there, deadly quiet, waiting our turn for the daily bath at three o'clock in the afternoon. I can still see myself: the soapbox, toothpaste, and toothbrush wrapped inside my towel and on my lap the pants that were far too long. Under my feet I feel the sand of the floorless section next to the tables and desks. I see the gigantic mango tree with its branches stretched above my head and the corrugated roof. During the hottest part of the day there was a large shadow under that tree. We loved sitting on the protruding roots, hard as iron, around the wide and crooked trunk. We would also sit there in order to be able to jump up as quickly as possible, during the mango harvest time when its clusters were yellow and tempting. We were hungry all the time. The three scant meals with a snack in between were not enough to relieve our hunger. The snack? At ten o'clock half of a 5-penny roll covered with butter: bread with butter. Or covered with guava jam, peanut butter, or goat muck, a sour milk product. The cheese was as transparent as nylon. The guava jam often had ants in it. The rice had maggots. A half-Jewish girl named Victorine collected them in a bottle. She showed her mother the bottle. After that she was gone. Some of us would not touch our rice, just like Victorine, and ate only the vegetables. That meant that you were even more hungry and would pace, like a kind of starving herbivore, under and between the trees on the playground. It was forbidden to eat a mango or a mammee apple that had dropped. Or a sapodilla plum. Instead, you were supposed to put them in a large wooden box. That was called "collecting fruit." When I discovered that the box was meant for the convent, I began to steal fruit in a variety of ways. I could aim well. The hood hindered the sister. She could not supervise the playing girls very well. Inconspicuously my sticks would reach the tree-ripe mangoes and sapodillas, the tamarinds, almonds, avocados. I hid the half-ripe fruit on the ground under withered leaves. I would regularly return to the spot where my fruit was hidden to inspect the ripening process. When the fruits felt soft, I would divide them among a number of accomplices. Girls who had kept watch for me. We would eat the fruit in the lavatories. You were safe in the lavatories. That was the only place where you could escape the watchful eye of the nun on surveillance duty. During the half-hour recess, you could stay there as long as you wanted. Who could prove you were not constipated? That is what I first believed. Later I realized how many informers I had to take into account. Some of us were finally pulled out of the lavatories, with leaking, half-eaten mangoes in our hands, the yellow juice dripping from our mouths. We would be punished. Locked up in one of the coops. We had transgressed against the fifth commandment: Thou shalt not steal. And we had stolen; we knew that.

But we were often punished for things we did not know about and for which not a single explanation was given. I know now that it was because of the sixth and ninth commandments. Thou shalt not do anything unchaste. Thou shalt not desire anything unchaste. How is it possible, I still ask myself. How is it possible that some girls underwent the medieval punishments without rebelling? Not that I was a heroine. I was skinny and deathly afraid of beatings and the loneliness of the punishment cells. Yet I did not tell on Magdalena Ramautarsingh. She had beautiful, pearly white teeth that she brushed at least three times per afternoon. She did that between hanging up our pants and gathering them again into full tubs. One afternoon, Mother Superior allowed me to help her. Before I went upstairs, Mother Superior whispered to me that I had to check what Magdalena did and that I had to tell her later. I told her that I had not seen anything. A lie. Magdalena had been waving to a young man in the Wulfinghstreet from behind the window of the attic stairs. I was locked up. From that day I was treated differently by several of the big girls. They had always attracted me. I thought of them as heroines and followed their rages and temper tantrums with an innate rebelliousness and a secret pleasure. I thought it just that they yelled ugly and angry things aimed at the Dutch. I sympathized when they resisted as they were slapped right on the face by the Mother Superior or by a sister from the kitchen. Too bad that most of them were orphans. They were at the mercy of their family's social and economic conditions or of a godmother. They were twenty and sometimes older when they left the boarding school. They would then end up in families who received them against their wills in the poor back alleys of the slums. They would become servants for ladies of colonial status. Or they would become hat weavers, with a salary of twenty-five guilders per month. They would seek refuge in a man's love. The love which was held up to us year in and year out as a mortal sin. A friendly approach. A few handkerchiefs. A few bars of chocolate. A piece of cloth. A pair of shoes. Enough to secure motherhood. They would be deserted. In the slums they would be called names and be driven away from the door and the yard with a broom. Those years behind the high metal fences of Mgr. Wulfinghstreet! I wonder if the convent chapel floors, the stairs, the classrooms floors, and the boarding school floors are still being scrubbed red and shiny before and during every vacation. Now that these girls are no longer there. How they wore themselves out to clean the desks, the stone steps, and the lavatories. To scrub. I also wonder if the proceeds of the needlework, the embroidered tablecloths and sheets intended for the mission continue to be as high. Yes, certainly. There will always be orphans.

"Put on your socks," in my mind I still hear the sister telling us. "With your face to the wall. Put on your clothes and cover your body. With your face to the wall. Do not talk to the outside children. They are bad."

Strange. We knew that money was collected every school day. Money for Petrus Donders. Money for the holy Antonius. Money for Saint Joseph. Money for Mother Maria. Money for the statue of Fatima. Money from outside children. The bad children. What then was the difference between us and the girls who lived at home with their parents? The difference between deceit and truth? I do not think there was a difference. In the outside world there was much covered up as well, forbidden, made out as bad. There was no difference. The nuns were only afraid that we, through contact with the outside children, would hear stories that had to do with boys. The word *boy* was taboo.

We rarely went out. Sometimes we went to the doctor to swallow oil—castor oil—to prevent worms. Sometimes we would walk in the city. The streets gave me the jitters. The large office buildings along the Gravenstreet and the houses too were not as large as those in my memory. We were allowed to speak to each other softly. When we passed the cathedral we had to make a sign of the cross respectfully and repeat a little prayer. We were not allowed to look at bad pictures. We had to stop close to the movie theater, and we were reminded that all eyes were focused on us. We were the example of a good upbringing. Of modesty. We were not allowed to look at the posters on the theater wall. I myself never looked. I did not care if there were others who did look, giggling, amusing themselves. After the boring walks through the town, several girls would be punished. According to the sister, they had looked at the dirty pictures and had also laughed. "That is not true at all, sister," the girls would say. "We did not look, let alone laugh." But the mother had no mercy. "Dirty street sluts, you would run with boys into the woods."

Resistance mounted. I had been in the boarding school one year. On the playground in those days the song about Indonesia was sung every afternoon. Indonesia shortly before its independence. "In the land of brown people. In the land of sugar cane. Where wealth knows no boundaries, all is riches where one looks. There one sees a brown man going to the fields. I often wonder to myself, what is a poor Java man. . . . In the fields, I see them struggling, up to their knees in the water. They humbly greet every white man who passes. If ever the greeting is answered, they gaze in amazement. I often wonder to myself what is a poor Java man. . . . Far away in the village lives a beautiful Java girl. The white man goes to her. He soon finds her. And Sarina who once sang so beautifully . . . Europeans, poor and rich, injustice also has its limits. Show your civilization. Treat the Javanese as human beings. For they are born here. This is their place. Who was it that took their rights away? It is the cruel, cruel European."

The thirst for freedom grew stronger. The big girls searched for an outlet. They found that in cracks and splits in the metal fences. Small holes would be made larger. By us. By the boys in the street. It often happened that a hole or crack was darkened by a boy's eye. There were whistles; names of the big girls would be called. The girls began to talk noisily. They would burst out laughing, pulling each other's braids and running around excitedly in the yard. Some would stand close to the fence and would dance to their own rhythm. They would try their utmost to move their hips under their wide skirts without anyone noticing. They preferred singing a song about the pleasures of alcohol. *Mi lob, mi lob mi sopi so'te, sere bamba.* Sometimes they were caught. They would be beaten and isolated for a few days in one of the coops. They did not get food, or it would be brought too late, when they were not expecting it.

It is difficult to sum up systematically the punishments we received. It is actually impossible. You could be punished for anything. Every five minutes you would risk doing something that was not permitted. At five o'clock in the morning, we would be awakened by the ringing of a copper bell. We slept on the floor but called it our bed. We had to shake out our bedding quickly, fold it, and put it on the lowest shelf against the wall. On the top shelf, the minimum of toiletries—a toothbrush, toothpaste, a hand mirror, Pond's talcum powder, a washcloth, and a towel. We would quickly grab our washcloth, toothbrush, toothpaste to be among the first at the sink. We ran past each other in long white nightgowns. We did not like to brush our teeth in tubs with water that had been used before. We hated to stand at the washstands full of spit and spit-out toothpaste. The water that was poured out over the washstand once in a while was not enough to rinse away the spit and toothpaste completely. Thrift was one of the major requirements in the boarding school. Therefore, I was surprised that some girls of the middle group went downstairs certain days of the week to wash themselves. I envied them. Much, much later, I understood that that was not a privilege but a hygienic measure. But at that age I could only be amazed at things around me. The punishments. The venom of the tattletales. Their scheming. They would hurry to the Mother Superior to tell her that there were girls who had "saved" their beds, as we euphemistically referred to it. While upstairs water ran over the washstands and the rinsing sounds of mouths and throats took turns, the cries of the girls who had wet their beds would resound in the lobby. They were beaten in front of the statue of Saint Joseph. The slat that was used was called John. Crying, their faces hidden behind their elbows, they returned to the dormitories, followed by a sister. They were lined up in the middle of the hall. On their heads the damp sheets that stank of urine. Off and on they were ridiculed by the tattletales who hissed between their teeth, "Piss the bed! Piss the bed!" No one was allowed to talk in the dormitory.

Piss the bed! Piss the bed! An important occasion. The story would go from room to room: Who was beaten and why? And how did they come back? And afterwards? And then? Everyone had her own opinion. The elder ones favored the girls who had wet their beds and became rebellious. But the majority of the middle group was silent. That is an opinion also. To be afraid is also an opinion. Norine was one exception. Like me she had been sent away to private school. We were in the same grade. She had trouble learning. Her parents were divorced. Maybe she was sad. Or maybe she was really stupid. But she possessed something that very few girls of the middle group did. She was honest, rude, and said exactly what she thought. She knew that I would get a cheese and peanut butter sandwich from a school friend each Monday morning. She never betrayed me. She knew I sent letters with complaints home. She never told on me. The tasks she was assigned to allowed her a lot of privileges. In retrospect I realized that she received preferential treatment because her father paid twice as much as most of the parents of the children who were not orphans. Maybe more. It was the time when people were throwing their money around in the Antilles, a time to get rich. I was not jealous of her. I was relieved that she did not report me. Yet I did not always feel at ease when I walked next to her and was conscious of my own presence. Norine wore totally different clothes than most of us. Her dresses were of American confection, very modern, and terrific for that time. The little shorts and culottes that I wore at home were deeply hidden in the closet of the boarding school. I wore pants made of cotton and unbleached cotton. Pants with long legs that stuck way out from under my skirts. Later my dresses were lengthened with a band of white cotton. That made me happy. Almost all the girls of the middle group disliked Norine. But everyone was afraid of her. She was the favorite of the sister who made the meals and cared for the sick. The wounded. The lice-infected heads. The toes with sand fleas. Norijnte, as the sister called her, took milk and chocolate milk to the little ones. She often ate with them. Sundays, she would often go out and then return in tears. Up to this day I do not know why she suddenly left for the Antilles. Without saying goodbye to me. I still remember so well her large, light brown eyes, the long eyelashes under her Panama hat which she wore with pink ribbons, pulled forward. "Square" we called this tilt of our hats and our berets. The fashion. I also had a Panama hat, slanted and pulled steeply forward to hide my eyes. That was easy. The main part of my head was hair. "You first see her hair, then her face," said the big girls with whom I studied in the afternoon.

The relationships among the girls in the middle group were not always as stiff and boring. Especially later when other students arrived. I also learned that it was safe for me to try to associate with the tattletales. I knew their weak spot. They too were hungry. I promised them a portion of the fruits that I poached or a potion of the potatoes that I snitched from the convent's cellar. I had found the way to the cellar through a nun who would come once in a while to look after us. I liked her and asked her during the cleanup if I could lug the brooms to the cellar. The sister saw that I snitched potatoes but pretended she had a bloody nose. The tattletales listened intensely when I told them that I had potatoes from the cellar. They tried to find favor with the nun. They had no success. The young sister smiled at them. Reserved. Ironic. They were not allowed to go to the cellar alone. Potatoes were a delicacy because we seldom got them on our plates. The tattletales needed me and made sure that I got salt to boil the potatoes. They stole salt from the cellar in the dining hall. During recess, I would boil the potatoes on the fire lit under the large iron kettles in which the convent clothes were boiled. The kettles were in one end of the laundry room. I hid behind the woodstack against the heated wall. I listened to the water simmering in the oatmeal canisters on the red-hot logs. But there wasn't always fruit or potatoes to soften up the tattletales. I received one bad mark after another.

It was not only forbidden to talk in the dormitories. You were not allowed to talk anywhere without permission. If you did talk, you received a bad mark. Every morning your name would be read from a list and you had to confess where you had talked. Five bad marks would be noted for talking in the dormitory. Seven for the bathroom. Seven for the lavatories. The one who had said something to someone in the line to or from chapel would receive two. At the end of the week the bad marks would be added up. Anyone with ten marks got no candy and no rusk with sugar on Sunday. Those with fourteen got the punishment cells. Punishment on Sunday also meant that you were not allowed to see your parents or other visitors. It happened often that my "nowhere, sister" was answered with a raised hand: "She did talk, sister," I would hear behind my back. "That is not true, sister," I would answer. "She's lying, sister." It did not help. I would get bad marks anyhow. Once I was so furious that I yelled right through the dining room, "everywhere, sister." I immediately received fourteen bad marks. No one investigated these accusations. You would be punished solely on the basis of an accusation. And yet, the sisters did not get much out of me. I hated to embroider and crochet. After my "everywhere, sister" I was locked up in the Clemens closet. It was dusty and cramped. My throat itched. I was thirsty. There were old convent mats on the floor, woven with pieces of black, red, and yellow fabric. Large spiders hung in the corners against the low ceiling. Light fell inside through the branches of the cherry tree onto the copper screen. I sat in a daze, staring in front of me. When I got tired, I lay down on the dusty mats, my hands behind my head. Later in the day, a few cherries fell through the holes in the screen. My dress got full of stains. The cherries were too large for the opening and burst as someone tried to push them inside. I recognized the hand, just as brown as mine. It was Agnes, Agnes Indian. I was happy. Someone had thought of me, someone had missed me on the playground. I was hungry; I devoured the cherries. I hoped that the door would open. That someone would bring me hot food. No one. I wasn't released from the coop until late in the evening. I was allowed to bathe. Afterwards I had to eat by myself in the dining hall. No rice. I did not like plantains. The girl who normally would give me her peelings in exchange for my plantain was already asleep. Eight o'clock. I washed my plate and my orange plastic mug in the back of the dining room. I dropped the plantain into the skull of the holy Joseph. I was eleven years old.

Things were never investigated. You would be accused, and once accused you were guilty. We were sitting in the catechism classroom one evening. We were sitting on long benches, painted brown. In front of us behind a table sat the Mother Superior of the boarding school, a middle-aged woman. She gave us religious instruction. The cream-colored statue of the baby Jesus stood on the table, surrounded by the flickering flames of three white candles. We crossed ourselves. Again and again. We crossed ourselves and prayed little prayers all day long. The long evening prayer on our knees had just ended. The Mother Superior had apparently forgotten that. She started her long-winded prayer again, first for the world and its sinners, then for the sick, the murderers possessed by Satan's will. We crossed ourselves again. The end of the invocation. We said "Amen." My name was called. Once before my name had been called during a religion class and without an explanation I had been told to stand in the darkness of the bleaching field. What would it be this time? My heart pounded in my throat. I walked up to the front. Maybe it had something to do with taking turns. "Dirty child," said the sister, "Dirty child." She pulled my skirt tight over my pants. I felt the heat of the stick, bit my lips, and then walked out of the catechism hall with bowed head. Years later I accidentally learned why I had been beaten. I was told by a girl with whom I had gone to high school. According to her, one of the others had told the sister that I had taken off my pants at night. The blood drained from my face. I was furious. It was a lie. Or had I dreamt that I was in the lavatory? I had trouble with nightmares. Sometimes I would lie awake, my body wet with sweat in the heat of the hall. We slept with the windows closed to keep the mosquitoes out. Other girls were also bothered by nightmares. I would see them get up and walk in their sleep. They would hide behind the closet door, stand in a corner of the hall, or walk toward the stairs. I often heard them scream. Sometimes the little ones would walk into our hall, looking for something. Calling out. I could not understand what they said. I could not make it out. There were so many other things I could not understand, that were not clear to me. Like the punishment I received on Saint Nicholas Eve.

A few days before the celebration, I was suddenly surprised by Zwarte Piet. He had little bells on his feet. With much tinkling, he jumped out of a window of a classroom behind me. I quickly looked around and immediately made myself scarce. I hid in the first lavatory of the playground. I locked the door. That same evening I found all kinds of untidy, scribbled notes on the place where I slept. Scribbles about my behavior, written in chalk and in clumsy Dutch. Zwarte Piet, Black Piet, the Moor, came from Spain, we were taught. Zwarte Piet with the bag. I had misgivings. Would Mother Superior lock me up again? I hated to embroider. During recess I would read a book. It was forbidden to be alone or with just one more person. Then you would think bad thoughts. Therefore, I must have thought bad thoughts. But which ones? I quickly covered the notes with my bedsheets, made my bed, and crawled under the blanket. I could not sleep. I did not care much for birthdays and religious celebrations. Happiness only came from within. To me parties were nothing but forced get-togethers. The Saint Nicholas celebration left me indifferent. I would get a present. Probably a puzzle. My father had little imagination in this respect. I knew all this. But I was afraid to have to stay behind, alone in the darkness of a hallway. The bleaching field, the staircase, or a coop. I put my hand under the mattress and rubbed out the scribbles. On the way to the auditorium I was picked out of a row of talking girls. "What did I do?" I asked while I was taken away by the shoulder. Mother Superior did not answer me. She locked me up in a broom closet. She moved away and turned off the light between the bathrooms and the lavatories. Voices, steps, fifteen minutes later. Light! I was put into a burlap sack. The Mother Superior and another sister tied the bag several times around my torso and tightened it around my legs. When I was bound and could no longer resist, they lifted me from the floor and carried me away. First I did not know where they were carrying me. I thought of the attic and went crazy with fright. My head dangled out of the opening of the bag. I screamed. The sisters walked through the dining halls. They went past the statue of the holy Joseph. I quieted down. Apparently they were not taking me to the bats. Nor to the black cloth with the skulls. I was locked up in a cupboard under the stairs to the chapel. I lay on the floor in the bag. I tried to free myself, got claustrophobic. In the cupboard hung a faint smell of coffee grounds and refuse of the convent kitchen. Again I began to cry. I screamed when I heard voices. They were already in the auditorium and were loudly singing: "Look, the moon is shining through the trees."

There was indeed a full moon. A white cat was sitting on the softly cream-colored sand. It meowed, its slender head turning to the clear sky. I saw it through a split in the wooden door. I tried again to take my arms out of the bag. After trying for a long time I managed to untie the top knot of the cord with my mouth. My arms were out. The rest was simple. I kicked the bag away. I jumped, staggered, and almost fell. I pressed my nose against the copper-screen window at the top of the door and looked outside. The evening was cool. The cat was still there. The lights behind the green shutters of the convent's dining hall were extinguished. At this hour the true mystery of convent life begins. Where were those women who tyrannized us? What were they doing now? And the other sisters? The shadows in the chapel. Shadows standing in a long line going to confession. Shadows seated one behind the other on the long shiny benches in front of the chapel. Shadows with black, sliding rosary beads between pale skinny fingers. Shadows that walked from one station of the cross to the next doing penance, kneeling with raised arms for the sins of the world. Penance for their own sins: *Mea culpa, mea culpa, mea maxima culpa . . . Et libera nos a malo . . .* Shadows that once every two weeks entered and left the confessional to confess their sins while saying "Reverend Father, please bless me. My last confession was . . ." Just like us. Shadows that chilled you when you ran into them unexpectedly in the darkness of the playgrounds. The schoolyard. Shadows that scared you stiff when you woke up at night. Because of their shaven heads and their long lilac-colored robes. Shadows you never heard laugh. Like us. Like the outsiders.

The lives of the sisters remained a mystery to me. I knew that they were people. Women just like our mothers. But the distance between us and most of the nuns was so great. There was something unreal about them, I thought. Something supernatural, something that I could not grasp. Sister Huperta was one of the few exceptions. When I stood in front of her or behind her or walked next to her, her hand in mine, I had the feeling that she was a school friend or one of our mothers. She was disturbed and in her eighties. She worked in the laundry room with another nun. She often walked away. It was my task to look for her and to take her back to the laundry room or to the chapel hall if it had gotten late. I had the feeling that I was walking hand in hand with Sister Huperta. I usually would find her by the grotto of Maria of Lourdes, among the green bushes of the Tears of Jesus. She always sang the same tune: "In heaven, in heaven we will be forever." Sister Huperta played a game with me. She would change her hiding place every time so that I sometimes had trouble finding her. Her last hiding place was the cemetery along the Sommelsdijck creek. I was happy she had found this hiding place. I loved the young tamarind trees, threw sticks at the branches before I would gently touch the shoulder of the childlike nun.

One morning she did not wake up. She was buried in the shadows of the tamarind trees. The end of a life, the end of a task I had been given because I usually finished my homework in half the time. I missed the deceased sister. She was dead. Nobody mentioned her anymore. Nobody laughed anymore about the punishments she meted out to the crucifix: "Well, well, how do you like it up there? Now it is your turn to be punished, right?" Sister Huperta had had the habit of leaving the crucifix in the corner of her cell. Now she was dead. I stayed in the study hall the whole afternoon. More than once I asked the nun who had to watch us do our homework if I could go to the lavatory. Then I locked myself in and cried over the dead nun.

Around that time the Mother Superior of the boarding school was suddenly gone. The big girls whispered among themselves that there was something funny going on. They believed that the Mother Superior had held her hood too close to the face of Father X, the priest for the orphans. "I'm glad that she's got what was coming to her," Eline said in the study hall. "The more pious the spirit, the more bestial the body," added Agnes Indian. Agnes was still furious over the beatings she had received when the Mother Superior had noticed how short her dress was. From cowboy books I had read I knew how proud an Indian can be of what he has and who he is. The Indian girls had short legs with solid muscular calves. They preferred the shorter length of their ponchos and hated long western dresses. They would turn up the hems of their dresses in the lavatories and in the darkness of the dormitories. Agnes Indian was the first one caught. She was beaten in the lobby after mass.

The new Mother Superior was called Selesia. The cruelest nun I have ever known. She was big and had broad round hips. Her face was as round as a ball, red as a chicken wattle. On some days during the month her cheeks were loaded with big pus pimples. Her mouth stank. "Her mouth stinks like the lavatory," was the going expression. We immediately stepped back when she stood in front of us. In the dining hall we would move our plates away as quickly as lightning. The spit from her mouth would spritz like water from a sprayer. We called her "Spritzer." I was under the impression that she was not pleased with her new position and that she hated children. She would pinch the skinny arms of the little ones with a sadistic expression on her face. She enjoyed it when they screamed with pain. Sister Selesia did not strike you with "John," the thick slat. She hit with her own heavy, masculine hand. The girls in my dormitory could not stand her, but they remained silent because they were afraid they would be sent away. They knew that they could not expect anything from their families. Life outside. They kept their mouths shut and offered their services, just as I had expected. During recess and on Friday evening, the only evening that we, the ones in the middle, were allowed to stay up, they embroidered more diligently than ever. I sat secretly reading a book in the corner, and once in a while I would pretend I was crocheting. Sometimes Sister Selesia's voice would scare us all. She would scold us because she thought we were acting like fishwives. After such rebukes came a *tjoerie*, a displeased sound with her lips. We started to form plots against Sister Selesia. Plans that were never executed. It never went beyond their mimicking in various tones her "Good morning, holy Joseph" and "My Jesus, full of grace" in the morning on the way to the chapel.

In the beginning the big girls were also scared of Selesia. They would act up against the nun on duty in the study hall. The sister was short, hunchbacked, and wore glasses with copper frames. Her nickname was "Penny Puff." She could not control the big girls. The girls would make all kinds of remarks about the food and asked her about freedom and fashion. The Sister liked me. She enjoyed hearing me recite my lessons. She would listen to my responses with great devotion. It was through her that I had been given the responsibility of looking for Sister Huperta and take her back to the laundry room. Now that the sister had died I was bored for at least an hour every afternoon, listening to the stories, the conversations, the remarks of the big girls. "Read," Agnes said one afternoon. She shoved her Dutch history book under my nose. Softly I started to read. "Loud," she said. "She won't do anything." I read out loud, "The East Indian

Company was founded in 1604 by Jan Pieterszoon Coen. The Dutch have always been sharp smugglers. The Dutch are . . ." There was a general "boo, boo, boo." The next afternoon I was called away immediately after I had recited my lesson. I was allowed to help in the garden. I pulled grass out of the flower beds and the vegetable beds diligently. My diligence began to wane by the following afternoon. I had discovered where I could best work and would not leave the radishes. I pulled them out and hid them in a paper sack. This went well for a few days. Then I got caught. I was not allowed to help in the garden anymore.

I got sick. A hundred-and-two-degree fever. I was given weak tea without sugar and dry soda crackers. I was happy to be sick, happy to be left alone. I was much relieved to have the whole dormitory to myself during the day. I could go to the lavatory whenever I wanted. In the chapel I would sometimes sit with a pale face, while the cold sweat would break out under my nose, because I had to go to the lavatory and the sister would not allow it. Now I was alone. I was finally spared the moralizing sermons in the dining room and the religious instruction hall. I did not need to pray. I was deathly ill.

When I felt a little better I looked after the little girls. They would go to bed at five in the afternoon. As soon as the Angelus bell sounded at six, the sister who had put them to bed would be relieved by the laundry-room sister. Every afternoon the big ones among the little girls would anxiously await this moment. As soon as the sister disappeared, they would jump wildly out of their beds. With the sheets over their heads they would run from one corner to the other. "Boo! Boo!" they screamed to scare each other. The littlest ones would wake up scared, rub their eyes, and look sleepily at the girls who would hide behind the closet door or who would all want to sit on the communal pot in the wooden box: "Auntie Alida! Auntie Alida! Auntie Alida! I do not like salt meat." The voice of a blond Antillean girl. I would laugh, and quickly run back when I heard the laundry-room sister.

I was well after two weeks. The first step on the stairs to the lobby, the green of the bleaching field and the leaves of the orange trees, the orange flowers, all made a fairytale-like impression on me. I had the feeling that this was my first day in the boarding school and that it would not last long. Everything would soon be like it used to be.

Translated by Hilda van Neck-Yoder

Myriam Warner-Vieyra was born in Guadeloupe, but has lived in Senegal for many years. The author of two novels—Le Quimboiseur l'avait dit and Juletane, both translated into English—and of a collection of short stories, Femmes Echouées, Warner-Vieyra is gaining increased recognition for her sensitive portrayals of Caribbean and African women in self-destroying conflicts with patriarchal institutions. Her novel Juletane has been praised for its keen analysis of women's limited choices. Warner-Vieyra works as a librarian and researcher at the University of Dakar.

MYRIAM WARNER-VIEYRA

Passport to Paradise

Eloise was a strong countrywoman, tireless and carefree as a carnival night. At thirty, she had a lovely family: four boys and four girls who were bursting with health. Her pregnancies had never stopped her from doing her work. She did not suffer from any of the usual discomforts other women experienced. Florette, her eldest, now almost nine, was already her mother's right hand. Eloise took her last baby, just three months old, to the field with her every day, in a basket which she carried on her head securely balanced on a *cotta* of rolled-up rags. She put down her baby in the shade, where she could see him, under the watchful eye of one of the bigger ones, who had been given this task, and attacked her work.

Their cane crop had all been harvested the day before, so that day she had begun to weed her vegetable garden. As she always did, she sang one of the old tunes which came from deep in her memory to keep time with her hoe as she dug up the weeds. She loved her man, her healthy children, her clean house; she was blessed with the strength and the courage to work. For her that was what happiness really meant.

Eugenio had just delivered his last cartload of cane to the Derousier factory. He would still have to wait several days before he could exchange the slip he had been given for a few bank-notes which would be barely enough to wipe out his debts at the store and allow the family to eke out their meager existence by the grace of God, until the next crop. He was tired. At forty, he had spent thirty years at hard labor in the fields, and *clairin*, that clear liquid which he constantly consumed, was certainly partly responsible for his being old before his time. But *he* did not know that. Besides, his physical weariness did not dampen his zest for life. His wife's good planning and her enthusiasm for work relieved him of all domestic chores. He loved her very much, but he was also a man with a craving. A fervent disciple of the god *Tafia*, he had, as a final will and testament, asked his wife Eloise to put a little flask of this firewater in his coffin, whenever he was ready to depart from this world.

That day Eugenio stopped in front of Miss Adelaide's rum shop at about five o'clock. He shouted "whoa" to his two mules and jumped down from his cart to have a few drinks with his regular companions before dinnertime. He rarely remembered the taste of this meal, because by then he was usually drunk enough to sleep with his eyes wide open on a pile of stones. "Trouble don't set like rain." He had hardly had time to swallow his first drink when an altercation broke out between two men. Eugenio, who was still quite sober, unlike the others, attempted to calm them down but to no avail. The quarrel grew louder and louder and they came to blows. The first was fatal; a bottle split open a skull: Eugenio's. He sank silently to the ground, died with one last hiccup, blood smelling of rum trickling from his mouth . . .

Eugenio's friends gave him a memorable wake, their favorite liquid flowed freely . . .

The next day, very, very early, Eloise dispatched a friend and neighbor to see "Monsieur le Curé," their village priest, to ask him if he would kindly come and bless the body. She did not have the wherewithall to give him a first-, second-, or even third-class funeral. Still, as a believer it was very important to her for the body to be blessed, and for the priest to recite one of his prayers in Latin, the key that would open the gates of heaven. The neighbor came back with the priest's reply, as serious as it was unjust: Eugenio, a notorious alcoholic, living in sin, had died without going to confession. No act of contrition, no absolution, no extreme unction, no benediction.

When she heard the news, Eloise felt the blood rush to her head. A multicolored veil, mostly red and black, blinded her vision. For a moment she could not even speak. Her man was going to burn in hell, not because of his sins, but because he was poor and black. The rich *békés* of the land openly kept several concubines; their skins and their eyes had the greenish tint of the absinthe which they drank like coconut water and which aged them as rapidly as the cartman's white rum. Yet, when one of them died, he was given the grandest of funerals. The whole clergy, in their robes, walked in procession before the hearse with crosses and banners. Masses sung in Latin were celebrated for months on end for the repose of their souls . . .

Faced with Eloise's deep depression, Eunice, her neighbor, remembered a stranger who had recently arrived from Asia. Everyone in the marketplace said he possessed the power to make amulets which were passports to paradise. You had only to lay the charm on the chest of the deceased and he was sure to go to heaven. Eloise was ready to try anything to save her man's soul, even if she had to give hers to the devil in exchange. She gave Eunice her most valuable possession, a ring that Eugenio had given her on the day that they had set up house together, ten years before.

Eunice set off in search of the magician, and one hour later she brought back the precious viaticum. It was a piece of goatskin on which there were strange markings, Chinese or Arabic characters, to the two women it was one and the same. Eloise kissed the sacred parchment, and entrusted it with her love as well, to go with the beloved on his journey. She placed it on Eugenio's bosom, under the only white shirt he had ever possessed in his whole life. At that moment she experienced the relief of having done her duty and she felt almost happy. Eugenio's soul would fly up to paradise in spite of the curé and on the day of her death, she would be reunited with him on high . . .

A week after the burial, the whole village in the little commune of Grand-Font-de-Sainte-Agnès learnt with great consternation that the vendor of tickets to the Great Beyond had been arrested by the police for fraud. A word which no one knew and which they had trouble pronouncing. It came out as flowd, frowd, frode, flawed. To cut a long story short, a high-up civil servant came from town and questioned the man about his powers. Of course, it had not occurred to anyone that to prove a crime had been committed it was necessary to demonstrate that the merchandise sold, in this case talismans, was useless. *That*, no one could prove, and no departed had come back to complain that the gates of heaven had remained closed to him. Therefore, for want of tangible evidence, there being no criminal act, they were obliged to release the prisoner. All the humble people in the village applauded heartily. The stranger set himself tirelessly to the task of giving every person in the village his celestial safe-conduct, ready for the moment of departure. Those who by day loudly proclaimed their disbelief, by night slunk along the fences secretly to procure their amulet, in order to hedge their bets. Even the *quimboiseur*, after invoking the gods of Africa, thought it prudent discreetly to get himself this additional assurance of a good seat on the sailing ship for the great voyage back to Guinea.

The last I heard, our Merlin of the islands was mixing lamb's blood with China ink to increase the effectiveness of the heavenly passport. The only dissatisfied people in the village were the members of the clergy, because, needless to say, now not a single soul came to ask them to say masses for the dead.

Heaven open to everybody and sin gone out of use. . . . Man's imagination can certainly go to unfathomable depths!

Translated by Betty Wilson

Mirta Yáñez was born in Havana in 1947 and received a degree in language and literature from the University of Havana. She has published poems and short stories in various Cuban publications, as well as two collections of short stories, Todos los negros tomamos café *and* La Habana es una ciudad bien grande, *and a novel,* La hora de los mameyes. *Yáñez's fiction draws primarily on her experiences as a* brigadista—a *member of the brigades of young Cubans who did agricultural work in the 1960s and 1970s—in a coffee plantation in rural Cuba, and gives testimony of her deep interest in cultural history and the Cuban peasantry.*

MIRTA YÁÑEZ

Of Natural Causes

Some men, estranged by one reason or another from their homeland, find themselves the object of people's wonderment, of constant curiosity concerning every peculiarity of their existence. Whenever these men form a small community, when they gather as if family, settle on a piece of land, or find a way to earn a living, neighboring people watch them with the amazement of children perusing the contours of a deserted island enclave on a school map.

The Haitians from the Mayarí Arriba mountains belong to that species of humans who are both attached and unattached to a place. They belong to their plots of land but at the same time they are marked by an air of rootlessness, by gusts of absence, and unknown seas.

For many years these men have lived in narrow barracks, men alone, so old that they have forgotten each other's ages, as their lives go on concocting stews, mumbling litanies in which an attentive ear could recognize a few words suspended in the air; men leaving at dawn with sacks on their shoulders, picking coffee in silence, and returning to their barracks, until early the next day.

Anyone who arrives at the village and stays near these shacks is sure to be cautioned about the Haitians' tolerance, an intimidating tolerance, especially when expressed in their own language, a tolerance which, fragile as an onionskin, could suddenly turn to abrupt, violent rage. Accustomed to hard work and hard lives, they are also burdened by legends of their brittle susceptibility, of certain virulences and passions, that contradict their peaceful and sagacious appearance, like those who have traveled all roads and know the innermost recesses of people.

But even if all this were mere rumor, it is true that I once saw a Haitian show his knife to a man, and this, according to superstitious neighbors, meant the man's hours were numbered.

The house I lived in while I was picking coffee was located on a *batey*, a settlement where two or three families from the village of Florida Blanca lived. At the foot of a hill, next to the remains of a fence destroyed by a cyclone, stood the Haitians' barracks, resisting by some miracle of nature the weather's pounding and past miseries. In the barracks lived five Haitians, their hair white from many decades spent in the mountains. Their dark skin showed through the layers of torn fabric they threw over themselves to fight the coolness of the sierra, and which, as the day wore on, they would remove from their bodies, as a snake sheds its old skin, and store over the coffee sacks they were filling with ripe beans; above their eyes and over their hair they would wear a colored handkerchief or a wide-brimmed peasant hat folded and refolded; sometimes they would wear both, the handkerchief and the hat over it; their hands were calloused and wide; their shoulders propped up as sails on an open sea. The five men would leave at the crack of dawn, way before we *brigadistas* began to cook our breakfast and got ready to leave. By the time we arrived at the coffee fields, it had already been quite a while since the five old men—as long as one of them was not sick or on his way to town to buy groceries—had scattered themselves across the plot of land and were working in silence, exchanging only a few brief phrases to specify their locations. Yulián was the oldest of the five. And I managed to find this out not from any sign on his face, or from hearing of his ailments, but from the attitude of the other four men, the way he was treated with a certain deference that revealed that Yulián was superior to them in some way, either in age or as the preserver of secret spiritual rituals. And one night it was Yulián who took a well-sharpened kitchen knife from within his many layers of coats and cloaks and ran along the foot of the hill to nail it into the heart of another man.

Although more than ten years have gone by since that time, I have the contours and details of these events securely engraved in my memory, like sharp photographs that capture forever an irreversible moment of life; stale images, but etched on metal with their contrasts settled in time, their chiaroscuros immobilized in memory.

If the Haitians' anger was proverbial, their extreme patience was also well known, as was their tenderness toward animals and children who did not fear the presence of these old men whose combined ages totaled more than three centuries. On cold nights, it was the custom to gather around the brazier's warmth where Yulián and his companions would cook, and to listen over and over again to tales brought from their faraway land, stories handed down from generation to generation, about when their entire country was ablaze and the blacks had taken power upon themselves, and of the wise men among them who made them men and no longer beasts of burden; they talked about all this way before the rebels had come to the sierra and had told similar stories. The Haitians related histories of their rebellions, of their hatred for the slave owners, who they vengefully impaled on pikes, and of how the poor people gained power, the ones who moments before had been slaves. But that was so long ago. Afterwards poverty had been so extreme—they never understood what had happened—and they were even forced to migrate in search of this promised land, a land of less hunger, who knows why. Their wives and children remained behind, now the kids were surely men, the wives old women, perhaps already dead, what had become of them all? More than fifty years without a word. And again to listen to legends of the great Mackandal, the one who managed to escape.

"Yulián," the kids from Florida Blanca would say, "tell us about the maimed one, the one without a hand, how he turned into a bird."

And Yulián would begin to narrate the endless stories about the great Mackandal transformed himself into a bird, flying away as in a sudden blaze of fire to escape from his enemies. Mackandal the unbelievable one, Mackandal transformed into an ugly bird, into a wolf. The great Mackandal.

I also sat down to listen and to watch how Yulián's eyes lit up when once again the mountains of his native land and the burning plantain fields passed before his eyes, and Mackandal doing his old tricks.

One night when Yulián had returned to recount his stories by the heat from the stove, something unexpected took place. From the small group of listeners someone burst out laughing, abruptly interrupting Yulián's intimate narration.

"Fancy that! A black man flying!" said the man, his voice coming from who knew where.

Later, we found out it was Cuco Serrano, a rich owner of land and tobacco drying sheds, who was furious those days because talk about land reform and intervention had begun. And he had it in for his neighbors, constantly holding grudges against them, spitting on the coffee beans they set out to dry, provoking everyone. I found all this out later, because at that instant a hush fell over all, followed by the silence and stillness that precedes catastrophes, a dead calm that shook my heart with the certainty of an impending cataclysm.

A second after, interrupted in the midst of his story, I saw Yulián lift his eyes in surprise, I saw them become darker and darker from astonishment, as if a cloud of blood was covering them, and I heard him say very softly, as if not a word had been spoken, as if giving Cuco Serrano a last chance to shut up, and himself, Yulián, a last chance to verify that he was not mistaken in what he had heard.

"Mackandal was a great man."

"Go to hell with your fucking Mackandal!" And then Yulián got up slowly, because the patience of the Haitians is an almost limitless patience, took the kids aside, and he confronted Cuco Serrano, with his chest thrust forward, his head leaning backwards, his hand moving like an animal as if it were separated from his body, beginning to search for that enormous kitchen knife lost between his many layers of clothing. And from then on everything happened like lightning, and this is the clearest part of my recollection: Yulián as in slow motion moving forward, his hand moving, while none of us knew at that point what it was searching for, Cuco Serrano stepping backwards without a fuss, and suddenly a metal blade shinning, reflecting the light from the burning wick, and Yulián, jumping straight ahead, finally having lost the patience of entire centuries, his whole body burning in a single flame, transformed into a wolf, like Mackandal; and Cuco Serrano, in one leap, vanishing into the coffee plantation, and the two men disappearing between the coffee plants without a single scream.

I looked around and I saw the four Haitians sitting, looking at the fire as if they had nothing to do with all this, and the kids running home screaming, "Yulián, the big knife, Cuco Serrano"; and I remaining next to the Haitians and asking them what would happen next.

"Yulián knows," they replied without lifting their eyes.

The entire night went by and Yulián didn't come back to the barracks and Cuco Serrano didn't go to his house to sleep.

By daybreak Yulián was picking coffee, behaving as if nothing had happened. No one dared make any comment, much less ask what had happened to the other man.

It was Rufinita, protected by her youth, who solved the problem. She went straight to where Yulián was working and confronted him with the question we all had on the tips of our tongues.

"Where did you stab him with the knife, Yulián?" Yulián took out the clean, stainless knife, and plunged it into the trunk of a tree, as he shook his head.

"Yulián is old, yes," he answered.

And I thought this time Cuco Serrano had escaped.

But that's life: three days later some co-workers came looking for Cuco Serrano, who had been in hiding since the night of the confrontation, and from them we found out that Cuco had not only hoarded lands and hatred, but also that during the rebellion he had denounced a rebel camp to Batista's soldiers, to one of the tyrant's patrols. To put it more clearly: he was an informer. This time not just Yulián but many were angered, and all the neighbors from the area set out looking for him, to take him out of wherever he was hiding, even from under the earth, and that was how they managed to find him curled up by the bed of a stream, stiff and already smelling badly. And, although everyone examined him over and over looking for a wound from Yulián's knife, after much checking they were convinced that Cuco Serrano died of natural causes—if one can call spending a night trembling by a river basin, waiting for the Haitian fury to descend upon him like a bolt of lightning at any moment, waiting with his heart in his mouth for Mackandal's revenge, death by natural causes.

Translated by Carmen C. Esteves

This selected bibliography is intended to aid the student and general reader in identifying fiction by writers included in this anthology, as well as critical appraisals of their work. We thus focus on short stories and novels (excluding poetry, theater, and essays due to space limitations) and, when possible, have limited the critical citations to English-language materials in readily accessible books and journals.

OLGA TORRES-SEDA

Selected Bibliography

GENERAL

Berrian, Brenda F., comp. *Bibliography of Women Writers from the Caribbean (1831-1986)*. Washington, D.C.: Three Continents Press, 1988.

Davies, Carol Boyce and Elaine Savory Fido, eds. *Out of the Kumbla: Caribbean Women and Literature*. Trenton, N.J.: Africa World Press, 1990.

Myers, Eunice and Ginette Adamso, eds. *Continental, Latin-American, and Francophone Women Writers*. Lanham, Md.: University Press of America, 1987.

Paravisini, Lizabeth and Barbara Webb. "On the Threshold of Becoming: Contemporary Caribbean Women Writers." *Cimarrón* 1, no. 3 (1988): 106-132.

Paravisini-Gebert, Lizabeth, ed. *Subversión de cánones: la escritora puertorriqueña ante la crítica*. New York: Peninsula, 1991.

Phaf, Ineke. "Women and Literature in the Caribbean." In *Unheard Words: Women and Literature in Africa, the Arab World, Asia, the Caribbean, and Latin America*, edited by Mineke Schipper, 168-200. London: Allison and Busby, 1985.

PHYLLIS SHAND ALLFREY

Novels

The Orchid House. London: Constable, 1953. Reprint. New York: E. P. Dutton, 1954. 2d ed. London: Virago Press, 1983. Reprint. Washington, D.C.: Three Continents Press, 1985.

Short Stories

"A Talk on China." In *The Windmill,* edited by Reginald Moore and Edward Lane, 52-56. London: Heinemann, 1944.

"The Tunnel." In *The Windmill,* edited by Reginald Moore and Edward Lane, 105-113. London: Heinemann, 1944.

Works About

Andre, Irving W. "The Social World of Phyllis Shand Allfrey's *The Orchid House.*" *Caribbean Quarterly* 29, no. 2 (1983): 11-21.

Campbell, Elaine. "Phyllis Shand Allfrey (1915-   )." In *Fifty Caribbean Writers,* edited by Daryl Cumber Dance, 9-18. New York: Greenwood Press, 1986.

Davies, Barrie. "Neglected West Indian Writers No. 1: Phyllis Allfrey, *The Orchid House.*" *World Literature Written in English* 2, no. 2 (1972): 81-85.

Nunez-Harrell, Elizabeth. "The Paradoxes of Belonging: The White West Indian Woman in Fiction." *Modern Fiction Studies* 31, no. 2 (1985): 281-293.

Ramchand, Kenneth. *The West Indian Novel and Its Background.* London: Faber and Faber, 1970, pp. 224-228.

DORA ALONSO

Novels

Tierra adentro. Havana: n.p., 1944.
Tierra inerme. Havana: Casa de las Américas, 1961.

Short Stories

Agua pasada (Autobiographical vignettes). Havana: Unión de Escritores y Artistas de Cuba, 1981.
Cuentos. Havana: Unión de Escritores y Artistas de Cuba, 1976.
Gente de mar. Havana: Gente Nueva, 1977.
Panolani: cuentos. Havana: Ediciones Granma, 1966.

Translations

"The Rat." In *Cuban Short Stories 1959-1966*, edited by Sylvia Carranza and María Juana Cazabón, 89-91. Havana: Instituto del Libro Arte y Literatura, 1967.
"Times Gone By." Translated by Myrthe Afelia Chabran. In *Fragment from a Lost Diary and Other Stories*, edited by Naomi Katz and Nancy Milton, 93-103. New York: Pantheon Books, 1973.

Works About

Alzola, Concepción Teresa. "Cuentística de Dora Alonso." *Unión* 1, no. 2 (July-August 1962): 89-106.
Shea, Maureen. "A Growing Awareness of Sexual Opression in the Novels of Contemporary Latin American Women Writers." *Confluencia* 4, no. 1 (1988): 53-59.

HAZEL D. CAMPBELL

Short Stories

The Rag Doll and Other Stories. Kingston: Savacou, 1978.
"See Dem Come." *Jamaica Journal* 6, no. 3 (1972): 37-39.
"The Thursday Wife." In *Caribbean New Wave: Contemporary Short Stories*, edited by Stewart Brown, 35-42. London: Heinemann, 1990.
"Tilly Bummie." In *Focus 1983*, edited by Mervyn Morris, 137-142. Kingston: Caribbean Authors, 1983.

Woman's Tongue. Kingston: Savacou Publications, 1985.

Works About

Earl, Claudette. "Review of *The Rag Doll and Other Stories.*" *Caribbean Contact,* July 1979, 3.

AIDA CARTAGENA PORTALATÍN

Novels

Escalera para Electra. Santo Domingo: Editora de la Universidad Autónoma de Santo Domingo, 1970. Reprint. Santo Domingo: Taller, 1975.

Short Stories

"La llamaban Aurora (Pasión por Donna Summer)." In *Puerta abierta: La nueva escritora latinoamericana,* edited by Carilda L. Silva-Velázquez and Nora Erro-Orthman, 75-77. México: Joaquín Mortiz, 1986.
Tablero: doce cuentos de lo popular a lo culto. Santo Domingo: Taller, 1978.

Works About

Figueroa, Ramón. "Nacionalismo y universalismo en *Escalera para Electra.*" *Areito* 10, no. 38 (1984): 41-43.
Mujer y literatura: Homenaje a Aida Cartagena Portalatín. Santo Domingo: Editora UASD, 1986.

MICHELLE CLIFF

Novels

Abeng. Trumansburg, N.Y.: The Crossing Press, 1984.
No Telephone to Heaven. New York: E. P. Dutton, 1987. Reprint. London: Methuen, 1988; New York: Vintage, 1989.

257

Short Stories

Bodies of Water. New York: E. P. Dutton, 1990.
The Land of Look Behind: Prose and Poetry. Ithaca, N.Y.: Firebrand Books, 1985.

Works About

Johnson, Lemuel A. "A-beng: (Re)Calling the Body in(to) Question." In *Out of the Kumbla: Caribbean Women and Literature*, edited by Carol Boyce Davies and Elaine Savory Fido, 111-142. Trenton, N.J.: Africa World Press, 1990.
Kaplan, Caren. "Deterritorializations: The Rewriting of Home and Exile in Western Feminist Discourse." *Cultural Critique* 6 (Spring 1987): 187-198.

MARIE-THÉRÈSE COLIMON-HALL

Novels

Fils de misère. Port-au-Prince: Éditions Horizons-Caraïbes, 1974.

Short Stories

Les Chants des sirènes. Port-au-Prince: Éditions du Soleil, 1979.

Works About

Condé, Maryse. *La Parole des femmes: essai sur des romancières des Antilles de langue française*, 91-97. Paris: L'Harmattan, 1979.

MARYSE CONDÉ

Novels

Hérémakhonon. Paris: Union Générale d'Éditions, 10/18, 1976. Reprint. Paris: Seghers, 1988.

Moi, Tituba, sorcière noire de Salem. Paris: Mercure de France, 1986.
Une Saison à Rihata. Paris: Robert Laffont, 1981.
Segou I: les murailles de terre. Paris: Robert Laffont, 1981. Reprint.
Paris: Robert Laffont, 1984.
Segou II: la terre en miettes. Paris: Robert Laffont, 1985.
Traversée de la mangrove. Paris: Mercure de France, 1989.
La Vie scélérate. Paris: Seghers, 1987.

Translations

The Children of Segu. Translation of *Segou II* by Linda Coverdale.
New York: Viking, 1989.
Heremakhonon. Translated by Richard Philcox. Washington, D.C.:
Three Continents Press, 1982.
A Season in Rihata. Translated by Richard Philcox. London: Heine-
mann, 1988.
Segu. Translated by Barbara Bray. New York: Viking, 1987.
Reprint. New York: Ballantine, 1988.

Short Stories

"Blurred Images." *Viva*, November 1975, 28-29, 42.
Pays Mêlé suivi de Nanna-ya. Paris: Hatier, 1985.
"Le Petit Garçon qui voulait voir la neige." *Bingo* 227 (1971): 100-
101.
"Solo." *Magazine Guadeloupéen* 4 (1982): 45-47.

Interviews

Clark, VèVè A. and Cecile Daheny. "Je me suis reconcilié avec
mon île/I Have Made Peace With My Island: An Interview
With Maryse Condé." *Callaloo: An Afro-American and African
Journal of Arts and Letters* 12, no.1 (Winter 1989): 95-133.
Williams, John. "Return of a Native Daughter: An Interview with
Paule Marshall and Maryse Condé." *Sage* 3, no.2 (Fall 1986):
52-53.

Works About

Bruner, Charlotte H. and David Bruner. "Buchi Emecheta and

Maryse Condé: Contemporary Writing from Africa and the Caribbean." *World Literature Today* 59, no. 1 (1985): 9-13.

Bruner, David K. "Maryse Condé: Creative Writer in a Political World." *L'Esprit Créateur* 17, no. 2 (1977): 168-173.

Case, Frederick Ivor. *The Crisis of Identity: Studies in the Guadeloupean and Martiniquan Novel.* Sherbrooke: Editions Naaman, 1985

Silenieks, Juris. "Beyond Historicity: The Middle Passage in Writings of Contemporary Francophone Caribbean Authors." In *Travel Quest and Pilgrimage as Literary Theme,* edited by Fran Amelinckx and Joyce Megay, 269-279. Ann Arbor: Society of Spanish and Spanish-American Studies, 1978.

Zimra, Clarisse. "Negritude in the Feminine Mode: The Case of Martinique and Guadeloupe." *The Journal of Ethnic Studies* 12, no. 1 (1984): 53-78.

———. "Patterns of Liberation in Contemporary Women Writers." *L'Esprit Créateur* 17, no. 2 (1977): 103-114.

———. "W/Righting His/tory: Versions of Things Past in Contemporary Caribbean Women Writers." In *Essays in Comparative Literature,* edited by Makoto Ueda, 227-252. New York: University Press of America, 1986.

HILMA CONTRERAS

Novels

La tierra está bramando. Santo Domingo: Biblioteca Nacional, 1986.

Short Stories

Cuatro cuentos. Santo Domingo: Editora Stella, 1953.
Entre dos silencios. Santo Domingo: Taller, 1987.
El ojo de Dios: cuentos de la clandestinidad. Santo Domingo: Ediciones Dominicanas, 1962.

Translations

"The Window." From the collection *Entre dos silencios.* Translated by Fernanda Steele. In *Her True-True Name: An Anthology of Women's Writing from the Caribbean,* edited by Pamela Mordecai and Betty Wilson, 90-93. London: Heinemann, 1989.

LILIANE DÉVIEUX

Novels

L'Amour, oui: La Mort, non. Sherbrooke: Éditions Naaman, 1976.

Short Stories

"Piano-Bar." *Conjonction* 171 (1988).

Interviews

Jonassaint, Jean. "Liliane Dévieux." In *Le Pouvoir des mots, les maux du pouvoir; des romanciers haitiens de l'exil,* 45-53. Paris: Éditions de l'Arcantere; Montreal: Les Presses de l'Université de Montreal, 1986.

Works About

Condé, Maryse. *La Parole des femmes: essai sur des romancières des Antilles de langue francaise,* 107-110. Paris: L'Harmattan, 1979.

RAMABAI ESPINET

Short Story

"Because I Could Not Stop for Death." *Tiger Lily* (November 1990).

Work Edited

Creation Fire: An Anthology of Caribbean Women's Poetry. Toronto: Sister Vision Press, 1990.

ROSARIO FERRÉ

Novels

Maldito amor. México: Joaquín Mortiz, 1986. Reprint. Río Piedras, P.R.: Huracán, 1988.

Sweet Diamond Dust. English version of *Maldito amor.* New York: Ballantine, 1988.

Short Stories

La caja de cristal. México: La Máquina de Escribir, 1978.

Los cuentos de Juan Bobo. Río Piedras, P.R.: Huracán, 1981.

El medio pollito: siete cuentos infantiles. Río Piedras, P.R.: Huracán, 1976.

La mona que le pisaron la cola. Río Piedras, P.R.: Huracán, 1981.

La muñeca menor. Río Piedras, P.R.: Huracán, 1980.

Papeles de Pandora. México: Joaquín Mortiz, 1976. 2d ed., 1979.

Sonatinas. Río Piedras: Huracán, 1989.

Translations

"Pico Rico Mandorico." Translated by Diana Vélez. In *Reclaiming Medusa: Short Stories by Contemporary Puerto Rican Women,* edited by Diana Vélez, 64-72. San Francisco: Aunt Lute, 1988.

"The Youngest Doll." Translated by Rosario Ferré and Diana Vélez. In *Reclaiming Medusa: Short Stories by Contemporary Puerto Rican Women,* edited by Diana Vélez, 27-33. San Francisco: Aunt Lute, 1988. Reprint. In *Her True-True Name: An Anthology of Women's Writing from the Caribbean,* edited by Pamela Mordecai and Betty Wilson, 93-98. London: Heinemann, 1989.

The Youngest Doll. Lincoln: University of Nebraska Press, 1991.

Works About

Chaves, María José. "La alegoría como método en los cuentos de Rosario Ferré." *Third Woman* 2, no. 2 (1984): 64-76.

Fernández Olmos, Margarite. "Constructing Heroines: Rosario Ferré's *Cuentos Infantiles* and Feminine Instruments of Change." *The Lion and the Unicorn* 10 (1986): 83-94.

———. "From a Woman's Perspective: The Short Stories of Rosario Ferré and Ana Lydia Vega." *Contemporary Women Authors of Latin America: Introductory Essays*, 78-90. Brooklyn, N.Y.: Brooklyn College Press, 1983.

———. "Luis Rafael Sánchez and Rosario Ferré: Sexual Politics and Contemporary Puerto Rican Narrative." *Hispania* 70, no. 1 (1987): 40-46.

———. "Sex, Color, and Class in Contemporary Women Authors." *Heresies* 4, no. 3, Consecutive Issue 15 (1982): 46-47.

Lagos-Pope, María-Inés. "Sumisión y rebeldía: El doble o la representación de la alienación femenina en narraciones de Marta Brunet y Rosario Ferré." *Revista Iberoamericana* 51, no.132-133 (1985): 731-749.

Mullen, Edward. "Interpreting Puerto Rico's Cultural Myths: Rosario Ferré and Manuel Ramos Otero." *Americas Review* 17, no. 3/4 (1989): 88-97.

Vélez, Diana. "Power and the Text: Rebellion in Rosario Ferré's *Papeles de Pandora*." *MMLA: The Journal of the Midwest Modern Language Association* 17, no. 1 (1984): 70-80.

MAGALI GARCÍA RAMIS

Novels

Felices días, Tío Sergio. Río Piedras, P.R.: Editorial Antillana, 1986.

Short Stories

La familia de todos nosotros. San Juan: Instituto de Cultura Puertorriqueña, 1976. Reprint. Río Piedras, P.R.: Editorial Cultural, 1989.

Translations

"Every Sunday." Translated by Carmen C. Esteves. In *Her True-True Name: An Anthology of Women's Writing from the Caribbean*, edited by Paula Mordecai and Betty Wilson, 98-101. London: Heinemann, 1989.

Works About

Barradas, Efraín. "*Felices días, Tío Sergio.*" *Revista de Crítica Literaria Hispanoamericana* 10, no. 20 (1984): 120-127.
Ferré, Rosario. "El tema de la cotidianeidad en *La familia de todos nosotros.*" *El Mundo* (San Juan, P.R.), 17 April 1977, 14A.
Rivera de Álvarez, Josefina. "El cuento." In her *La literatura puertorriqueña: su proceso en el tiempo*, 897-898. Madrid: Partenón, 1983.

ÁNGELA HERNÁNDEZ

Short Stories

Alótropos. Santo Domingo: Editorial Alas, 1989.

JEANNE HYVRARD

Novels

Canal de la Toussaint. Paris: Des Femmes, 1985.
Les Doigts du figuier. Paris: Éditions de Minuit, 1977.
Mère la Mort. Paris: Éditions de Minuit, 1976.
La Meurtritude. Paris: Éditions de Minuit, 1977.
Les Prunes de Cythère. Paris: Éditions de Minuit, 1975.
Le Silence et l'obscurité: requiem littoral pour corps polonais, 13-28 decembre 1981. Paris: Montalba, 1982.

Works About

Corzani, Jack. "Un Désespoir quasi total." In *La Littérature des Antilles et Guyane françaises*, vol. 6, 262-270. Fort de France: Désormeaux, 1978.

Toumson, Roger. "Un Aspect de la contradiction littéraire afro-antillaise: l'école en procès." *Revue des Sciences Humaines* 174 (1979): 105-128.

Zimra, Clarisse. "W/Righting His/tory: Versions of Things Past in Contemporary Caribbean Women Writers." In *Essays in Comparative Literature*, edited by Makoto Ueda, 227-252. New York: University Press of America, 1986.

JAMAICA KINCAID

Novels

Annie John. New York: Farrar, Straus and Giroux; Toronto: Collins Publishers, 1985. Reprint. New York: New American Library, 1986.

Lucy. New York: Farrar, Straus and Giroux, 1990.

Short Stories

At the Bottom of the River. New York: Farrar, Straus and Giroux, 1983. Reprint. New York: Vintage Books, 1985.

Works About

Dutton, Wendy. "Merge and Separate: Jamaica Kincaid's Fiction." *World Literature Today* 63, no. 3 (1989): 406-410.

Ismond, Patricia. "Jamaica Kincaid: 'First They Must Be Children.'" *World Literature Written in English* 28, no. 2 (1988): 336-341.

Mangum, Bryant. "Jamaica Kincaid." In *Fifty Caribbean Writers*, edited by Daryl Cumber Dance, 255-263. New York: Greenwood Press, 1986.

265

OLGA NOLLA

Novel

La otra hija. Río Piedras, P.R.: Universidad de Puerto Rico, 1992.

Short Stories

"Un corazón tierno." *Caribán* 1, no. 2 (1985): 20-21.
"En esta casa no puede haber polvo." *Sin Nombre* 5, no. 4 (1975): 32-42.
Porque nos queremos tanto. Buenos Aires: Ediciones de la Flor, 1989.

Works About

Trelles, Carmen Dolores. "Cuentos de Olga Nolla." *En Grande* (San Juan, P.R.), 14 January 1980, 12.

OPAL PALMER ADISA

Short Stories

Bake-Face and Other Guava Stories. Introduction by Barbara Christian. Berkeley: Kelsey Street Press, 1986.
"Duppy Get Her." In *Caribbean New Wave: Contemporary Short Stories,* edited by Stewart Brown, 1-11. London: Heinemann, 1990.

VELMA POLLARD

Short Stories

"Cages." *Bim* 16, no. 22 (1977): 107-116.
Considering Woman. London: Women's Press, 1989.
"The Dust—A Tribute to the Folk." *Caribbean Quarterly* 26, no. 1/2 (1980): 41:48.

"Gran." *Jamaica Journal* 11, no. 3/4 (1978): 35-42.

PAULETTE POUJOL-ORIOL

Novel

Le Creuset. Port-au-Prince: Henry Deschamps, 1985.

JEAN RHYS

Novels

After Leaving Mr. Mackenzie. London: Jonathan Cape, 1931. Reprint. New York: Alfred Knopf, 1931; London: A. Deutsch, 1969; Harmondsworth: Penguin, 1971, 1977, 1980; New York: Harper & Row, 1972, 1982; New York: Vintage Books, 1974.

Good Morning, Midnight. London: Constable, 1939. Reprint. London: A. Deutsch, 1967; Harmondsworth: Penguin, 1969; New York: Harper & Row, 1970; New York: Vintage Books, 1974; New York: Perennial Library, Harper & Row, 1982.

Jean Rhys: The Complete Novels. Introduction by Diana Athill. New York: W. W. Norton, 1985.

Postures. London: Chatto & Windus, 1928. As *Quartet: a Novel.* New York: Simon and Schuster, 1929. Reprint. London: A. Deutsch, 1969; New York: Harper & Row, 1971; Harmondsworth: Penguin, 1973, 1977, 1981, 1982; New York: Vintage Books, 1974; New York: Perennial Library, Harper & Row, 1981.

Voyage to the Dark. London: Constable, 1934, 1936; New York: Morrow, 1935. Reprint. London: A. Deutsch, 1967; New York: Vintage Books, 1974; New York: W. W. Norton, 1968, 1982; New York: Popular Library, 1975; Harmondsworth: Penguin, 1969, 1975, 1978, 1980.

Wide Sargasso Sea. New York: W. W. Norton, 1966, 1982; London: A. Deutsch, 1966. Reprint. Harmondsworth: Penguin, 1968,

1969, 1970, 1975, 1976, 1977, 1979, 1980; New York: Popular Library, 1976.

Short Stories

The Collected Stories of Jean Rhys. New York: Norton, 1987.
Jean Rhys: Tales of the Wide Caribbean. London: Heinemann, 1986.
The Left Bank and Other Stories. London: Jonathan Cape, 1947.
Sleep It Off Lady. London: Andre Deutsch; New York: Harper & Row, 1976; Harmondsworth: Penguin, 1979, 1980, 1981.
Tigers Are Better Looking. With a selection from *The Left Bank.* London: Andre Deutsch, 1968; Harmondsworth: Penguin, 1973, 1977, 1981, 1982; New York: Harper & Row, 1974; New York: Popular Library, 1976.

Works About

Abel, Elizabeth. "Women and Schizophrenia: The Fiction of Jean Rhys." *Contemporary Literature* 20 (1979): 155-177.
Angier, Carole. *Jean Rhys.* Harmondsworth: Penguin Books, 1985. Reprint. New York: Viking/Penguin, 1985.
———. *Jean Rhys: Life and Work.* Boston: Little, Brown and Company, 1990.
Braybrooke, Neville. "Jean Rhys." In *Contemporary Novelists*, 1061-1064. New York: St. Martin's, 1972.
Brown, Beverly E. "Mansong and Matrix: A Radical Experiment." In *A Double Colonization: Colonial and Post-Colonial Women's Writing*, edited by Kristen Holst Petersen and Anna Rutherford, 68-80. Denmark: Dangaroo Press, 1986.
Bruner, Charlotte H. "A Caribbean Madness: Half Slave and Half Free." *Canadian Review of Comparative Literature* 11, no. 2 (1984): 236-248.
Casey, Nancy. "Jean Rhys' *Wide Sargasso Sea*: Exterminating the White Cockroach." *Revista Interamericana* 4, no. 3 (1974): 340-349.
———. "The 'Liberated' Woman in Jean Rhys' Later Short Fiction." *Revista Interamericana* 4, no. 2 (1974): 264-272.
———. "Study in the Alienation of a Creole Woman." *Caribbean Quarterly*, 19, no. 3 (1973): 95-102.

Cummins, Marsha Z. "Point of View in the Novels of Jean Rhys: The Effect of Double Focus." *World Literature Written in English* 24, no. 2 (1984): 359-372.

Dash, Cheryl M. L. "Jean Rhys." In *West Indian Literature*, edited by Bruce King, 196-209. London: Macmillan, 1979.

D'Costa, Jean. "Jean Rhys." In *Fifty Caribbean Writers*, edited by Daryl Cumber Dance, 390-404. New York: Greenwood Press, 1986.

Fayad, Mona. "Unquiet Ghosts: The Struggle for Representation in Jean Rhys's *Wide Sargasso Sea*." *Modern Fiction Studies* 34, no. 3 (1988): 437-452.

Frickey, Pierrette. *Critical Perspective on Jean Rhys*. Washington, D.C.: Three Continents Press, 1984.

James, Louis. *Jean Rhys*. London: Longman, 1978.

Jones, Angela. "Voodoo and Apocalyse in the Works of Jean Rhys." *Journal of Commonwealth Literature* 16, no. 1 (1981): 126-131.

Kubitschek, Missy Dehn. "Charting the Empty Spaces of Jean Rhys' *Wide Sargasso Sea*." *Frontiers* 9, no. 2 (1987): 23-28.

Lai, Wally Look. "Jean Rhys: *Wide Sargasso Sea*." *New World Quarterly* 4, no. 2/3 (1968): 17-27. Reprint. In *New Beacon Reviews*, Collection One, edited by John La Rose, 38-52. London: New Beacon, 1968.

Leigh, Nancy J. "Mirror, Mirror: The Development of Female Identity in Jean Rhys's Fiction." *World Literature Written in English* 25, no. 2 (1985): 270-284.

Luengo, Anthony E. "*Wide Sargasso Sea* and the Gothic Mode." *World Literature Written in English* 15 (1976): 229-245.

Mellown, Elgin W. "Character and Themes in the Novels of Jean Rhys." *Contemporary Literature* 13 (1972): 458-475. Reprint. In *Contemporary Women Novelists*, edited by Patricia Meyer Spacks, 118-136. Englewood Cliffs, N.J.: Prentice-Hall, 1977.

———. *Jean Rhys: A Descriptive and Annotated Bibliography of Works and Criticism*. New York: Garland, 1984.

Morrell, A. C. "The World of Jean Rhys' Short Stories." *World Literature Written in English* 18, no. 1 (1979): 235-244.

Nebeker, Helen. *Jean Rhys: Woman in Passage*. Montreal: Women's Publications, 1981.

Nunez-Harell, Elizabeth. "The Paradoxes of Belonging: The White West Indian Woman in Fiction." *Modern Fiction Studies* 31, no. 2 (1985): 281-293.

Ramchand, Kenneth. *The West Indian Novel and Its Background*. London: Faber and Faber, 1970.

Scharfman, Ronnie. "Mirroring and Mothering in Simone Schwarz-Bart's *Pluie et vent sur Telumee Miracle* and Jean Rhys's *Wide Sargasso Sea*." *Yale French Studies* 62 (1981): 88-106.

Staley, Thomas F. *Jean Rhys: A Critical Study*. London: Macmillan; Austin: University of Texas Press, 1979.

Thieme, John. "Apparitions of Disaster: Brontean Parallels in *Wide Sargasso Sea* and *Guerillas*." *Journal of Commonwealth Literature* 14 (1979): 116-132.

Tiffin, Helen. "Mirror and Mask: Colonial Motifs in the Novels of Jean Rhys." *World Literature Written in English*, 1, no. 1 (1978): 328-341.

Wolfe, Peter. *Jean Rhys*. Boston: Twayne Publishers, 1980.

Wyndham, Francis and Diana Melly, eds. *Jean Rhys: Letters 1931-1966*. London: Andre Deutsch, 1984.

ASTRID H. ROEMER

Novels

Levenslang gedicht: roman. Haarlem: In De Knipscheer, 1987.
Neem mijn terug Suriname. Haarlem: In De Knipscheer, 1974. 2d ed. The Hague: Pressag, 1975.
Nergens, ergens. Haarlem: In De Knipscheer, 1983.
Schoon en schofterig. Haarlem: In De Knipscheer, 1985.

Short Stories

De Orde van de dag: novelle. Schoorl: Conserve, 1988.
Het Spoor van de jakhals: novelle. Schoorl: Conserve, 1988.
Waaron zou je huilen mijn lieve mijn lieve: novelle. Zoetermeer: Z &

Co., 1977. Reprint. Haarlem: In De Knipscheer, 1976; Schoorl: Conserve, 1987.

Works About

Phaf, Ineke. "Interview with Astrid Roemer." In *Unheard Words. Women and Literature in Africa, the Arab World, Asia, the Caribbean, and Latin America*, edited by Mineke Schipper, 201-210. London: Allison and Busby, 1985.

OLIVE SENIOR

Short Stories

Arrival of the Snake Woman and Other Stories. Essex, England: Longman, 1989.
"Ascot." In *Over Our Way*, edited by Jean D'Costa and Velma Pollard, 146-160. Kingston: Longman Caribbean, 1980.
"Ballad." *Jamaica Journal* 11, no. 1/2 (1976): 35-43.
Summer Lighting and Other Stories. Essex, England: Longman, 1986.

ANA LYDIA VEGA

Short Stories

Encancaranublado y otros cuentos de naufragio. Havana: Casa de las Américas, 1982. Reprint. Río Piedras, P.R.: Editorial Antillana, 1983.
Pasión de historia y otras historias de pasión. Buenos Aires: Editorial de la Flor, 1987.
Vírgenes y mártires, by Ana Lydia Vega and Carmen Lugo-Filippi. Rio Piedras, P.R.: Editorial Antillana, 1981. Reprint. Río Piedras, P.R.: Editorial Cultural, 1982.

Translations

"Cloud Cover Caribbean." Translated by Mark McCaffrey. From the collection *Encancaranublado y otros cuentos de naufragio*. In *Her True-True Name: An Anthology of Women's Writing from the Caribbean*, edited by Pamela Mordecai and Betty Wilson, 105-111. London: Heinemann, 1989.

"Lyrics for Puerto Rican Salsa and Three Soneos by Request." Translated by Mark McCaffrey. *New England Review and Bread Loaf Quarterly* 7, no. 4 (1985): 550-554.

"Three Love Aerobics." In *Reclaiming Medusa: Short Stories by Contemporary Puerto Rican Women*, edited and translated by Diana Vélez, 143-148. San Francisco: Aunt Lute, 1988.

Works About

Fernández Olmos, Margarite. "From a Woman's Perspective: The Short Stories of Rosario Ferré and Ana Lydia Vega." *Contemporary Women Authors of Latin America: Introductory Essays*, 78-90. Brooklyn, N.Y.: Brooklyn College Press, 1983.

Vélez, Diana L. "Pollito Chicken: Split Subjectivity, National Identity, and Articulation of Female Sexuality in a Narrative." *Americas Review* 14, no. 2 (1986): 68-76.

BEA VIANEN

Novels

Geen Onderdelen. Amsterdam: Bezige Bij, 1979.
Het Paradije van Oranje. Amsterdam: Querido, 1973.
Ik eet, ik eet, tot ik niet meer kan. Amsterdam: Querido, 1972.
Sarnami, hai. Amsterdam: Querido, 1969.
Strafhok. Amsterdam: Querido, 1971.

MYRIAM WARNER-VIEYRA

Novels

Juletane. Paris: Présence Africaine, 1982.
Le Quimboiseur l'avait dit. Paris: Présence Africaine, 1980.

Short Stories

Femmes Echouées. Paris: Présence Africaine, 1988.

Translations

As the Sorcerer Said. Translation of *Le Quimboiseur l'avait dit* by Dorothy Blair. London: Longman's Drumbeat Series, 1982.
Juletane. Translated by Betty Wilson. London: Heinemann, 1987.

Works About

Bruner, Charlotte H. "First Novels of Girlhood." *CLAJ* 31, no.3 (1988): 324-338.
Midihouan, Thecla. "Des Antilles à l'Afrique: Myriam Warner-Vieyra." *Notre Librairie* 74 (1984): 39-53.
Ngate, Jonathan. "Reading Warner-Vieyra's *Juletane.*" *Callaloo* 9, no. 4 (1986): 553-564.
Okpanachi, Sunday. "Le Couple afro-antillais: le jeu de l'apparence et l'évidence," *Peuples Noirs, Peuples Africaines* no. 47 (1985): 24-37.

MIRTA YÁÑEZ

Novels

La hora de los mameyes. Havana: Editorial Letras Cubanas, 1983.

Short Stories

Havana es una ciudad bien grande. Havana: Editorial Letras Cubanas, 1980.
Todos los negros tomamos café. Havana: Editorial Arte y Literatura,

Instituto Cubano del Libro, 1976.

Translations

"We Blacks All Drink Coffee." Translated by Claudette Williams. In *Her True-True Name: An Anthology of Women's Writing from the Caribbean*, edited by Pamela Mordecai and Betty Wilson, 38-41. London: Heinemann, 1989.